Comparing Political Systems

Comparing Political Systems

JEAN BLONDEL

PRAEGER PUBLISHERS
New York · Washington

BOOKS THAT MATTER

Published in the United States of America in 1972
by Praeger Publishers, Inc.
111 Fourth Avenue, New York, N.Y. 10003

Library of Congress Catalog Card Number: 72-88041

Printed in the United States of America

For Dominique and Nathalie

Contents

Contents

Preface

Comparing Political Systems is designed to be of use to all those who feel more and more that political life must be studied on a worldwide basis. Until recently it was possible to concentrate, often in great detail, on the institutions and problems of a few countries, possibly because others seemed less important, possibly because it was assumed, consciously or not, that all would eventually converge toward the "models" that the United States, Britain, France, and later the Soviet Union had devised for the world. Yet, in becoming smaller, the modern world has become more complex politically. The governmental structures of these large countries have indeed been used as models by newer nations, but in the course of imitation alterations were necessarily made until, with the passage of time, the copies became very different from the original blueprints. It is no longer realistic to believe that we can understand all governments by studying only a few countries; nor is it reasonable to expect that the few "more important" polities will continue to be guides and models for others.

In analyzing governments across the world, one has to simplify and summarize, particularly in a short book; I shall therefore concentrate here on the central features of "structures of government" in order to analyze the fabric of political systems. But one needs also to consider the ways in which these structures interact to give a special flavor to real-life political systems. After having examined structures, therefore, I shall describe political systems under a number of broad models or types, knowing that not all countries fit precisely within one of these types but recognizing the broad similarities in both present organization and direction of future development.

This is why this book should be viewed as a preliminary survey of the field, of its approaches and its findings. It will, it is hoped, be helpful in preparing the ground for further and more detailed work in comparative government, whether studies of particular structures or of general arrangements. It is also hoped that it will be of some value to those who wish to concentrate on one particular country or one particular model, for the study of one government can only be fully meaningful if it is contrasted to the over-all panorama of contemporary politics. And, above all, it is hoped that this book will give to some or even to many a taste for the study of contemporary government, which, though among the oldest of mankind's discoveries, since it led Aristotle to some of his most profound thinking, is also very modern by virtue of the new approaches it uses and very important in terms of the problems it tackles.

                                                           J. B.

Mourillon, Toulon, France
July, 1972

Comparing Political Systems

1

The Scope and Purpose of the Study of Comparative Government

This book is about the way in which men in the various countries of the world organize their governments and conduct public policies. It will concentrate on contemporary governments; and although it is not about any particular government or any particular country, it will tend to draw its examples from some governments and from some countries more than from others for purely practical reasons. But its primary aim is not to describe the characteristics of these governments. It is rather to try to account for such phenomena as the prevalence of military rule in some countries, to examine whether liberal democracy can be expected to bring about change while maintaining freedom, or to assess whether the Soviet "model" necessarily entails severe restrictions for the citizens of Communist countries. In order to simplify the analysis, we shall classify political systems and describe the main models or types which are currently in existence; but we shall also try to go further and examine the general variables that, by their interplay, lead to variations in the arrangements of governmental systems.

By concentrating on variables and on types of government, we do not imply that the study of individual governments is uninteresting or unimportant; but conceptually the general study of governments on a comparative basis should precede the study of individual governments. We cannot expect to understand how *one* government works if we do not have a framework of comparison. It is sometimes suggested that comparative analysis is difficult, which it is, or even impossible, which it is not, but the study of individual governments is far more difficult, or indeed impossible, unless models or theories in some form are drawn from the study of comparative government and applied to particular cases.

Let us consider this point a little more closely. It is sometimes stated that a broad and general study of governments is difficult or impossible because we do not have the ability to measure many aspects of political life or because political phenomena are unique. These difficulties undeniably exist for a variety of reasons, which will become clearer as we look at the various aspects of government. It is sufficient to note at this stage that they occur at many levels: Sometimes we are hampered because we cannot find the facts we require to draw adequate comparisons; sometimes we are hampered because we do not have the theory or have not refined the concepts we need for our analysis. Some political scientists go further and deny that we can be comparative in a systematic and truly "scientific" fashion. It is said that a government is the product of the experiences of generations of men who live a *unique* history; the institutions, customs, and ideals of Americans are so different from those of the Chinese, for example, that only if we study the history and the culture of each of these countries can we hope to understand the organization and life of their governments. Events such as the French or Russian Revolution or the World Wars shape nations in ways that are viewed by some to necessitate individual studies of the consequences of these events.

The point is not to deny the importance of such events or to claim that the study of individual cultures will not help us a great deal to understand government. The point is really that, if we begin to analyze how we study individual governments or types of governments, we quickly become aware of an underlying broader framework that gives significance to individual events.

The Russian Revolution may or may not be directly contrasted with the French Revolution; it is always examined in the light of "revolutions"—their aims, their techniques, their development. If it were not assessed in this way, it would merely be a sequence of disconnected happenings without meaning.

We have to recognize that any analysis of government is, in the deepest reality, either implicitly or explicitly comparative. It is explicitly comparative if we give ourselves the task of seeing whether an institution, for instance a legislature or a party, is organized in the same way and does the same things in two or more countries; it is implicitly comparative if we look only at one institution of the government and try to assess what it does, in what way it does it, and if it does it well. There is no point in asserting that we are not comparing when we describe in great detail the operations of a particular committee of the United States House of Representatives: We are unconsciously comparing that body with other committees elsewhere, or other committees of the House, and we have in our minds some idea of how committees work and should work. We may have a precise model in mind or have only a vague view of the blueprint with which to compare the reality; we may concentrate so much on the details of the mechanics that the comparative element will be minute and concealed. This is why it is sometimes felt that there is opposition between *description* and *systematic analysis,* which includes the conscious building of models. But in reality the two are closely related, because any real world analysis uses descriptions and models in sequence and together.

This book therefore approaches governments comparatively to try to order the reality of the contemporary world on the basis of models and theories that up to now have seemed to explain at least part of the reality. We should no more concentrate exclusively on models than we should attempt merely to describe the unique events of the contemporary world. The ultimate aim is to understand why governments have some characteristics, why parties emerge, what are the conditions of military rule, and why, in a given country and at a particular moment, a government has some characteristics. Indeed, without wishing to be overpractical, the purpose of the study of comparative government must also be to help not only to understand but, where possible, to redress and change those aspects of government that seem to some or to many to be objectionable. To do this, we must examine particular situations in the light of the models of government that seem best able to account for the reality.

Political Activity and the Study of Comparative Government

Where do these models come from? What are the problems requiring solution that the organization and life of governments have raised and continue to raise? The answers can only come in an indirect way, by seeing the study of government in the more general context of the study of politics. Governments exist at the level of the nation, and this is the study with which we are concerned here; but governments at the national level are only a part, even if an important part, of the whole series of governments that exist among mankind. There are differences in scope and powers between the governments of nations and the governments of small clubs and large associations. But all these governments are concerned in reality with the same problem, that of making decisions for the communities they serve or control. On the whole, the governments of local authorities and of private institutions have been studied less systematically and for a much shorter period than have national governments, but political scientists have now come to recognize that the problems are theoretically the same and that the study of national governments is isolated only for reasons of convenience.

We shall continue here to concentrate on national governments, in the main, because national governments happen to have great importance for the lives of individuals. But if we consider for a moment all the governments that exist in the world in all the communities where decisions have to be taken, we are able to discover the first element of the model we need in order to understand the structure and role of governments. Governments exist as a means of taking *collective* decisions applicable for a whole community. When a common policy has to be devised, either because it is not possible for everyone to do as he pleases or because it is thought inadvisable for everyone to do as he pleases, the activity that leads to the decision (whether the decision is positive or negative—for instance, merely a "nondecision") is a *political* activity. *Economic* activities are all those activities which relate to the allocation of resources (of a scarce character), to the extent that these activities pass through or are regulated by the *price mechanism;* political activities are all those activities which relate to the allocation of (scarce) resources (and more generally values), through some mechanism of collective decision-making for the whole community. This is why it is sometimes said that politics relates to the "authoritative allocation of values."[1] This allocation is "authoritative" in that it is made in the name of all and is applicable to all. The government is the mechanism through which the allocation takes place.

Any follow-up of this line of reasoning shows that political activity can relate to any problem, not to a specific type of question. Governments—the government of any community—may be confronted with the most varied issues and not only with questions defined in advance.[2] The questions that will come before governments, those having a political flavor, are those for which there is a need to decide on one policy (rather than another—again, even if the decision is merely negative). Clearly this will happen only if there is some controversy over the issue in question, for if there were no controversy, the issue would not even come to be raised. It therefore follows that, because in a given community and for a particular government the controversial problems will be the ones raised, these are likely to differ from one government to another, and comparisons may be difficult as a result.

But if we follow one step further the problem of controversy, we encounter a distinction that will be one of the most important in the study of governments. We just noted that the con-

---

[1] Politics has been defined in this way by David Easton in *The Political System* (New York: Knopf, 1953), pp. 129–48. Considerable similarity can be seen to exist between problems faced by economists and those faced by political scientists. In both cases there is a question of allocation and of deciding between alternatives. In economics, this is within the framework of monetary considerations; in politics there is no such framework, and the scope is therefore wider.

[2] One can easily see that any group or community may be faced suddenly with problems that have been totally overlooked or unanticipated. Witness, for example, the problem faced by many athletic organizations trying to avoid the "racial issue" and yet confronted with the question of whether to allow all-white South African teams to compete in their games.

troversy, the conflict, which the government had to solve by taking a decision and which had led to a particular political activity, could be over any issue. It could be said that politics was therefore essentially of a procedural—we should perhaps say a *processual*—type. But in reality there are two types of conflict in such a controversy. One relates to the character of the decision to be taken, for instance, should there be free medicine in a polity? Such a question is substantive. Only the other is truly procedural, being concerned with the *way* in which the decision is to be taken: Should it be by referendum, majority vote, or a throw of the dice? Any political activity refers, therefore, or may refer, to two types of matter: the substance of the issue and the procedure by which the issue will be resolved. As can intuitively be felt (but would need to be examined at a greater depth than is possible here in order to be fully argued), the development of government is largely a means of solving once and for all, or at least for a long time, the problem of the *procedure* for conflict resolution. This is what happens if it is said in an association that decisions shall be taken by majority rule. But as can also be easily felt, the procedure for solution is not wholly unconnected, to say the least, with the substance of the problem: No one is prepared to accept majority rule to solve *any* problem. Thus, (1) we are confronted with governments that exist in order to solve conflicts by taking decisions over an infinite variety of issues, but (2) these governments also attempt to solve, once and for all, or at least for a long time, the procedural questions common to all these problems.

Norms, Structures, Behavior

While distinguishing between two types of objects of controversy, the problem and the procedure of solution, we encounter the role of the time element or of repetitiveness in the field of political activity. If a procedure—for instance, a referendum—is adopted for the solution of a whole category of conflicts, this means that a decision taken in the past about a procedure will be followed, and followed in numerous instances, in the future. The same argument could be made if we considered not a procedure but an *institution* such as a legislature or a party; indeed, we can extend the argument to decisions on the substance of problems, for instance, when a law declares that there will be free medicine available to all the citizens of a given polity. We have thus encountered two types of "happenings" relating to political activity: those occurring *once,* which constitute the true happenings, and those occurring on the basis of some procedure or under the rules of some institution. In practice, this dichotomy is exaggerated: The happenings, or the behavior of the various elements of the polity, are shaped by the institutions and procedures. This, indeed, is why procedures and institutions exist. Happenings relate to institutions and procedures in the manner of a ball bouncing against the six sides of a squash court. Conversely, institutions and procedures are modified by the happenings: If the wall or ceiling of a squash court is in bad condition, it can be damaged by the ball.

Over the years, in any community but particularly in a nation, there comes a slow (and at times rapid) modification of the *structures* (that is, the institutions and procedures) by the happenings in the polity. Of course, efforts may be made to maintain the institutions and procedures in their original form. As we shall see, this may be possible only for a limited period, and the consequences of clinging to outmoded structures may be serious for the whole polity. Change is very difficult to analyze, and some suggest it poses a limitation on the effectiveness of the comparative method, because the pace of change and the interaction between structure and behavior are bound to be different from one polity to another. But the fact that the problem is difficult to solve is no justification for refusing to analyze its character. The study of comparative government thus includes the examination of the way in which procedures and institutions come to change, the reasons that make for the changes, and the pace at which these changes take place under various circumstances.

One can immediately discover a number of reasons why such changes can take place. New men, new social conditions, new attitudes all contribute to changes in behavior; sources outside the polity itself can have an impact on behavior, either because men may change under the influence of others or because circumstances may enable a particular nation to impose on another (forcefully or in a subtle fashion) modifications of structures and behavior. Imitation is a common source of structural innovation across the world, as witness the development of constitutions modeled on the British or U.S. pattern in newer nations or the appearance of single-party systems on the Soviet model, by imposition or by imitation, in Eastern Europe and large parts of the Third World. This is a further source of difficulty for the analysis, since even imitation has to take into account pre-existing attitudes and leads to an almost infinite variety of patterns of changes of behavior, of structures, and of the relation between structures and behavior.

This complexity can be somewhat reduced if we begin to examine under what conditions institutions and procedures tend to emerge. An institution is created or simply exists if it corresponds positively to the views of the population, or at least if it is tolerated by having the passive acquiescence of that population (or through the fear of the consequences of change among that population). Thus institutions and procedures correspond to the *ideals* or *norms* that prevail in the polity as a whole. In the most straightforward cases, institutions and procedures are created in order to embody these norms. If majority rule by the *whole* people is the norm that prevails, the procedure of the referendum would seem to have to be adopted. In cases that are less clear-cut, the norms and the structures correspond to each other in a less precise fashion. To use a mathematical expression, in the best cases there is a functional relationship between norms and structures, while in other cases it becomes more difficult to deduce norms from structures, and vice versa.

Let us explore the reasons why the relationship between norms and structures is not always simple. It may be because there is conflict over norms; it may also be because there is conflict over which institutions and procedures are best capable of implementing accepted norms. For instance, it is not clear to everybody that referendums are the best embodiment of the notion of popular majority rule. Both types of problem may lead to vast confusion. But the situation is further complicated if we introduce a time element in the model: We can assume that norms will change over time (people will change their views and ideals, new immigrants will come, influences from outside will be different, and so forth). As norms change, there will be some pressure on the structures and institutions, but these will also offer some resistance: Thus behavior may no longer correspond entirely to the institutions and procedures as they were created. We started from the proposition that institutions and procedures developed (or were created) in order to resolve conflicts over procedures once and for all. The outcome may be that, over time, a further conflict is created in the pressure to change a procedure or an institution that no longer corresponds to the prevailing norms.

One type of problem often arises in this context, and it is truly a special case of the general difficulty we encounter in relating norms, structures, and behavior. This is the question of the role of the *law* in the governmental process. Everyone knows the important part played by laws in public decision-making, and in particular the role of the *fundamental law* of a country, its constitution, in the structure of government itself. If we follow our previous developments, we can see that the *lawmaking process* and the constitution-making process are means by which procedures and institutions are created in order to shape future behavior; but these laws and constitutions are also made (or at least are deemed to be made) to implement some norms or ideals held by the lawmakers at the time of the drafting of the law. If there is conflict over the norms to which the law refers, it is very likely that implementation of the law will be difficult and that the behavior of citizens will create a discrepancy between *law* and *practice*. We can therefore expect numerous difficulties while considering the extent to which laws (particularly constitutions) are implemented in given polities. Indeed, we can even postulate that no law (or constitution) will be fully implemented, as full implementation would suggest no conflict whatsoever about the question, and in particular no change in norms over time. There will therefore be cases of limited implementation, variations of interpretation about implementation, and many other situations, in particular when *customs* come slowly to modify the law (or constitution), just as barnacles tend slowly to take a firm grip on the hull of a sunken ship.

The study of comparative government therefore has to be undertaken within the framework of a complex relationship between institutions and procedures, which generally shape the course of behavior, on the one hand, and, on the other, pressures for change stemming from conflicts between norms and values in a vast number of situations and through a whole maze of problems. We shall have to try to reduce the number of these problems to manageable proportions if we are to understand at least the broad outlines of the movements, but we should remain aware of the complexity of the question at hand, not in order to foreclose the analysis (can mankind cease to try to understand?), but in order to remain modest and somewhat tentative in the conclusions. On balance, we shall concentrate on structures and on norms, because the complexity of happenings of course precludes any systematic analysis in the course of so short a text. But we need to remain aware of the extent to which changed norms modify behavior and in turn structures, and to assess the conditions under which changes are most likely to be rapid or, on the contrary, modify only slowly the structures of the polity.

In the first part of this book, we shall look at the problem generally and examine the role of different types of structures, the types of norms and ideologies that prevail in the world, and the kind of support norms and structures need in order to give a government a chance to survive. In the second part, we shall have a closer look at the more important structures, such as groups, parties, executives, legislatures, bureaucracies, the military, and the judiciary, to see how they develop and what forms they tend to take under different conditions. In the third part, we shall try to see how structures relate to each other in different broad models of types of political systems, corresponding to different normative arrangements, and to assess which of these systems are likely to be maintained and which do not appear, at least under normal conditions, to be viable.

PART ONE

The Framework of Analysis

2

The Political System:
Structures and Functions

Governments are concerned with decisions on problems requiring *authoritative* solutions for all the members of the community. The decision-making process is carried out by means of institutions and procedures that can be called "structures," as they give some rigidity to the arrangements existing in the polity, though changes of course affect these structures more or less rapidly. We need therefore to explore a little more closely the nature and roles of these structures. We need to see how structures operate in the decision-making process and thus discover what each structure actually achieves. This is also, of course, the only way in which it will be possible to compare structures from one governmental system to another.

Let us start by having a closer look at the nature of political activity in a community such as the nation, focusing exclusively on political activities that are national in scope and therefore involve the national government. It is permissible to describe the sequence of political activities identified in this way as a political *system,* as there is continuity of the process over time and a whole variety of problems are dealt with by the same mechanisms and possibly by the same people. It could, admittedly, be argued that each decision is made by somewhat different people and with slightly different processes and that there is therefore no one political system in any polity. But if we are not quite so strict, if we simply consider the extent to which some groups of people, some institutions, some procedures are used repeatedly, and if we note the large overlap that occurs among these men or among these groups, it is not inappropriate to view as a system the set of interactions leading to decisions of a national character in which governments find themselves as important actors.

The Political System and Its Characteristics

Let us look a little more closely at what this political system does, generalizing for the system as a whole the characteristic features of political activity described in the preceding chapter. It appears immediately that, through a series of decisions that are authoritative and applicable to all (or potentially to all, at least negatively), a number of problems are solved (or shelved— but this should be considered a form of decision); the *operation* or *function* performed is then specific to the political system. It is admissible to designate as *outputs* of the political system the decisions taken—though a difficulty soon emerges as we begin to reflect on the distinction between the *stating* of a decision and its *implementation*.

But this decision, whether implemented or not, does not come wholly "out of the blue"; it is a decision on a matter that was felt to be a problem by some members of the polity, however minute the section of the population may have been (perhaps it is the decision-maker alone who thought of the problem, but this will happen infrequently in a large political system). It is therefore permissible to suggest that, even if we grant that the process is complex, outputs are in some fashion preceded by *inputs* into the political system stemming from a section of the polity. From this follows a model of the political system that owes much to David Easton's analysis, which describes the process as one in which the political system is subjected to demands, which are turned into inputs (and for which various types of support are needed, as otherwise the demands would not be pressed), and these inputs are turned into outputs through the decision taken (and implemented) by the polity.[1]

The function of the political system as a whole is thus to convert inputs into outputs. Though this is undeniably what happens in all political systems, the word "function" has been criticized in this usage, while other criticisms have been leveled at the apparently mechanical fashion in which the conversion of demands into decisions has sometimes been viewed.[2] It is important that we not have an oversimplified view of this process. The word "function" must be seen here as meaning no more than an operation; the whole matter has an axiomatic character. Decisions have to be taken, even if they are negative (nondecisions). From the fact that decisions are taken on the basis of problems that are raised, it follows that a *sequence, operation,* or function does indeed take place. Moreover, *demands* and *inputs* must not be seen as necessarily injecting a *democratic* principle in the process. All that is suggested is that, if a problem does not arise, there will be no decision; for a decision to occur, the problem must have arisen. Nothing is said about the numbers of people who raise the problem, nor about the time lag. The input may be due to the whims of very few people or to a large group, to some individuals meeting together or to an organized party. The decision may follow the input almost immediately, or years may elapse between the moment when the question is first raised and the decision. Moreover, as Easton noted from the start, previous decisions will affect inputs at a later period. A feedback process has to be taken into account, and we can see already that this is one of the ways by which decision-makers may attempt to shape the environment.

Finally, and most importantly, it is essential to distinguish between inputs and demands, on the one hand, and *desires* or *hopes,* on the other. Demands that become inputs in the political

---

[1] See especially David Easton, *A Framework for Political Analysis* (Englewood Cliffs, N.J.: Prentice-Hall, 1965); *idem, A Systems Analysis of Political Life* (New York: John Wiley, 1965); and Easton's other works.

[2] See Gabriel A. Almond and G. Bingham Powell, Jr., *Comparative Politics: A Developmental Approach* (Boston: Little, Brown, 1966), esp. pp. 29–33, for a presentation of the model. For a critique, see Robert T. Holt and John E. Turner, *The Political Basis of Economic Development* (Princeton, N.J.: Van Nostrand Reinhold, 1966), Chapter I.

system and affect the decisions taken constitute only part of the hopes and desires of the members of the polity. For a desire to become significant, there must be considerable support in the political system, not necessarily in terms of numbers but in terms of the intensity of the support or pressure brought to bear. It follows that desires and hopes of persons who have access to the decision-makers are much more likely to become demands and be inputs in the political system than are desires and hopes of people far away from the centers of decision. It may be that some political systems allow larger numbers of people to make their desires felt; this is one of the ways in which *democratic* systems can be distinguished from others, as we shall see. But even in the most democratic systems, some desires will be repressed because they are not vocal enough, and because engrained habits militate against them.

The Specific Functions of Political Systems

By distinguishing desires and hopes from demands, we have begun to move a little closer to a detailed analysis of the process by which problems are resolved in all political systems. If we are to consider the ways in which institutions and procedures help this process to occur, we need to distinguish between the various *subfunctions* or *suboperations* that take place. In this task, political scientists have been markedly helped by the work of Gabriel Almond, who, on the basis of Easton's work, described these suboperations under five headings.[3]

Two of these operations are conducted on the input side of the political system. The first, which was called *articulation* by Almond but might perhaps more aptly be called *selection,* is the process by which problems are, so to speak, chosen by the political system. Only a fraction of the desires and hopes of the citizens of the polity will become problems at a given moment, though we can expect these matters to be more numerous if the polity is fairly open; we can also imagine, without being overtly cynical, that in some political systems efforts will be made to depress the level of demands through efforts made by the leaders of the political system, for instance by propaganda. Independent of these

---

[3] Almond and Powell, *Comparative Politics,* p. 29.

conscious activities, desires and hopes will be repressed by members of the polity through the weight of the culture under which they live. This is why political scientists have become increasingly interested in questions of political socialization, and in particular in the political socialization of the young, since the ideas and hopes of young people will be at the root of demands that will be made on the polity at a future point in time.[4]

The second operation that occurs at the level of inputs is *combination,* or "aggregation" in Almond's terminology. Demands made by an individual or group of individuals will often be in competition or at least at some variance with the demands of others, so a process will be needed by which these demands become coordinated or compromised. It seems fairly logical to suggest that, at least in the large majority of cases, demands will become pressing only if made in association with other demands. The function or operation of combination is thus as important and as natural and general as the function or operation of selection.

On the output side of the political system, Almond described three operations or functions, but the distinction has sometimes been criticized as paralleling too closely that existing in the constitutional arrangements of Western Europe and North America. These are the functions of rule-making, rule-implementing, and rule-adjudicating. In reality these three operations can be deduced logically from the nature of the over-all operation of the political system, if we follow the problems raised by ouputs from their conception to their final implementation.

We noted already that there is some ambiguity in the word "decision": While it is agreed that the political system is concerned with the making of decisions, these can be viewed merely as the expression of authoritative rules that are universally applicable (at least potentially) or as the effective action that takes place as a result of these rules. It is clear that it is not sufficient for a rule merely to be stated for it to have an impact on the polity; but it is also clear that the fact of deciding on a general rule, whether it is implemented or not, is of some importance.

---

4 See, in particular, Fred I. Greenstein, *Children and Politics* (New Haven: Yale University Press, 1965), and David Easton and Jack Dennis, *Children and the Political System* (New York: McGraw-Hill, 1969).

Thus it is natural to distinguish between *rule-making* and *rule-application* and to view these two aspects of the over-all operation of decision-making as conceptually distinct, even if there may be cases when these two operations follow each other immediately. As we shall have occasion to notice later, the distinction is difficult to draw in practice and is often a question more of degree than of kind.

Indeed, the distinction should be viewed in relation to two dimensions according to which decisions can be classified, one ranging from general to particular, the other ranging from normative arrangements, relating to principles, to arrangements aimed at handling, somewhat technically, a special situation. Rule-making is concerned with questions that are both highly normative and truly general, while rule-application is concerned with a series of matters that tend to be both less normative and more particular. If we draw a diagram on which the two dimensions are represented (Diagram 1), rule-application will tend to occupy a corridor ranging from relatively general and normative questions to highly particular and behavioral matters. However, while decisions on general matters always have a normative content, decisions on particular matters may also have a normative content. Hence a third type of operation of the political system (named rule-adjudication by Almond), which might be better termed double-checking, the point being to see whether a norm is indeed implemented in relation to a particular problem. Judges, for instance, tend to look at the extent to which a particular decision follows the normative rules previously adopted in the polity. This is not implementation in the strict sense; judges do not deduce a more specialized rule by looking at the sequence linking the general to the particular; they examine one particular action and see whether it does properly relate to a general rule. This gives rule-adjudication a double-checking aspect, which is much more specific in character than rule-implementation.

Rule-adjudication is truly at the border between inputs and outputs, however, and it can also be seen as one of the elements of the feedback process. It would therefore be incorrect to believe that rule-adjudication exists only where the political system allows for it. Like the other operations we have described, rule-

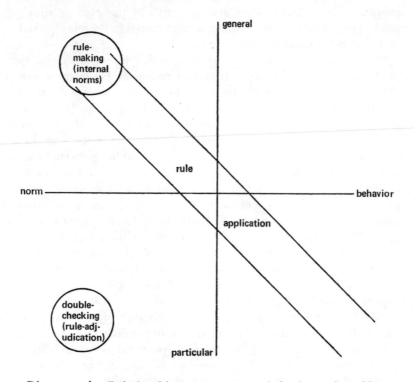

Diagram   1   Relationship among norms, behavior, rule-making,
rule-implementation, and rule-adjudication.

adjudication exists in all political systems, but, also like other
operations, it exists to a different extent in different political
systems. We noted the point specifically in relation to the selection
operation, but it can be made for all operations. Because it was
not specifically stated, at least in the earlier versions of Almond's
analysis, that the extent to which these operations are carried out
can vary, much criticism occurred about the generality of the
model he suggested. One way of measuring, or at least noting in
a somewhat impressionistic fashion, the extent to which these
functions are carried out is by referring to the capability of the
political system, though capability should not be seen merely in
terms of the extent to which the system *is able* to process inputs
(because of the size of the "machine," to use an analogy with a

computer, for instance) but also in terms of the *bias* by which
some types of rules will be made, implemented or double-checked
better or more quickly than others.[5]

One element that plays a large part in developing the capacity
of the political system, as well as in developing biases by which
the system "listens" more to some hopes and desires than to
others, is the communication system. Communication has sometimes been viewed as an operation or function of the system.
More truthfully, Almond came to conclude, it was not a function
but the general means by which inputs came to be converted into
outputs, and outputs came to be implemented and in turn led to
further outputs.[6] The nature of the communication system in a
given polity is highly indicative—though up to now only im-
pressionistically—of the types of biases that characterize a system.
It has to be seen in terms of all the media existing in the polity,
in particular in terms of both private and public communication.
In more traditional societies, for example, communication tends
to be private, in that information about decisions as well as
inputs occurs through personal discussions; the capacity of the
system to process inputs appears to be relatively small, and selection will be very narrow. Where means of public communication
are numerous, there may be greater opportunities for citizens to
press demands on the political system; but as there may be more
inputs, the effect on the combination mechanism may be such
that the proportion of these inputs which is processed is not
necessarily larger. Moreover, the leaders of the political system
may feel in a better position to attempt to influence inputs by
generating decisions that affect the selective mechanism: Propaganda (in particular through the mass media) is often aimed at
affecting the *socialization* process and in turn the nature of the
inputs into the political system. The problem does not stop here,
as the propaganda issued through means of public communication will be effective only if it corresponds, at least in part, to the
attitudes and habits of the population; if not, communication
may not occur at all. The propaganda may not affect the population because of some lack of understanding. One can thus define a maximum amount of influence that leaders of the political

5 Almond and Powell, *Comparative Politics,* Chapter 8, pp. 190–212.
6 *Ibid.,* Chapter 7, pp. 164–89.

system can have—a point (noted empirically) where the effects of propaganda are seen in the long run to be generally smaller than originally hoped for by supporters and feared by opponents of the regimes using it.

There are, therefore, a number of general operations of all political systems. We have begun to notice that the extent to which these operations are fulfilled depends on the views and norms of leaders and citizens: Selection may be more or less narrow; outputs may or may not attempt to modify views. We shall have to consider these norms, but before doing so we need to see how these operations or functions are implemented in different political systems through the numerous structures, and particularly institutions, that exist, since we can expect structures to be the means by which norms are translated into decisions and by which the effort is made to reduce conflict levels and thereby maintain the political systems.

Structures and Operations

When we describe the institutions of, for instance, the American federal government, we tend first to describe a number of structures of a constitutional character. As our description becomes more searching, we begin to see that in addition to the legislature, the executive, and the judiciary, we should also describe the political parties, the bureaucracy, and many interest groups such as trade unions and business lobbies. But these descriptions are not satisfactory, as we said at the outset of this book, because we need to know what each of these institutions, bodies, or structures does if we are to pass any meaningful judgments about them. We can see, then, in what way the need to relate structures to functions or operations occurs: If we are interested in groups, parties, legislatures, or the bureaucracy, one of the questions we shall have to answer is the extent to which these structures help to select and process demands. This is why structures are always described in terms of their "purpose" or "role," even in the context of individual country studies.

Almond's determination of these functions or operations was prompted by the specific desire to be truly comparative, because a general comparative analysis implies going beyond a mere description of structures without reference to operations. Ethiopia does not have political parties, nor does Saudi Arabia; the interest groups that prevail in such countries as the United States or the United Kingdom are absent in other countries, though groups of some kind do always exist. Legislatures vary in influence and types of functions from one country to another, and in some polities (Saudi Arabia, for instance) there is no legislature. Comparisons on a worldwide basis, and even comparisons between countries with relatively similar structures, need to refer to operations or functions. The comparison may start from operations and lead to discovering the structures that perform these operations. It may start from the structures and lead to the examination of the operations these structures perform in different polities. But comparative analysis does require an examination of the relationship between structure and function.

It is difficult to discuss structures and functions without becoming involved in a debate over the philosophical purpose of such an analysis, however. The discussion of structural-functionalism that has taken place in other disciplines has spilled over into political science, largely because it was suggested or at least implied, somewhat unwisely and truly unscientifically, that some types of structure-function relationship were "better" in some way than others, and that countries displaying such and such a relationship were more "developed" than others. We shall see in the next chapter what can be said about the use of the concept of development in the field of politics. Clearly, only if it were proved that some particular type of structure-function relationship in fact leads to greater development would it be scientifically justifiable to suggest that there is anything "superior" in one type of relationship. Moreover, as we have already noted, the use of the word "function" has been unfortunate; it has led at times to an anthropomorphic view of the political system whereby structures help regimes to be maintained and prevent change from taking place. Political systems do not appear to have self-steering mechanisms of this kind. Some regimes are more stable than others, but many aspects of these regimes change in the midst of over-all stability. The reasons for the greater stability of some systems can be found in the interplay of some variables and in the types of structures and norms that characterize the system. There is no need to postulate that political systems have some propensity to maintain themselves or that the functions of the political system are directed at achieving a particular result. The functions or operations must simply be viewed as types of activities that are more or less fulfilled by different structures; the main value of discovering these activities is that we are then able to compare the structures, both cross-nationally and internally.

If we examine the polities of the contemporary world (and indeed, polities in the past) we can distinguish six broad types of structure, some of which do not exist everywhere and all of which have different characteristics from one polity to another, as we shall become increasingly aware in the course of this book. First, there are *groups,* which range from bodies of a general and even all-embracing type, such as religious or tribal organizations, to small organizations with very specific aims, such as environmental pressure groups. Some polities are more likely to generate broad and far-reaching groups, while others are characterized by narrow-gauge interest groups, but all polities have groups of one form or another. As we shall see in Chapter 5, all of these groups are, to a varying degree, involved in politics. Second, there are political *parties,* which do not exist everywhere but have become increasingly common in the course of the last hundred years (though not a creation of the contemporary period: Ancient Rome and Renaissance Italy had political parties). Moreover, even in countries that do not officially have parties, it is often possible to detect the existence of factions that have the characteristics of political parties. We shall discuss in Chapter 6 the question of the definition of political parties. It is sufficient for now to define them as bodies theoretically open to all that have policy aims covering the whole field of government and have the over-all purpose of achieving power.

Third, all countries have *executives,* or governments in the narrow sense, though the characteristics of these bodies of course vary widely from hereditary monarchs to elective presidents and from one-man to collective leadership. Fourth, executives have often to rely on the support, at least the passive support, of an *assembly,* though these bodies are not universal, at least if we consider assemblies in the precise constitutional sense. Assemblies

are indeed the constitutional body *par excellence:* The demand
for an assembly was one of the major demands of liberal reform-
ers in Europe in the eighteenth and nineteenth centuries; consequently, absolutist regimes—of which there are now very few—do
not have assemblies in this sense. But in practice assemblies have
varying powers, whatever the constitutional arrangements decree
about their status. Moreover, a truly comprehensive analysis
should include, along with assemblies in the constitutional sense,
those bodies which, though merely advisory, do in fact, even in
absolutist regimes, "represent" a section of the population and
pass on requests to the executive. In this sense, it is probable that
no regime has ever functioned without some form of assembly,
and informal assemblies should increasingly be taken into account in a truly comprehensive comparative analysis.

Fifth, all governments have a *bureaucracy,* national as well as
regional and local, and, within this bureaucracy in the broad
sense, there are almost everywhere *armed forces,* which have special characteristics and which, as is well known, often play a large
part in the making and unmaking of governments. Although
these structures are created as part of the governmental machine,
in the long run, they often acquire an *esprit de corps,* an internal
unity of a social or even ideological character, which makes them
somewhat similar to groups in much of their outlook. Sixth, also
in every polity, but organized in different ways and with varying
strength and influence, there are *judiciaries,* which play an important part in a number of aspects of the political system. The
judiciaries must be distinguished from the bureaucracy, at least
in principle, even though their functions, to which we are now
coming, may not always be distinguishable in practice.

The examination of operations or functions can help markedly
in the examination of structures. Progress in comparative analysis will increasingly demonstrate the role of this structure-function
relationship. Ideally, and if comparative government theory was
truly advanced, one could relate structures to functions in a rigorous fashion and thus "define" a country by the precise way in
which a particular function is fulfilled through given structures.
The idea was first suggested by Almond in 1960 in *The Politics
of the Developing Areas,* when he mentioned the possibility of a

"probabilistic theory of the polity."[7] Even though such a precise definition is not obtained yet, we can at least note, first, that it is very likely that the same structures will fulfill different functions in different countries and, second, that a given function or operation will be fulfilled in a given country by more than one structure. For instance, both socio-economic groups and political parties can be engaged in the operation of selection and in the operation of combination; the bureaucracy may be involved in selecting demands in one country while political parties are more likely to do so in another.

Criticisms leveled at the type of structure-function relationship that emerges from Almond's analysis stemmed from the implication that, in some ideal fashion, some structures were better suited to fulfill some functions. It can be seen that a simple scheme would link structures and functions in the following way:

Functions	*Structures*
Inputs:	
Selection	Groups (socio-economic)
Combination	Political parties
Outputs:	
General and norms (rule-making)	Assemblies and councils
Particular decisions (rule-implementation)	Executives, bureaucracies
Particular and norms (rule-adjudication)	Judiciaries

Such a vision of the relationship seems to be biased in favor of Western states, in large part because the constitutional arrangements of these states are often based on the notion that the three output operations are to be performed by assemblies, executives, and judiciaries, respectively. Yet in practice not even Western

[7] Gabriel A. Almond and James S. Coleman, *The Politics of the Developing Areas* (Princeton, N.J.: Princeton University Press, 1960), Introduction, pp. 58–64.

polities can be described adequately on the basis of this model. Executives make many general rules; bureaucracies are involved in selection and combination as well as rule-implementation. It is probably true that other polities are even more likely to show different configurations of structure-function relationships, particularly those involving political parties and bureaucracies. A party such as the Communist party of the Soviet Union, for example, is involved in the implementation of decisions and in double-checking (rule-adjudication) as much perhaps as in the combination of demands, though it is concerned with that as well.

Two points can be made, however, that are of some practical importance, at least until a more exact probabilistic theory of the polity is devised. The first concerns the distinction between the input and output functions of a particular type of structure. It may be quite valuable to distinguish political parties in one country from those in another by the extent to which the former are more involved in, say, the input aspect of politics and the latter more involved in the output aspect. Though it is not possible to give a precise value to the extent to which input or output functions are performed, it is possible to note broad variations and, as we shall see, possible also to note some consequences from the standpoint of the structure and maintenance of these parties. The same could be said of other types of structures, for instance, groups and bureaucracies.

The second point relates to the problem of the extent to which structures have well-defined characteristics and can therefore be differentiated, as this may have some influence on the extent to which functions are performed. It seems to have been postulated by Almond that "modern" countries (and to some extent the idea of development has been based on this idea) had more well-defined structures (a greater degree of differentiation) than developing and traditional countries.[8] As political parties do not exist everywhere, it can be argued that the presence of parties increases this differentiation; because the bureaucracy of traditional countries is much smaller than that of industrial countries, there, too, is an element of greater differentiation in the latter. But Almond's suggestion went further: It postulated that modernization led to a differentiation of the structures along the functional lines

8 Almond and Powell, *Comparative Politics*, pp. 213–18.

mentioned earlier; this has not been proved, nor is it even supported by much empirical evidence. Moreover, differentiation should be considered jointly with the question of the extent to which a particular function is fulfilled. Is selection less narrow, for instance, if socio-economic groupings are in charge of the selection process, or do the demands and hopes of the population have better representation if political parties or the bureaucrats participate in the selection process? In relating structures to functions or in analyzing the extent to which some structures fulfill some functions, we should examine, therefore, the extent to which, over all, the system allows for a particular function to be more fully implemented and for problems to be solved more rapidly and more adequately for the polity as a whole.

The problem of the relationship between structures and functions thus poses ultimately the question of the *efficiency* of political systems—a problem that has scarcely been tackled at all and that seems almost intractable, because the parameters and variables are numerous and ill-defined. On the surface, a system would seem to be more efficient (not necessarily effective, as we shall see later) if, for a given set of demands, it succeeds in achieving a decision and implementing it as quickly as possible and with the greatest economy of resources in cost and manpower, as well as with the least political tension and conflict. It is not efficient to take a decision that leads to civil war unless it can be proved that, in the circumstances of tension in the polity, civil war was unavoidable. Measurement of the efficiency of political systems needs to be achieved, for it is often noted that a particular polity or government is, in common parlance, unable to do what another system is presumed able to do. But, for the time being, such a measurement is unlikely. We should therefore be very careful in comparing political systems on this basis, especially because increased demands in a particular system will have the immediately apparent effect of reducing the system's efficiency, which leaves us with the consequent paradox that the most efficient political system would be one in which no demands at all were made!

The analysis of structures and functions provides a general configuration of political systems that makes comparisons possible in principle, even if these comparisons in many cases must at this stage remain somewhat impressionistic. Without this instrument, it would be impossible even to begin to give some reality to the claim of a systematic examination of political systems. This is why we shall concentrate on the characteristics of structures and on the functions they perform in the bulk of the second part of this book. But, although there is a relationship between structures and operations, there is also a relationship between structures and norms: Some structures have been expressly created in order to implement some norms (for instance, such constitutional structures as assemblies); other structures emerge differently. In all cases, however, they correspond to some norms. Thus different types of structural configurations clearly correspond to different types of normative standpoints. We need therefore to turn to norms and to see how they can be classified in order to find how they might suggest distinctions between types of political systems.

3

The Norms of Political Systems

In all political systems, leaders holding certain values, or norms, act in order to achieve the policies they believe (or at least feel) to be the *best* policies in the circumstances. The norms are related to the policies, even if the relationship is not always clear and direct. A close examination of the behavior of leaders would make it possible to deduce the values, policy goals, or norms they uphold. In the same way, one could discover the norms and policy goals of various sections of the population, even if they are often held unconsciously or are disguised or concealed. The problem is not that norms or goals cannot be found if one wants to find them; it is that the instruments by which to measure them and their impact on policy are difficult to devise. Such measurement requires in the first place a classification of all possible types of norms. This classification is complex: For instance, some leaders may wish to achieve "progress" autocratically, some leaders may be more "tolerant" than others, "progress" may mean different things in different polities, and so forth.

In all these cases, two elements seem of paramount importance. First, a number of different types of norms can be held jointly or separately. One should therefore distinguish among *fields* or *areas* of norms, such as the area of tolerance, the area of progress, and so on: Second, the areas can be ordered in terms of "more or less": Leaders may be more or less tolerant, more or less autocratic. By taking these two points together, one comes to the idea of separate normative *dimensions* that can be discovered. Once this is done, we shall need to see how to measure concretely the norms of a given political system and, then, how to compare political systems and the impact of norms on these systems.

The Dimensions of Norms and Policy Goals of Political Systems

Norms and policy goals are closely related. Norms are the general values on the basis of which reactions to events occur; goals are the aims—ultimate or intermediate—on the basis of which action takes place. In practice some goals may become impossible because some norms are held, in which case the contradiction will have to be resolved in some fashion. But both norms and goals express the general vision individuals have (consciously and clearly or not) of what the "good life" should be. To that extent they can be examined together.

It is possible to consider the norms and goals of individuals and, by some form of extrapolation, of collections of individuals, hence of groups such as parties or of a political system. Two qualifications have to be made, however: (1) In all cases, norms and goals are considered at one point in time; changes can and do occur, and one of the important problems of political analysis is precisely to see under what conditions these norms and goals may come to change. This is true of individuals, but it is of course truer of collections of individuals and of groups. (2) The norms and goals of a political system, for instance, or of a political party can be discovered only by reference to either an *average* or some subgroup of individuals who are deemed to play a major part in the decision-making process. Thus the norms of a political system correspond to the norms of the members of this political system, or, if only a segment of the population is found to play a part, of the norms of that segment. Yet one can easily see that there might be conflict between the norms of one important subgroup, such as the leadership group, and those of the "average" population. Whereas we shall be discussing here the ways in which the norms of political systems can be analyzed and the ways in which political systems can be classified as a result, we shall have to see later the effect that clashes over norms between the leaders and the led may have on the characteristics of the political system. This is the purpose of the following chapter.

The first step is to try to discover the dimensions according to which the norms of political systems, groups, or individuals can be ordered and classified. These dimensions can be found if we list the main types of questions that political activity raises, that is, the questions that can be asked about a decision relating to a community. There are three such questions: Who took the decision? In what way was it taken? What was it about? If we extrapolate from one decision to a whole series of decisions taken by a group or a political system, the same questions arise: Who were the participants in these decisions? What was the process of decision-making? What were the purposes of these decisions? These three questions help to identify three broad dimensions of analysis that we need to examine in turn, the question of participation, the question of the "means" of government, and the question of the "ideology" or purpose of decisions.

1. Participation: Democracy Versus Monarchy or Oligarchy

Participation is the first dimension to come to mind when considering the process of decision-making in any group, and in particular in a polity. It is also by all accounts the easiest to analyze and even to "operationalize." Clearly, it is an important dimension, and it is distinct from the content of a decision and even the procedure by which it is prepared. One can also easily see that there are two extremes: full *democracy*, which means (as Rousseau suggested) that *all* participate in the decision or decisions considered, and full *monarchy* (or strictly, "monocracy"), where only one member of the group or polity decides. We can readily pose that neither extreme is in fact real, at least for a polity of any size, both full monocracy and full democracy being technically impossible. We are therefore confronted in practice with various degrees of *oligarchy*.

The operationalization of this dimension raises difficulties, but some rough indicators can at least be suggested. Clearly it is not sufficient to take into account percentages of voters in a polity, for instance, to determine the extent to which that polity is democratic. Voting is only the final stage of a series of preliminary decisions. Voters usually play little or no part in the selection of candidates for election, and they play an even smaller part in the determination of the party programs on which elections are fought. Realistic indicators should therefore take into account not only numbers participating at the final stage but also numbers participating at various intermediate stages of the decision process. Alternatively, one could examine the major decisions taken by a group or a polity over a period of time and determine the numbers of persons involved in making them. The time spent by individuals is an important indicator, as it constitutes, at least ostensibly, a measure of the extent to which these individuals participated in the various segments of the decision.

2. MEANS OF GOVERNMENT: LIBERALISM VERSUS AUTHORITARIANISM

Decisions may be taken after long discussions, involving all aspects of a problem; alternatively they may follow very quickly the initial stage of selection. Moreover, perhaps more importantly, some decisions may not be taken because the problem is not discussed or is not allowed to be discussed. Hence a dimension of means, which relates to the common contrast between an authoritarian approach and a liberal approach to decision-making. Here, too, however, the distinction has a continuous character. The political system (or any group) may be *more or less* liberal, that is to say open with respect to the discussion of problems. Opposition may be restricted to a limited number of questions or to a limited area of each question. Pressure toward conformity may arise from strict rules and blatant imposition, or it may be the result of more subtle action, stemming in particular from the socialization process of all generations, especially the young.

It is clear that measurement of the degree of liberalism in the polity is more difficult and therefore more imprecise than measurement of the degree of democracy. One common index of liberalism is the existence of an institutionalized opposition; another is the existence of freedoms, such as freedom of movement (especially in and out of the country), freedom to print, to demonstrate, and so on. But the boundaries of effective liberalism are of course often very different from the boundaries of "legal" liberalism: newspapers may not be prepared to be critical for fear of possible reprisals; there may be *de facto* arrangements between leaders of various opposing groups and parties by which some problems are kept under cover and find little expression.

3. THE PURPOSE OF GOVERNMENT: THE NOTION OF IDEOLOGY

The norms and goals of leaders and led, and of the political system as a whole, relate also (some might say primarily) to the purpose of government. What is to be achieved? Is there to be change in the polity and, if so, in what directions? The question is difficult, as the political system might be confronted with a large, if not an infinite, number of problems. Moreover, the study of policies, which proceed from goals, and of ideology might be viewed as going beyond the study of comparative government, in particular of governmental systems, with which we are concerned in this book. Political activity refers to the decision-making process, and the political system is concerned with the structures that help these decisions to be taken. The content of decisions has often appeared to be a matter for economists and sociologists, not for political scientists, whose concern is with the framework within which policies are decided.

Though we cannot of course consider the content of policies in much detail, the general direction of policies—the goals of the government—are of considerable importance in shaping the character of the political system. This is so because no government is ever constituted irrespective of its policy goals. Proponents of universal suffrage and of democracy do not press for greater participation in the polity merely for the sake of participation; they press for it in the hope that, as a result, new legislation might be passed that will benefit, for instance, manual workers or other underprivileged groups. Those who oppose universal suffrage often do so precisely in order to avoid these legislative changes. Many further examples suggest themselves in which participation or means of government are related to policy goals. Thus, policy goals can affect markedly the behavior of leaders and of citizens in relation to other norms.

The problem that immediately arises, however, is that of the way in which these policy goals can be ordered. On each issue, one can see that participation, means of government, and aims of policies constitute the three dimensions that account for the shaping of the views. But it would be impossible in practice to classify political systems if we had to be concerned with an almost infinite number of aims relating to each issue, to each social, economic, or cultural problem. We can simplify the analysis markedly, however, if we note that, in contemporary societies, policy goals are united—or very nearly united—through the part played by ideologies relating to socio-economic questions. In a broad fashion, it is possible to distinguish between views that tend to promote greater social and economic equality among the citizens and those opposed to such equality. We shall use the words conservatism and radicalism to refer to this distinction. The ideology may be tightly knit, as is Marxist ideology, or it may be more "pragmatic," but the distinction does remain. To be sure, political life is concerned with a variety of problems that may be said to be only loosely connected with the question of the more or less even distribution of social and economic benefits. Cultural questions and racial oppositions are in part (though only in part) divorced from social and economic matters.

Yet, over all, the *dimension* of more or less inequality in the distribution of social and economic benefits (in our terms, more conservatism or more radicalism) is unquestionably predominant in the large majority of the important political questions of contemporary societies. Indeed, the difficulty is perhaps something else: The dimension of policy goals relates to goals, and not achievements alone. The political system is likely to be affected not only by what has been achieved in the polity but also by the rate at which these achievements are taking place and by the aims of leaders and citizens for the future. Clearly, goals and ideology must be real goals and real ideology. There must be some movement in the direction of these goals, for otherwise they will not be recognized as goals in the long run. Expectations and their relationship to realizations are at the root of the dimension of policy goals.

Though we can thus identify the dimension of policy goals, the operationalization of the dimension is more difficult than in the cases of participation and means of government. Political scientists will have to rely on approximate measurements derived from the postures of leaders, attitudes of citizens, and from somewhat impressionistic comparisons between countries and organizations. But it is at least possible in principle to locate leaders, groups, or bodies of citizens on a continuum ranging from full conservatism (which at the limit would place all socio-economic benefits in the hands of one man) to full radicalism (which, again at the limit, would mean a "perfectly" even distribution of social and economic benefits, a difficult concept to visualize in theory). Groups and individuals who tend to be located toward the middle of this continuum will be defined as "center," a term used commonly in political parlance to refer to leaders and groups that aim at a "happy medium" between full inequality and perfect equality.

The distinction between "conservatism" and "radicalism" overlaps, but is not wholly coextensive with, the notion of socio-economic *development,* which refers more to the *amount* of economic goods and social services that exist in a polity than to their *distribution.* We cannot discuss here the empirical relationship between amount and distribution, but many leaders of the contemporary world take the view that equality can be realized only when "plenty" has been reached, with the result that populations are expected to hope for a better distribution of benefits as a consequence of socio-economic development. We shall therefore use goals of socio-economic development as one of the indicators of the goal of "greater social and economic equality" and a tendency toward radicalism.

The Classification of Groups, Parties, and Political Systems

Men naturally tend to classify political systems, as they classify political leaders and groups, according to the norms and goals they profess and implement. Ever since the early beginnings of political science, and in particular ever since Aristotle, efforts have been made to arrive at a sound classification. Even if the efforts have not always been successful, the failures as well as the achievements have often been quite revealing.

Failures have tended to be of two types. First, many classifications of political systems (or groups) have been partial, that is, they have mainly or exclusively taken into account one or two only of the dimensions of norms. This is particularly true of the classifications that can be labeled "constitutionalist," devised in eighteenth- and nineteenth-century Europe under the influence of Locke and Montesquieu.[1] It is well known that political systems are often divided into parliamentary and presidential, as well as dictatorial (though constitutional lawyers sometimes prefer a division into separation-of-powers, parliamentary, and convention governments—a distinction we shall find again in Chapter 7). Such a classification does not take into account the content of policies; indeed, it scarcely even takes into account the extent of participation. It concentrates instead on the opposition between authoritarian and liberal regimes and on subdivisions among liberal regimes. It was as if, for such thinkers, despotic regimes were a thing of the past that characterized primitive polities; no attention had to be paid to them, any more than economists need to pay attention to primitive economies in studying economic systems. This view certainly does not appear empirically warranted, nor is it logically acceptable in view of the importance of policy goals and participation in the norms of government.

The second type of failure is the tradition of dichotomies or trichotomies. Until recently, classifications of political systems have always been of this type. Even a classification such as Aristotle's, the oldest of all and the most comprehensive, in that it takes into account policy goals and participation, remains unsatisfactory because it appears not to recognize that systems can be *more or less* oligarchical, liberal, or radical.[2] Only when the idea of a number of continuous dimensions began to emerge, in part through the work of Dahl and Almond, did classificatory schemes become flexible enough to take into account the many variations

[1] For a presentation, see Douglas V. Verney, *The Analysis of Political Systems* (New York: Humanities Press, 1960; London: Routledge & Kegan Paul, 1959), Part I, pp. 17–93; see also Gwendolen M. Carter and John H. Herz, *Government and Politics in the Twentieth Century* (New York: Praeger Publishers, 1965), pp. 28–63.

[2] Aristotle, *Politics*, Book 3, Chapter 7.

The Norms of Political Systems 39

in norms that exist along these dimensions and the interplay between positions on these dimensions.[3]

If we return to the three dimensions of norms we have identified in this chapter, we can see that political systems can be classified according to them, that a truly infinite number of positions is allowed for, and that variations, for instance, over time, may occur along one, two, or three of the "axes" that represent these dimensions. The questions facing political scientists are thus: First, is it possible to locate each political system, party leader, and so forth at a particular point on the basis of the means of operationalization that we have? Second, what relationship, if any, is there between positions occupied on these three axes? Can one expect that movements over time along one of the axes will have an effect on the positions occupied along the others? For instance, if a regime becomes more liberal, is it also likely to become more democratic or more radical?

Improvements in operationalization will occur gradually, but, as we noted in the previous section, we have some means of locating leaders, parties, or political systems on each of these axes. It should be noted that the location of a body has only to be relative to the location of others. But because the operationalization is imprecise, we should not try at this stage to embark on distinctions that are overrefined. Consequently, for practical reasons in part, we shall discuss political systems as if they belonged to broad types, this "typology" being based on broad similarity, not on identity.

This question deserves to be increasingly studied, however, as the existence of *types* of political systems has a direct bearing on the problem of the dynamic relationship between positions occupied by a system on the three axes. Let us examine the two extreme opposite possibilities. On the one hand, it could be that political systems, political parties, or leaders are distributed at random in the three-dimensional space corresponding to the three types of norms. This would mean that no one position in relation to one axis (for instance, the axis of participation) is likely to be related to a position on another axis (for instance, the axis of liberalism): Relatively democratic countries could be

[3] Almond and Powell, *Comparative Politics*, and Robert A. Dahl, *Modern Political Analysis* (Englewood Cliffs, N.J.: Prentice-Hall, 1963), pp. 14–38.

very authoritarian, very liberal, or occupy intermediate positions. It would follow that a change of position on one axis would be unlikely to have an effect on the other axes. There would be no grounds for predicting *a priori* that some particular change would occur at the next point in time. If, on the other hand, we find that political systems (or parties or leaders) tend to cluster at particular positions in the three-dimensional space, the converse becomes true: A position on the axis of participation would tend to correspond to a position, or a small number of positions, on the axis of liberalism or on the axis of ideology, for instance; it would follow that a change occurring at one point in time

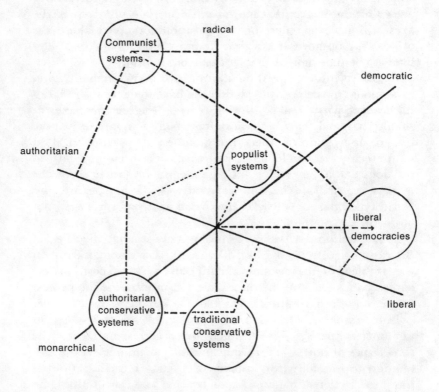

Diagram   2   The three dimensions of norms.

along one axis would make changes likely at subsequent points in time on the other axes.

The limited amount of empirical information at our disposal seems to suggest that such clusters exist in the contemporary world and indeed have existed in the past—a further reason why we shall examine types of political systems in the third part of this book. If we oversimplify the distinction somewhat and give the *ideal-type* characteristics of these political systems, we find five forms of broad normative arrangements into which the polities of the contemporary world appear to fall.

1. Some countries, which can be termed *liberal democracies,* are characterized by an emphasis on liberalism in public decision-making. Perhaps not all problems are discussed fully, and the socialization process also plays a part in selecting some ideas over others. But liberalism, based on the constitutionalist principles elaborated by Locke and Montesquieu, has "priority." Early in the nineteenth century, participation remained low, but since the twentieth century began a democratization process has taken place in these countries, and they are therefore located fairly near the liberal and democratic ends of the two axes of means and participation. Meanwhile, only a limited stress has been placed on greater equality in the distribution of social and economic benefits; endeavors toward this goal have tended to be slow and "pragmatic." These countries should therefore be located toward the middle point of the dimension of policy goals.

2. It is interesting to contrast Communist systems with liberal democracies with respect to the three dimensions of norms. In Communist systems, priority is placed on equality of social benefits and, secondarily, on participation of the whole population (though with limited effect, since the Communist party has a special role to play in these polities). On the other hand, very little stress is placed on liberal means. In recent years, a small amount of liberalization has taken place, but the extent of discussion of over-all goals remains narrow. Communist polities should therefore be located at the radical end of the conservative-radical axis and toward the authoritarian end of the authoritarian-liberal axis. They are *radical authoritarian* systems; as

participation is large (seemingly no smaller than in liberal democracies), both liberal democracies and Communist systems should be placed about the same distance from the democratic end of the democratic-oligarchic continuum.

3. A third type of political system, very common in the past though less frequently represented in the contemporary world, is the *traditional* polity. This is usually ruled oligarchically and is conservative, as the distribution of social and economic benefits is typically very uneven (although the over-all amount to distribute may be relatively small, the rich are often as rich as some of the wealthiest elements in more economically advanced countries). The goal is not redistribution; it is on the contrary maintenance of the *status quo* of social and economic inequality. Traditional polities are more difficult to locate on the liberal-authoritarian continuum. They appear authoritarian when considered from the outside; pluralism is limited and disagreements are few. But the pressure to conform is internalized through the weight of tradition on members of the polity, and the real extent of authoritarianism may therefore be low, much lower, for instance, than in Communist radical authoritarian systems, precisely because the latter have had to break tradition. As long as there is no challenge to the system, traditional polities may not need to be authoritarian; they remain "paternalistic" and occupy a position a considerable distance from the authoritarian end of the liberal-authoritarian dimension.

4. We come therefore to systems that in the postwar period have been called developing polities, largely because they have attempted (though in different ways from Communist systems, in the main) to pursue goals of greater equality of social and economic benefits, either directly or through an increase in the absolute amount of goods to be distributed (as we indicated at the end of the previous section). Like Communist systems, developing systems lay less stress on the position to be occupied on the other two axes, though there is some emphasis on participation. Developing polities are in any case farther away from the monarchical or oligarchic end of the participation continuum than are traditional systems. They may be, on the other hand, fairly authoritarian, as authoritarian means may be required to achieve greater equality. These *populist* systems are therefore character-

ized by a relatively democratic form of government, authoritarian means, and policy goals that are "center," rather than radical or conservative, the objectives and realizations being a less uneven distribution of social and economic benefits (for instance through the redistribution of land and through industrialization) rather than full equality.

5. Where there is enough resistance to moves toward greater equality and greater participation (or even more liberalism), the polity may be ruled by a system that can be termed *authoritarian conservative*. The goal here is to maintain social and economic inequalities as in traditional systems, but the means may have to be more forceful. The same can happen if an effort is needed to prevent a liberal democratic system from "sliding" in the direction of radicalism. These regimes may therefore have as their primary goal the maintenance of policies as conservative as possible; positions on the participation and means axes seem to follow from these views on policy goals.

As we were describing the characteristics of these ideal types, we noted that some internal pressures—the logic of priorities, for instance—entailed that a position on one axis depended on a position on one or both of the other axes. This is true at a given moment in time; it is also true over time. It is of course difficult to do more than hypothesize the direction, much less the rate, of the changes, given the lack of adequate measurement of norms and policy goals. Yet such hypotheses have often been advanced in the past, for instance by historians wishing to explain the political evolution of a particular country. If we say that slow changes on the axis of liberalism lead to slow changes on the axis of participation, we are simply restating more generally a point that has repeatedly been made about the evolution of polities in the nineteenth century, for instance in Britain and, though less neatly, in other European countries. From the examination of these countries, it indeed seems possible to infer that, if rates of change in the direction of liberalism or of democracy are rather slow, the polity will tend to move fairly smoothly in both directions at the same time. The same evidence seems also to suggest that if, on the other hand, rates of change are rapid on one axis, demands will build quickly on the other axis and counter-pressures will follow. Similar relationships appear to exist between movements on the axes of means and of policy goals: If liberalism increases in a polity, demands for greater equality in the distribution of social and economic benefits emerge and a shift toward the radical end of the policy goals continuum takes place; however, demands for the maintenance of the *status quo* are also likely to emerge, and after a time, particularly if the shift toward radicalism is rapid and large, the system is likely to become authoritarian, in order either to maintain the radical achievements or to force a return to more conservative goals.

The difficulties of locating countries on the three dimensions are compounded by a need to measure rates of shifts over time, hence a need for more precise instruments than the ones we possess. The impressionistic evidence resulting from the evolution of European countries over the last hundred years and of Communist and Third World countries since World War II does seem to suggest that interconnected shifts do occur, whether we consider authoritarian reactions in Nazi Germany and Fascist Italy, the crises of "liberalization" in countries such as Czechoslovakia or Poland, or the apparent shifts between Right and Left in Latin American, Asian, or African states. What has to be noted, however, is that this analysis does not prejudice in any way the fundamental *causes* of movements that occur: We are not stating here that shifts toward greater equality are *due* to certain political leaders, to basic social forces, or to economic conditions. We are simply stating that, if a shift occurs on one axis and if it takes place at a given rate over a period, some consequences will occur on the other axes. This model is not "voluntaristic" in its approach, nor does it suggest that socio-economic forces are the only ones that account for changes in societies. Indeed, it does not even suggest an order in which the types of shifts occur: Movements may take place on the axis of participation either before or after movements on the axis of means—empirically, both situations seem to have occurred. As we noted, and as we shall see again in the coming chapters, major differences can be discovered if we remember that, on balance, in liberal democracies shifts on the axis of means have tended to take priority over shifts on the other axes, while the converse is true for many other systems, particularly for Communist and populist systems.

That is why we should avoid the expression "political development," which has been commonly, but very imprecisely, used in political science literature. Socio-economic development does have a clear meaning, but political development could only be meaningful if related to achievements, for instance, to what might be termed the "efficiency" of the political system (how much it processes, how many demands it turns into outputs, and so on). But we have noted already the conceptual difficulties relating to efficiency; a do-nothing system can appear quite efficient! Still, unless some objective element of this kind is used as a criterion there can be no agreement on the concept of political development. Labeling systems "more developed politically" because they are democratic or radical makes development dependent on the value standpoint of the observer. By using a three-dimensional framework of norms, we avoid giving seemingly objective preference to one system rather than another and thus avoid the insoluble difficulties in which proponents of the concept of political development have been immersed.[4]

By suggesting that the political systems of the contemporary world may be classified under five main types, we are simply noting that, on the available evidence, these are the types that appear to exist in the contemporary world. Indeed, there are variations within each type, as we shall find when we consider the types in greater detail in the third part of this book. We should expect such variations, since we are considering what are, in effect, five locations in a three-dimensional space; these types have not always existed in the past, the idea of development (of a socio-economic kind) being in large part the product of industrialization. There may therefore be different types in the future. Variations around the cluster points may also increase or decrease. One should not view these positions as equilibrium positions in a strong and permanent sense; they happen simply to be occupied by a large number of countries in the present.

[4] See Lucian W. Pye, *Aspects of Political Development* (Boston: Little, Brown, 1966), pp. 31–48, giving various definitions of "political development."

Different conditions in these countries may—indeed almost certainly will—change the positions occupied.

By examining norms and goals in this way, we can see both the importance of structures and the reasons why structural configurations are likely to vary from one type of system to another. Positions on the axis of means will affect the *selectiveness* of the system and will therefore lead to some groups being stronger or weaker, while the converse happens for other groups. Before going further and examining more closely the interplay between structures, we need to study the characteristics of these structures, which is what we shall do in the second part of this book. Yet one last general problem needs to be considered, and we have already referred to it in passing. This is the question of the likely consequence of vast conflicts over norms among members of the polity. We noted earlier that we could describe the norms of a political system or of a party by reference to those held by the citizens or by the leaders. But the result is likely to be different if the norms of the population and of the leaders cluster near the "average" or if conflicts are vast between citizens and leaders holding extreme positions. We can hypothesize that, in the latter case, serious difficulties will be encountered by leaders in pursuing their policies. We now turn to this problem by examining the legitimacy of political systems and the extent to which norms can be *imposed* on a divided population.

4

Legitimacy, Imposition, and the Question of Dictatorship

If norms can differ widely on a worldwide basis, they can differ also among members of the same polity; if they are in sharp conflict internally, tension is likely to arise and it seems reasonable to assume that, the greater the conflict over norms, the greater the tension. At the limit, tension may be such that civil war will occur, though civil war is not likely to solve the problem unless supporters of different normative standpoints can split geographically; if people holding very different norms are located territorially in the same areas, the outcome of armed conflict will have to be (barring mass murders or mass migration) subjection of one group by another.

Such a situation is likely to occur more frequently in a new than in an old country, as the very existence of a country for a long period entails that conflicts, especially conflicts over norms, are less intense. Yet new conflicts can arise if a new problem acquires some importance in the political system. Large-scale immigration can provide the basis for such new problems, as it has in the course of the history of human societies. The subjection of indigenous populations has often taken place. Change in norms

47

can also occur through what might be called the "immigration of ideas," whereby some members of a polity first come to be aware of and later endorse views and policy goals distinct from the population at large. It may be that values held traditionally, and thus quite passively, cease to be accepted and are reassessed and reviewed. The spread of education is one means by which this review can take place.

Sooner or later, developments of this kind tend to weaken the basis of the political system. The leaders of the polity, in particular, may find their decisions increasingly challenged. Indeed, support may come to be so low that the leaders, unable to run the polity, are easily ousted by opponents. Or else, the challengers, wishing to "quicken the pace of history," may succeed in replacing the traditional leaders by violent overthrow. In either situation—that of the decaying system where support is dwindling or that of the regime that comes to power suddenly and is confronted by supporters of the past—the problem of legitimacy arises as a major source of difficulty. A large extent of coercion upon the population might have to be invoked to maintain the system. We now turn to this problem in an attempt to see how legitimacy grows and decays, what forms of coercion need to be used, and, in particular, the nature of *dictatorships,* as regimes which use coercion have often been labeled.

The Concept of Legitimacy: Natural Support and Transfer of Support

Political leaders and political systems need support. Hence the concept of legitimacy is of primary importance if we are to understand why some political systems and leaders are more able to maintain themselves than others. But the notion of legitimacy has a wider application: It relates not only to political systems but also to any group that exists in a society. This is indeed important, in turn, for the political system, as the evolution of the support granted to groups may account for the maintenance of the political system and the legitimacy of the political system as a whole; more precisely, the legitimacy of the political system as a whole is intertwined with the legitimacy of the groups that exist in the polity.

Let us start by looking at this concept at a given point in time. Legitimacy can be defined as the extent to which the population accepts naturally, without questioning, the organization to which it belongs. However, as it is clear that the legitimacy of an organization or community relates in some fashion to its activities, an organization could be legitimate in relation to some matters and not legitimate in relation to others. Consequently, the broader the area of acceptance, the more legitimate the organization. These points apply to political systems as well as to other groups. Though the area of activity of political systems is very wide and generally recognized to be wide, it is not infinite. There are matters on which members of the polity will feel (at least in general) the polity should not act, and if it were to act in them the legitimacy of the system would be questioned, as in, for instance, matters of personal conduct. We shall have occasion to return to this point in the next chapter, when considering distinctions between groups.

It seems perfectly clear that legitimacy should not be conceived as dichotomous, or an "all-or-nothing" matter. There are, in fact, two ways in which it would seem possible to talk about the extent of legitimacy, or a "dimension" of legitimacy. One relates to the numbers of persons (or more precisely the percentage of the population) who support the political system or group. The greater this percentage, the more legitimate the political system or group would seem to be. The other relates to the intensity of support: Members of the political system or group may be very passive, almost neutral, or else intensely opposed or intensely in favor. When the two aspects are linked, it becomes conceivable (if in most cases impossible in practice) to measure the legitimacy of a group or political system by considering its weighted support minus the weighted "rejection." If the figure were near zero or even negative, the group would have no legitimacy and would be in considerable danger of not maintaining itself.

The measurement is not simple, however. The support given to a system for positive reasons may not necessarily be stronger than "unthinking" and "traditional" support. A system may be legitimate because members of the polity feel that it is realizing their expectations, for instance in relation to socio-economic development; but it may be no less legitimate if traditions are not questioned and are just accepted. There may not even be any awareness that alternative norms and goals could exist. The support for the system (or group, such as a tribe) can be very large in these circumstances, although it is not *positive* in the sense of resulting from choice. The situation is merely *normal*.

Whether the political system (or a group) has normal support or whether it fulfills the expectations of those who belong to it, levels of legitimacy can change over time, as the membership of the groups that support the system changes or as the intensity of the support changes. But, understandably, the loss of legitimacy is delayed, as the level of support enjoyed by a body at a particular moment in time helps it to maintain itself during the following period. Legitimacy should therefore be seen to embody changes in the *capital* of trust an organization has acquired in the past. Members of a political system (consciously or not) expect it to perform in the same way in the future as it has in the past. If its performance is viewed as either normal or positive, the capital of trust enjoyed by the organization will enable the system to maintain itself through rather difficult periods during which realizations are not as high or expectations are frustrated. Only after a time will the over-all capital of legitimacy of the political system or group begin to diminish; similarly, it will take time for this capital to be gradually rebuilt, even if the expectations are fulfilled after a period of disappointment. One can therefore see that a political system (or group) supported without question might not lose its capital of trust as easily or quickly as a system based on expectations; but it is also impossible to build normal or unquestioning support for a new polity or a new governmental system.

Increases and decreases in support for a group or a political system are not merely functions of the realization of expectations. One of the main ways by which support is gradually created is through the transfer of support from one group to another. In the political arena, we have noted, institutions are the means by which decisions are made and continuity is maintained. When institutions are created—that is, when a new association or sub-group is formed outside the political arena in the narrow sense —the support the new bodies enjoy depends almost exclusively on the support enjoyed by the bodies that helped to create them, which can be termed their "parent" bodies. The situation resembles the development of subsidiaries by a firm. Indeed, the reasons for creating a new group are often similar: Subsidiaries are created because a firm is too large to handle all the business from the center, or because the product being manufactured is of a special type, or because expansion abroad has created new legal requirements. Similarly, a new group or new institution may be created because a particular section of the community is to be catered to (as when a political party creates women's or young people's auxiliaries) or because social conditions in a country change (the church creates a political party because it finds it cannot intervene directly in politics any longer), or for

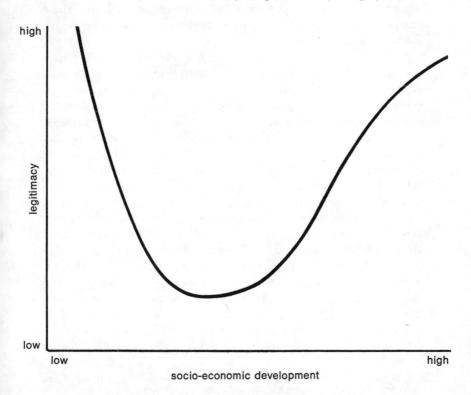

Diagram 3   Legitimacy and socio-economic development.

other such reasons. In cases of this kind the new organization has to rely on the parent body for support. In the first instance, the allegiance the new group gains passes through the parent body; in the second, members of a religion will vote for the religious political party not because of the political party but because the church says they should vote for it. The indirect support for organizations that can be deemed "dependent organizations" is one of the principal ways by which the legitimacy of groups is created and can change. Without it, new groups would be very difficult to start, the necessary capital of trust being at the outset quite small, and pressure from existing groups being very large. Gradually, dependent organizations acquire support of their own; the religious political party, for instance, may achieve results that in themselves satisfy the churchgoers. Slowly these organizations "become" legitimate, instead of owing their legitimacy to the support of others.

This type of development can occur also in relation to a political system or governmental system; indeed, it can occur in relation to a nation, though the magnitude of the support required makes failures much more likely than in connection with other groups. But some states have been built in this indirect fashion. Israel is perhaps the clearest case in the contemporary period, though many African states have developed around one major tribal organization, which acts as the intermediary for the development of support for the polity (the drawback, however, is that other tribes may not support the national unit and as a result may constitute an element of disloyalty, contributing to a drop in the level of legitimacy). It is not possible to examine here all the conditions under which states are likely to develop through the support of some large group, such as a tribe or a religious body. It is sufficient to note that it logically should happen (and does in fact happen) and that the conditions that must be fulfilled are such that it is unlikely to be successful except in a small number of cases and after a long period of time.[1]

Similar developments occur with respect to specific types of

[1] When comparing European states to developing nations, the difference in time scale must never be forgotten. It has taken centuries for many of the European countries to build their nationhood, and various internal and external crises have marred the history of all of them.

government. When there is conflict over norms between groups in a given polity, a group that wishes to achieve power will attempt to increase its legitimacy by "borrowing" support from groups having a large capital of legitimacy in the polity (as well as by trying to reduce the legitimacy of groups opposed to them). This, too, may be a very slow process whose success or failure will depend on the relative legitimacy of the groups that support and oppose the various political elements, be they parties, factions, etc. If a political faction that upholds policy goals of a progressive or radical character wants to maintain itself in power, for instance, it might find itself opposed by elements that base their support on tribes or religious organizations; and if such a radical political faction has support only among a very small segment, precisely because the norms it upholds are at considerable variance with the norms of the tribes, the maintenance of the radical group in power becomes problematic.

Legitimacy can therefore be transferred and is indeed commonly transferred from one group to another and from groups to the political system and vice versa. A similar process of transfer involves political leaders, as well as leaders of groups. Leaders quite commonly receive their support indirectly, through the support enjoyed by the groups they lead. Obedience to leaders is typically based on such an indirect transfer, a phenomenon so widespread that the point is seldom made. But the amount of support that is transferred in this way is often quite small, hence political leaders remain dependent on the political system or on a group for their legitimacy. If they cease to be leaders of the political system or of the group, they are no longer followed. However, the support transferred can sometimes be large, and leaders who benefit in this way are known as charismatic or "personalized." Members of the polity or group then support such leaders irrespective of their status and give allegiance to them alone.

A situation of this kind occurred commonly in polities of a feudal character, though of course there were also cases when allegiance to the leader was not truly personal. In the contemporary world, leaders who have achieved success in some particularly difficult situations, such as during a war or in the country's attainment of independence, may acquire a personal following, a greater following, in fact, than the state, the nation, or any political party might have. Indeed, allegiance to such leaders may be so great as to permit the converse of the usual process: The leader may find himself able to "build" a new group, a political party, or even a nation by attempting to transfer the support he has for himself to the group, party, or nation. Charismatic leaders have indeed helped to build nations. Washington was probably one of the first modern leaders to have this role, at least in part. In contemporary Asia and Africa, a similar process has taken place, often with markedly less success. Failures there have sometimes resembled that of Bolivar, who tried to build a "nation" over vast areas of South America.

Thus groups, parties, nations, and governmental systems can have two forms of legitimacy. One is the direct support of members of the group or polity based on tradition or expectations that have been realized. The other is indirect and is more a legitimization process than legitimacy in the strict sense. While the process takes place, the legitimacy of the dependent body is contingent on the continuing support of groups that are legitimate and on the maintenance of support for these parent groups among the whole population. In fact, by building a new group or a new party, the parent group is likely to lose some of its own capital of support. The new group has to be justified to, or impressed upon, supporters of the parent group. Any lapses in so doing will contribute to a decrease in the legitimacy capital of the parent group and thus will either prolong or encumber the process of legitimization.

However, both the groups, parties, or political systems that are legitimate and those in the process of legitimization can be said to develop in a natural fashion as long as, and to the extent that, opposition to the maintenance or continuation of the process is small. If a tribal organization becomes the nucleus of a new nation, if a religious organization creates a political party, if a political party creates a women's or youth auxiliary, these developments are "natural" if the parent bodies have considerable support and are not challenged, at least internally. If an internal challenge occurs, the process of legitimization may be prevented, and indeed the legitimacy capital of the parent group may decrease. The maintenance of the leadership of these bodies and, ultimately, the survival of the organization therefore become dependent on the use of various forms of compulsion—and the organization becomes "imposed" to a degree that varies in proportion to the extent of challenge within the organization.

We noted that political systems or groups were not legitimate to the same degree and that their legitimacy depended on the extent and intensity of the support they enjoyed. When opposition to the group or political system is widespread, the organization will not maintain itself unless it attempts to silence the opposition by coercion and, by doing so, to increase support for itself in the long run. These systems can be said to be imposed on the population. They occur when the level of support is low (for instance because the norms of the leaders are at considerable variance with the norms of the members of the polity, or because most of the legitimate groups are opposed to the leaders); their maintenance depends on the creation of a capital of support in the long run. Creating support can be very costly. The leaders of the political system are likely to attempt to increase their support more rapidly through operations of socialization, characteristically by the development of new groups and organizations that will be dependent on them but might, after a period, find some support in the polity. Clearly, there are limits to the extent to which a system that has little support can maintain itself. Where imposition is very pronounced, tension may well be strong, and the political system or regime may be constantly in danger of being overthrown. But, below this limit, it might be possible to build support in the long run while maintaining the regime in the short run through coercion. Hence the question of dictatorships and authoritarian rule in general, the recourse of leaders of political systems whose support is small but who hope in various ways to increase it.

Authoritarian and Liberal Government: Dictatorships and Their Spread

The examination of legitimacy has shown that time is one of the main requirements for building support for a political system or a group. There can be some shortcutting of the process if the political system or the group is dependent for a period on the

support another group enjoys; but even then the time requirements cannot altogether be abolished. Yet many studies of government have failed to give the time dimension its deserved
importance; indeed, the question of the build-up of legitimacy is
often ignored. The analysis of constitutional government which
developed in the eighteenth and nineteenth centuries apparently
rested on the assumption that populations would instantly support the norm of liberalism, that liberalism, once discovered,
would be adopted by all as a universal first priority. For eighteenth-century writers who propounded liberalism, despotism
was merely a mistake stemming from the ignorance of populations subjected to absolutist rulers. Once the curtain was lifted,
the virtues of constitutional rule would become universally recognized.

But, as the examination of norms in the previous chapter
showed, there is *a priori* no reason why individuals and political
leaders should give priority to liberal values rather than, for
instance, radical policy goals or democratic participation. If,
indeed, the expectations of a large part of a population give
achievements in the socio-economic field more importance, the
proponents of liberalism find themselves in a dilemma: Either
they will have to agree that liberal values must be shelved, or
they will have to impose liberalism on the polity on the assumption that in time the population will come to accept the new
values. Of course, in practice it is difficult if not impossible to
impose liberalism, a fact demonstrated by the experience of upholders of liberalism when confronted with political leaders
and/or large numbers of citizens whose main goals are socio-
economic development.

It has sometimes been implied that there is something natural
in the priority to be given to liberal goals; it has been argued
that political activity is mainly procedural, and that once all
have agreed on the procedures (liberal procedures) to be followed,
any kind of policy aims can be implemented. Thus, constitutionalists often allege that the establishment of a constitution should
have first priority in a new polity. But it has not always been sufficiently appreciated that this stand is profoundly normative.
Others might feel, on the contrary, that the establishment of a
constitution would slow the pace of change or that (as Marxists

have argued) basic socio-economic conditions have to be created before "true" liberalism can be instituted. These positions are as normative as those upheld by constitutionalist liberals, being based on the assumption that the preference for socio-economic achievements over liberal procedural rules is natural. They exist nonetheless, and their presence accounts for differences in priority scales among the members of a polity and raises anew the problem of imposition.

The analysis in the previous section showed that imposition should be distinguished from authoritarianism. If a system is "natural," if it has support among the population, possibly because of tradition and a lack of perceived alternatives, this system is not imposed. Yet it may be authoritarian, as have been many absolutist regimes in the past and as some traditional regimes of the type outlined in the previous chapter are still. A system is liberal if it allows for various forms of questioning and opposition. A population may very well "accept" naturally a system that does not allow for such questioning; it may indeed believe the situation that exists to be the only one that can exist. Clearly, if questioning and opposition begin to grow, the system will become gradually less natural and increasingly imposed. But as long as questioning does not occur and the population accepts the tenets of the system, it can be both quasi-authoritarian and natural. Thus, while it seems difficult for a system to be both truly liberal and imposed, authoritarianism can be, and is empirically in some cases, dissociated from imposition. It is when authoritarian systems *are* imposed that they are normally referred to as "dictatorships"; as there can obviously be degrees of imposition, regimes can be more or less dictatorial, one special and all-embracing form of dictatorship being referred to as "totalitarianism."

Factors Influencing Imposition and Dictatorial Government, and the Role of Socio-economic Conditions

Since legitimacy results from the convergence of the norms of the population as a whole with the norms of the government and political leaders (which may not be consciously felt), the tendency toward imposition will increase as the distance between the norms of leaders and the norms of the led grows. This may occur in two ways. The norms of the leaders may change while those of the population remain the same, or vice versa (because the leaders themselves change or, as we noted, because the population changes markedly through immigration). On the other hand, discontent in one form or another may occur as a result of changes in the norms or with respect to realization. This is why the activities of a government will affect legitimacy levels in the long run though over the short term the capital of trust enjoyed by the political system may maintain high levels of acceptance based on previous accomplishments. Moreover, in a liberal democratic system in which opposition is institutionalized, the unpopularity of a particular government may simply mean increased support for the opposition; the whole political system will be affected only if all the potential leaders of the government are equally unpopular and expectations about their potential achievements are low.

Because these factors affect legitimacy levels, socio-economic conditions can have, indirectly, a profound impact on the extent of imposition in a country. In traditional systems, expectations are likely to be relatively low; the population is accustomed to the *status quo* and does not hope for different arrangements. If the socio-economic conditions of the country do not change (if education remains the same, if the population remains distributed occupationally in the same way from generation to generation), legitimacy levels will not change and imposition will therefore tend to be relatively low. However, if changes in socio-economic conditions increase the number of members of the polity who become aware of other possible conditions and who start questioning traditional arrangements, levels of imposition are likely to increase. Thus, at least in a first stage, changes in socio-economic conditions are likely to affect levels of imposition and indeed to increase them. This is true whatever happens to the political system. The new norms that spread through some sections of the population will be opposed by those who continue to uphold the traditional values. It is therefore logical that imposed regimes, among them dictatorial regimes, should tend to be more common as socio-economic conditions create new expectations among some segments of the population. Even if the regime in power is sympathetic to the new norms or upholds them, its realizations are likely to fall short of the new expectations. The revolution of "rising expectations" will thus tend to increase discontent among the very people who hold these expectations.

As levels of socio-economic development increase beyond the take-off point, the amount of opposition stemming from upholders of the traditional system will decrease and the population as a whole will become accustomed to change in its socio-economic conditions. Moreover, though the matter is still in dispute and no final conclusion can be given at this stage, it seems at least permissible to hypothesize that the expectations of given populations are in part the consequence of realizations elsewhere. Thus the existence of rich countries, where the main problems have to do with a more equitable sharing among the whole population of a superabundance of commodities, seems in part to cause the expectations to rise in Third World polities. On the other hand, North American and (to a lesser extent) European populations have no model of a richer type of polity that they might expect to realize. While discontent is far from absent in these areas, it tends to be concentrated among minorities that are economically, geographically, or culturally underprivileged or among the young who have not yet been integrated into the system. The absence of better conditions elsewhere may therefore be one of the reasons why, in socio-economically developed polities, levels of acceptance and, hence, legitimacy are higher than in developing countries or in polities at the take-off stage.

Dictatorships are most likely to occur at intermediate stages of socio-economic development and are least likely to be found in either very traditional societies or countries that are economically advanced. This situation occurs in the contemporary world and can also be found in previous periods of history. One should expect levels of legitimacy to drop when changes in socio-economic conditions lead to a break in traditional patterns of allegiance and create conflicts between upholders of different norms. This was the case when Ancient Greece confronted the impact of commercial developments in the Mediterranean on the civilization of its "colonial cities," and again at the end of the Middle Ages, particularly in Renaissance Italy, when the traditional societies

were broken up by commercial developments.[2] Indeed, the contemporary situation is part of a century-long change beginning
with the Industrial Revolution, which has led to many forms of
dictatorship, first in Europe and later in the Third World. This
is not to say that all dictatorships arise from the same cause:
Alongside dictatorships that stem from socio-economic changes,
which can be termed "structural dictatorships," there are also
"technical dictatorships," which result from occupation, colonization, or other kinds of subjugation. Though these developments are not wholly "accidental," in that they arise from
differences in socio-economic development between two types of
powers, they are not the direct result of changing conditions in
one country alone. In fact, technical dictatorships are the result
of a form of imposition based on the force of a different political
system. They are therefore to some extent immune from the legitimacy problems that characterize "internal" or structural
dictatorships, though in the long run they, too, have to face the
question of support if they wish to rely on internal support as
well as outside might.

NORMS AND GOALS OF DICTATORSHIPS AND
THE TOOLS OF DICTATORIAL RULE

As we have repeatedly noted, imposed regimes arise from the
desire of one part of the population, and in particular the leaders, to maintain or bring about norms and goals that might not
otherwise prevail. Dictatorships can be imposed in order to pursue a variety of norms or policy goals—all types of norms, in fact,
except liberalism. Dictatorial governments thus can be of the
Right or of the Left. Because of the great variation possible in
policy goals, it would be interesting to know whether dictatorships
characterized by certain policy goals are more likely to occur in
certain circumstances. Given the relationship between socio-
economic development and the spread of dictatorships, are some
types of socio-economic development more likely to lead, for instance, to left-wing dictatorships than to right-wing dictatorships?

The empirical analysis of the situation in the contemporary

2 See M. Duverger, *De la dictature* (Paris: Julliard, 1961), for an incisive
analysis.

world is somewhat confused, although theoretically the elements of the problem are relatively simple. If we start from the premise that imposed governments, particularly dictatorships, will tend to occur as changes in norms and values come about through socio-economic development, and the further premise that expectations arise while realizations tend to fall short of these expectations, it follows generally that left-wing or radical dictatorships are likely to occur during the first stages of development, while right-wing or conservative dictatorships will tend to occur at later stages. During the first stages, the bulk of the population and the groups will remain attached to traditional norms, and the implementation of new norms and values will require imposition. When the levels of socio-economic development are higher, there is, conversely, rejection of old values.

These broad relationships are complicated, however, by anticipation and imitation, which play a considerable part, and, of course, by the fact that "technical dictatorships" arise out of occupation or colonization. As left-wing dictatorships displace right-wing regimes in some polities, other right-wing regimes strike pre-emptively, rounding up or even annihilating the opposition before it can prepare a coup to displace the traditional leaders. In this way a traditional authoritarian system can become a dictatorship. Then again, the counter-coup may come not from the leaders of the traditional regime but from another right-wing group. On the other side, once in power a left-wing dictatorship may maintain itself beyond the take-off stage in the face of pressures toward liberalization arising out of the development of new ideas within the dictatorship. This has been very marked in some of the technical dictatorships of Eastern Europe and explains why the Soviet Union has had to intervene in various ways there since World War II. Moreover, imitation seems to have contributed substantially, in one way or another, to the development of several dictatorships, past and present, in Latin America and Africa. All these variables make it extremely difficult in practice to assess the true effect of socio-economic development on the ideology of a dictatorship.

Given that dictatorships are not accepted, at least not by broad sections of the population, they are in need of tools with which to maintain themselves. Conceptually, this problem has two aspects, though of course a real-world situation will show that the two are intertwined and that leaders are not always conscious of the implications. First, imposition implies the repression of elements that might come together to topple the regime, hence the need for short-term tools to maintain a dictatorship. Second, a long-term effort to change the norms of the population and of subgroups within it might serve to win support away from the opponents and diminish the need for repression. The leaders of the political system, after all, may not wish to govern a hostile population (reactions from abroad may not always be easily dismissed), besides which the use of short-term controls is costly in the long run in terms of material resources and in terms of the capital of trust the system enjoys among its supporters. The allegiance of these supporters needs to be maintained. Indeed, they should not always be used as the policemen of the system, for if they are allowed to feel that they are indispensable, they may find it opportune to take over the regime for their own advantage.

The short-term tools at the disposal of dictatorships are essentially, as is well known, the army and the police, as well as various paramilitary organizations, through which elements of the population can be controlled. A dictatorship needs in the first instance to be able to count on these elements; if they are not loyal, they have to be purged and constantly kept under control. That is why, if the dictatorship is not the product of the military itself, emphasis must be placed on new institutional structures created by the dictatorship itself among its loyal supporters, of which the type *par excellence* is the single political party. We shall consider in Chapter 6 various types of single-party systems, not all of which are dictatorial, let alone totalitarian, in character. But if the problem is to control the population, and if army and police cannot be entirely or permanently relied on, the only means of control are either existing groups (tribes, religious groups) or a new party. Where the dictatorship is left-wing or radical and proposes to change the traditional system, the likelihood is that it will be unable to rely on, and indeed will combat, the traditional groups. For this reason, reliance on the single party is usually greater in left-wing dictatorships than in right-wing dictatorships. This is, incidentally, why radical regimes often seem "harsher" than conservative regimes: Radical dictatorships are more likely to create new groups and to repress traditional groups than conservative dictatorships.

But the party (and in some cases the existing groups) is primarily used for the long-term purpose of changing the attitudes of the population as a whole. Particularly in left-wing dictatorships, where the aim is to quicken the revision of values, the party is a very useful—indeed the best—instrument to "educate" the population and socialize it into new values. One can therefore understand why parties of this kind tend to be very widespread, with many branches, regional organizations, and cells, and to be composed of essentially those elements of the population that are truly in favor of the regime. Indeed, the regime is likely to assess the loyalty of party members constantly and to involve them in recurrent purges. Moreover, alongside—or, perhaps more truthfully, below—the party, it is useful to create further "tentacles" designed to spread the new values, for instance, women's, youth, professional, labor, athletic, and other organizations. A whole network of associations dependent on the party for support will be maintained and will contribute to the educational effort of the dictatorial system.

This description in part characterizes the developments that have taken place in Communist states, as well as in some of the Third World states, particularly in Africa (e.g., Guinea), where emphasis has been placed on changing the values of the population. Where the emphasis is not on change, a party may still be created (e.g., in Portugal or Spain), but to help maintain the old values (as well as in part to imitate other states and create an impression of legitimacy). The party then becomes an umbrella under which the traditional social groups—tribal, family, religious —can attempt to regain control of a population among whom new elements have started questioning the traditional values. Moreover, the situation in contemporary dictatorships does not necessarily vary only according to the degree of imposition they require. One important variable, which we mentioned in the first section of the chapter, is the personal popularity of the country's leader. A leader who is very popular is likely to be able to build a party fairly easily, and this party may include a wide variety of men holding widely divergent views (as in Egypt or

Tanzania). Of course, less "education" of the population may take place as a consequence, and, in the long run, value change may be fairly small. But the need to impose may also be lower: The norms of the leader may be such that he does not give as high a priority to policy goals, or else reliance on short-term means of imposition (police or army) may be impractical for a variety of reasons. In the matter of dictatorships, as in the questions encountered earlier, we must always conceive developments in terms of a continuous range of degrees: Dictatorships are more harsh or less so; they can go from the extreme of totalitarianism, where the tolerance of criticism is almost zero while the demand for such questioning is fairly large, to a moderate form of authoritarianism, where the leader is very popular, demands for changes in norms are limited, and expectations remain fairly low.

We have now examined the various elements at the root of the development of political systems. The decision-making activities of governments lead to the creation of structures, whatever the aims of the decision-making process. But the aims of the decision-making process—its norms and policy goals—are what creates a given "temperature" of conflict in the system, either because the leaders want to go where the population no longer wants or does not yet want to go or simply because the leaders fail to realize the population's expectations. Where tension rises, the political system may topple; efforts are made by political leaders to maintain themselves and their regimes, which may result in forms of imposition that can be very harsh. To achieve this aim leaders use some structures—we have encountered specifically the army, the police, the party, and social groups—but they also use to some extent the rest of the bureaucracy, the judiciary, and even assemblies and other councils.

We now must turn to the examination of the structures that constitute the "bones" of political systems, the agencies by which norms are implemented. We shall therefore proceed to an analysis of the anatomy of political systems before considering again some types of political systems in the third part of this book.

PART TWO

The Structure of Government

5

Groups and Their Role in Political Systems

It may seem unjustified to begin the study of structures of government with a study of groups and an examination of the various types of groupings that may exist within political systems. Ostensibly, while some groups are deeply involved in political developments, others, perhaps most, are not political in character: The political involvement of a bridge club is not obvious at first sight.

Yet there are two main reasons why groups are crucial to the political system. Firstly, the most important groups are very active in politics, whether overtly or not. The political influence of religious organizations is usually quite apparent; many trade unions have direct links with political parties; and some groups are created expressly to exert influence on the process of decision-making, such as environmental groups, peace groups, or organizations for the defense of minorities. These groups need not be in "party politics," for they may choose to put pressure on any and all parties, in power or out; but they are certainly political in the broad sense.

Secondly, it must be realized that all groups are involved, to a varying degree, in the fabric of the political system. We saw in the previous chapter that the legitimacy of the political system depends in large part on the support of groups. Moreover, the same group may, on different occasions, become more or less politically involved. For instance, even a bridge club can be involved in political issues, if the local authorities take steps to close down its meeting place, or if decision-makers take action against certain kinds of games, because, say, money changes hands as a result. We have therefore to consider generally the conditions under which groups are involved in politics, either in the form of broad support (or lack of support) of the political system or in the form of pressure for changes in policies. This makes it imperative to begin a study of structures by a study of groups and of their relation with the political system.

We shall therefore examine here the consequences of the development and activities of groups for the political system. We shall first look generally at the various categories of groups, with emphasis on the importance of groupings of a broad kind as against more precisely structured associations. This will enable us then to see how groups can influence the structure of political life in general, stressing in particular the role of some major groupings —tribes, ethnic groups, religious and class bodies—in shaping the characteristics of many political systems.

The Distinction Between Communal and Associational Groups and Its Consequences

The role of groups in political life is no longer questioned or, as sometimes in the past, considered harmful.[1] But their role is sometimes viewed too narrowly; the development of interest groups or pressure groups in liberal democracies has sometimes obscured the part played by a variety of other bodies in all types of societies. When considering the role of groups, we should not

---

[1] The evils of "faction" were described in particular by Jean Jacques Rousseau in *The Social Contract* (1762) and in Number 10 of *The Federalist Papers*. Modern "group theory," in contrast, has upheld the positive role of groups; see, in particular, Arthur F. Bentley, *The Process of Government* (Cambridge: Harvard University Press, 1967), and David B. Truman, *The Governmental Process: Political Interests and Public Opinion* (New York: Alfred A. Knopf, 1950).

exclusively, or even mainly, concentrate on bodies created expressly for the purpose of catering to a particular interest and applying pressure in a special way. Our earlier definition of the role of groups in politics suggests that what is important is the extent to which a grouping, body, or organization is involved in the development of political life. In industrial capitalist societies, a firm may be involved in political activity even though it is not primarily an interest group. In a traditional or developing society, a tribal group may be so influential that the government is composed solely of its members. Everywhere, leaders of religions have been known to be involved, openly or covertly, in elections and in legislative or governmental decision-making. Were we to concentrate on interest or pressure groups, which have been created in some countries, particularly liberal democracies, to lobby governments or to defend particular interests before the public, we would leave many aspects of the role of groups out of consideration and would run the risk of distorting their influence in politics.

If we are to look both at *groupings* and formally organized groups in the broadest fashion, we must introduce some distinctions and a classification. A distinction can easily be drawn if we consider the way groups tend to develop and the part played by aims and goals in their creation. Families, tribes, religious groups, and some class-based groups are made up of people whose common link is an accident of birth. Other groups are created specifically for a purpose, which can be to play bridge, to defend workers, to protect sites of natural beauty, or to make money by selling a product. These are two extreme poles, and many groups appear to fall somewhere between them in aims and creation. Trade unions, as we shall see, often occupy a position halfway between bodies that simply express existing human relationships and voluntaristic bodies that correspond to a particular aim. But it is clear that the distinction exists in principle and leads to important consequences.

Let us call *communal* the groups that tend to express a pattern of relationships, and *associational* those that have a particular aim or set of aims. It follows from the principle of the distinction that communal groups are bodies in which members are linked together by the relationship itself. The group is a network;

achievements are not explicitly part of its activities and are not the reason for the linkage. In associational groups, on the contrary, the members are bound together as a consequence of an aim, which may not always be precise and may cover a variety of activities over a long period, but which none the less constitutes both the limit of the relationships between the members and the ultimate *raison d'être* of these relationships. If we translate the distinction in terms of legitimacy or support, members of a communal group support that group and hold it as legitimate to the extent that they believe in the existence of the bond that links them to other members. A family or a religious body is legitimate on this basis. In an associational group, the legitimacy or support given to the group is dependent on the group's achieving results or at least being involved in activities relating to the purpose of the group.

These variations in the nature of support suggest that the scope for action of a communal group will be larger than that of an associational group. An association created for purposes of defending a particular sector of the community will not be able to extend its activities to other sectors, or at least not before its members have agreed to do so, which ordinarily takes a long time. On the other hand, a communal group will undertake activities in a variety of directions, all of them held to be perfectly normal, as long as the bond among its members remains solid. The danger might be more that the bond will disappear altogether (as with tribes or even ethnic groups in many societies) than that members will feel the group has overstepped its original purpose. The difference shows itself as well in the scope given to leaders. In an association, leaders are constrained by a goal; they risk losing the support of the group if, for instance, they involve the association in borderline activities (especially if they get it involved in politics). This will not happen with communal groups.

We have already said that this distinction allows for a variety of intermediate situations, where groups truly belong to both camps. Besides, the same group will vary over time, and there will be a tendency for associations to become more communal in character. The example of trade unions, already noted, could be extended to many other groups. As long as a trade union is concerned only with the wages and working conditions of its members, it is wholly associational. But if a trade union tends also to tie members with bonds of comradeship and feelings of class unity or class solidarity against employers, the tie between the members will go beyond associational relationships. At the same time, one can intuitively perceive that such a trade union will become more able, hence more likely, to involve itself in matters more general than wages and working conditions for workers in a particular trade. Trade union federations are naturally in a better position to do so than small, independent trade unions representing only a limited group of workers. The claim of the federation to represent the whole of the working class is more credible, and therefore the leadership is in a better position to act on a wide variety of questions. In all groups, what might be termed the "ratio of associationalism to communalism" varies over time. Associational groups have a propensity to become more communal, because, with time, patterns of relationship naturally emerge between members. Conversely, under the influence of associations with specific aims, communal groups become somewhat more associational in character, though the form this evolution takes is probably the creation of dependent associations by the communal group, a process to which we are now coming.

As the aims of associations are circumscribed while those of communal groups are not, the activities communal groups cover can be much broader. Communal groups become concerned with new problems as they arise, while, typically, a new problem will give rise to a new association. As long as the bond of allegiance among members of a communal group is strong, these bodies have a surplus of support or capital of trust, which they can draw upon for new purposes. At one limit (for instance, in a tribal society, where the tribe has an all-purpose character) a communal group has such a surplus of allegiance that it can extend its activities to any matter. At the other limit, an association that is truly *associational* has such a narrow aim that it cannot extend its activities at all beyond the purposes of its creation. However, in practice the two types of group tend to stay away from their extremes. Existing communal groups will be in competition with each other, at least in societies that are not wholly closed and isolated from outside influence. Specialized aims will engender associations, which will branch out from communal groups as dependents, in the manner described in Chapter 4.

All communal groupings, when confronted with new aims or new interests among the population, will be led gradually but naturally to the creation of dependent bodies, which at first will owe their existence to the communal group and will be maintained in existence by the allegiance it commands. A religious body, for instance, will cater to the special interests of some of its members by creating special organizations, first informally, and later increasingly formally. Athletic and hobby clubs, young men's associations, and so forth are the means by which a religious body will find it can maintain the support of its members and retain them in their faith in the face of competing efforts from other communal groupings or, indeed, associations. Parties of a religious character have just such an origin. Slowly, as we found in Chapter 4, these dependent bodies will acquire a legitimacy of their own. In the case of the church athletic club or youth organization, the church member will join the group and stay in it out of interest in its activities, in its aim. The association will cease to be dependent and will become simply an association like any other, with a fairly narrow aim and consequently a limited area of legitimacy, but an area of legitimacy that is its own.

We can see both the origins and the development of this situation in the contrast between what might be termed a "communal society" and an "associational society." No society is fully communal, though a perfectly tribal system approximates such a model. No society is perfectly associational, since there is an underlying propensity for associational bodies to develop social relationships among their members. But societies can be more communal or more associational, depending on how many bodies have communal characteristics and on the extent to which associations tend to be dependent. Moreover, the situation changes over time. Communal bonds are eroded, possibly through the influence of new communal groups, and as a result competing dependent associations are created and come slowly to acquire some legitimacy. Meanwhile, the associational character of societies is also modified. Unless new associations are created with specific aims uniquely their own, existing associations will acquire increasingly communal characteristics. It would be wrong to suppose that there is a "linear development" that moves societies inexorably away from communalism. Changes occur slowly, gradually, and in both directions. Admittedly, industrialization and educational development probably tend to break most traditional ties of a purely communal character; but it has not been proved that the new ties replacing them are all associational. Besides, as we have said repeatedly, associational ties in the true sense are eroded by the creation of patterns of relationship within formal associations.

When associations depend on communal groups that are themselves legitimate, the process of group formation remains natural on the principle discussed in Chapter 4. If, on the other hand, the parent communal groups lose their legitimacy because of a slackening of the ties among members, or if a communal group attempts to cover the needs of people not tied by its bonds (for instance, if a religious group tries to extend its strength beyond its adherents), the group pattern becomes imposed. The situation is similar when, for the broad communal group, we substitute the political system or the apparatus of a regime: If its support is not very large, it becomes imposed and has to use the tools of dictatorial rule discussed in Chapter 4. In particular, it will be tempted to create dependent associations, which will also be imposed and will have to be supported and maintained, in this case even against the natural tendency these associations will have to develop their own support, as all associations do beyond the ideology of the political system and its leaders. This tendency explains why dependent associations in an imposed situation themselves have to be controlled, purged, and at times disbanded. It explains also why the development of independent, or at least semi-independent, associations is very difficult to check.

Types of Communal and Associational Groups

Seen in this light, both the static and the dynamic configurations of groups account for the ways in which groups can be inserted in political systems. It is possible to arrange types of groups on a continuous dimension ranging from *full commu-*

nalism to *full associationalism.* Toward the former pole are communal groups that might be called *customary,* which correspond to immemorial or, at least, very old relationships among men. Leaving aside the family in the narrow sense (though families can play a large part in the political process as well as in long-term political allegiance), tribes, ethnic groups, and regional groups are perhaps the best examples of customary communalism. There are variations in the degree to which tribal, ethnic, and regional groups are communal, as they tend to have associational characteristics in some societies. Groups formed to defend the rights of black people or Jewish people in Western societies have many associational characteristics, though the bonds among the members go beyond their specific aims. Associations formed to promote the interests of certain regions or national minorities, such as the ones that flourished in the 1960's in Canada, Belgium, parts of France, the United Kingdom, Spain, and elsewhere, are also in part communal and in part associational. Where the claims of other associations or other communal groups upon their members are small, these broad groupings are near the communal end of a communal-associational dimension.

Two other types of customary groupings that have developed in many societies are religious and class-based bodies. Religious bodies, like regional or ethnic bodies, also range from the highly communal, with an embracing influence and little associational organization, to highly associational groups whose role is concentrated on limited matters. Roman Catholicism contrasts sharply in this respect with many of the smaller Protestant sects in being more communal. Class-based bodies tend to be associational in outlook and organization. Their spread is relatively recent, though organizations representing occupational groups have existed for a long time in many parts of the world. As we noted before, such class-based bodies as trade unions are not wholly associational. They vary over a wide range, but apart from a minority of specialized unions, they generally embody patterns of relationships expressing the solidarity of men who had relatively little influence and did not share fully the benefits of society.

Customary groups are not the only communal groups. As class-based bodies sprang from the development of societies into social classes, so have other groups emerged from the development of a number of structures in the political and social system. Those *institutional* groups, of which the most important are the bureaucracy and the military, start out merely as bodies with a particular function or as no more than collections of individuals each with a special task. With the passage of time, these men and women often acquire an *esprit de corps,* which the government (especially as regards the military) tends to foster in order to maintain the loyalty and discipline of members. As a result, they begin to acquire common attitudes, and those who, in some fashion, become the leaders of these groups start claiming the loyalty of members for a variety of tasks. Indeed, these institutional groups have often been instrumental in breaking up the solidarity of older customary groups; tribal loyalties are sometimes held by the military to be a hindrance to discipline (though some armies are also the instruments of the domination of one tribe over another, as in Nigeria at the time of the Biafran secession). When a regime finds that regional or ethnic loyalties prevent the development of a sense of national identity, the government relies on the bureaucracy (and the army) to help break up communal groups based on these loyalties. This is why, in polities where communal groups are strong, institutional groupings often appear "progressive," as we shall see more in detail in Part Three of this book.

As we move away from communal groups toward associational groups, we also find a range of bodies that are associational to a varying degree. One type of distinction commonly adopted to distinguish between associations is that of *protective* versus *promotional* groups. Protective groups defend the interests of a particular section. Their area of protection is sometimes large, but the membership is restricted to those who are being protected. The archetype of this kind of group is the trade union, but employers' associations, veterans' associations, or groups defending a particular racial or regional section also fit this category. These groups, as we noted earlier, often begin as dependent associations of communal groups, but their aims are usually narrower. Their protection extends to particular aspects of the life of the individuals protected. However, one can see that such protective groups begin at some distance from the associational end of the continuum and have a fairly high propensity to become more communal as they gain the allegiance of the population to which they cater.

Promotional groups aim at changing a policy on a given issue. A peace group, a group for the liberalization of abortion laws, or an antipollution group would fit this category. Typically, promotional groups are open to everyone in the community, unlike protective groups. Typically, too, they are fairly narrow in their aims, though some of the more political ones try to extend their aims. However, they usually fail, which shows precisely the difference between associational and communal groups and the importance of time in the build-up of allegiance. Peace groups in several Western countries attempted in the 1960's to extend their aims beyond the particular problem on which they were originally focused. This led to disunity among leaders and members and gradual disaffection. We can see that this disaffection occurred probably because leaders overextended themselves in selecting goals, their groups not yet having formed a pattern of relationships sufficiently solid to unite followers behind such an extension (that is, the promotional groups were still too associational and not communal enough). However, it is unlikely that the groups would have been able to extend themselves much beyond their original aims even with the passage of time, as competing associational or communal groups come into existence and pre-empt the other fields of political life. Promotional groups are thus the most associational of the groups to be found, more so than most protective groups (though here, too, differences exist, and protective groups as well as promotional groups extend along a wide section of the communal-associational continuum).

One can at least visualize a way of locating the various groups of a given society at the appropriate points between full communalism and full associationalism and deducing from the resultant pattern the extent to which that particular society is, over all, communal or associational. The procedure would be valid for only one point in time, but, if repeated, it would give an impression of the direction and rate of the society's movement. Even if such a precise measurement is precluded by the instruments at our disposal, we can at least compare and contrast countries in a somewhat impressionistic fashion by noting the extent to which some of the broad patterns of relationships influence political life or whether, on the other hand, associational groups (autonomous, that is, and not dependent) are markedly involved. Broadly speaking, industrial liberal democracies would appear to be characterized by a large number of associations, many of them autonomous; Communist countries and populist systems tend to develop dependent associations; and traditional systems are more markedly based on communal groups—though, as we shall see in Part Three, there are variations. At this stage, it is

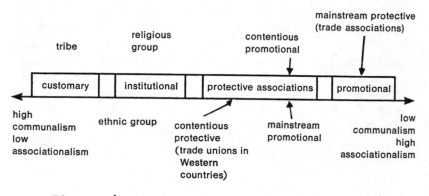

Diagram 4 Associationalism and various types of groups.

more important to concentrate on the broad groupings, since they have everywhere played a major part in building support for the political system and in developing political parties.

The Organization and Development of Major Communal Groupings and Their Dependent Associations

As we saw, communal groups, especially customary groupings, are likely to create dependent associations in order to maintain and even expand the support they enjoy. The creation of dependent associations is related to the over-all extent to which the society is associational or becoming associational and the extent to which competing customary and institutional groups exist in the polity. It is particularly important to follow this development in relation to the broad groupings that exist in all polities and to see under what circumstances dependent associations are likely to be numerous, how they gradually become independent, and the main characteristics of their organization.

As long as a communal group is not challenged, its organization will remain informal; decision-making processes will be based on established—though somewhat complicated—patterns of leadership and of communication between leaders and led, which also will not be challenged. Custom will account for the role of elders in a tribe, for instance, and regular meetings of the various leaders will suffice to provide an element of participation. When the communal group is challenged, it needs to act more positively so as to prevent opposition to the leaders and their decisions. The nature of the decision-making mechanism comes into question, and the creation of dependent associations is one way of establishing more formal types of leadership and communication. One of the major questions to arise with the creation of associations will be that of *centralization*. If an association is to remain dependent, it must be centralized, but if it is to gather support from its members and extend its membership, overcentralization is a danger. Centralization is one of the main indicators by which it is possible to study differences in organization among associations dependent on communal groups, whether the parent body is an ethnic pattern of relationship or (as more frequently happens) a religious or class-based body.

Let us concentrate here, however briefly, on religious and class-based groups. Religious bodies are unlikely to succeed in building class-based bodies if they are not themselves relatively centralized. A Protestant sect of a highly individualistic type will ordinarily have seceded from another religious body on the grounds of overcentralization. Its area of legitimacy among its supporters is likely to be relatively narrow—hardly less so, in extreme cases, than that of some of the promotional bodies described in the previous section of this chapter. A body such as the Roman Catholic Church, on the other hand, which has traditionally been highly centralized, is likely to attempt to mobilize support among its followers, as soon as there is challenge in the society, by creating dependent associations, closely controlled by the hierarchy, which will thus need to be highly centralized.

However, if the challenge is strong in the society (coming from other religions, for instance, or from a relatively strong anti-religious group), Roman Catholic organizations will slowly grow more independent and will acquire a degree of "liveliness" of their own. It could be shown that the liveliness of these dependent organizations will reach its maximum at a point when support for the church is large (but not overwhelming) for if support for the church dwindles, the dependent organizations will either cease to be dependent on the church or, on the contrary, themselves dwindle. This can be applied to political parties created by churches. Political parties will be created mainly by centralized churches: The Roman Catholic Church has been at the origin of many political parties in Western Europe and Latin America. These political parties will be most lively when they achieve a degree of autonomy that allows their members to be truly active and not to depend on the hierarchy, but when the church none the less continues to be the source of the maintenance of the party.

The development of trade unions follows a similar pattern, though complicated by its arising from the development of class feeling (or at least opposition to employers and a desire to improve the conditions of workers) and by the attempts of other communal groups, particularly religious bodies, to retain their hold over the trade union movement. The trade union movement is therefore more likely to be divided into opposing factions where centralized religious groups exist (the same could be the case, and is the case to some extent, where ethnic feelings are strong) than where the churches are not very strong or are not centralized. This accounts for the fact that the trade union movement has typically been more divided in countries where Roman Catholicism is strong (though not overwhelming) than where it is not. Secondly, the degree of centralization of trade unions is directly associated with the extent to which one group purports to embody class feelings. This accounts for the greater centralization of Communist trade union movements, even in countries not controlled by a Communist government and where imposition plays only a minor part. The Communist ideology—and the ideology of other radical groups—stresses the lack of "consciousness" of large sections of the working class; it tends naturally toward a belief in the need for a centralized organization that will embody this class feeling and that trade unionists will be asked to follow. On the contrary, where, as in most of Northern Europe and North America, class feelings are translated into a variety of organizations that have grown up piecemeal and have corresponded to particular sections of the community (thus being somewhat more associational in character, though with differences from country to country), the trade union movement is much more decentralized. It tends also to be more *united* in these countries, for in a country where associationalism is lacking, one can expect many trade unions to be merely dependent associations of a party or a church, in which case (as in Communist countries and many parts of the developing world), unity can be preserved only through imposition.

Similar developments could be found to exist, though less clearly, among groups created by ethnic or religious bodies as well as, though this happens more rarely, by military or bureaucratic organizations (usually as part of the state machinery). This is how communal groupings continue to play a major part in all contemporary societies, even where associations appear to dominate the scene, as in some Western and Eastern countries. The strength and attractiveness of trade unions, whether class-based or based on religious or ethnic groups, and the part played by "defense" groups, such as veterans' organizations or leagues to promote private schools (which in many countries mean Catholic church schools), and other nationalistic or cultural bodies are evidence of the influence of customary communal groups everywhere. In polities where imposition is strong, as in Communist countries, the pull of communal feelings is attested by the extent to which these countries must rely on force to limit the role of communal feelings; attempts to eliminate these feelings altogether have not been completely successful (as for instance in Poland, where the Roman Catholic Church has kept considerable support among the population).

The role of groups in political systems thus varies widely, depending on the origin and breadth of the support they enjoy while they are helping to shape the character of the political system. There is a constant two-way process: Communal groups have to create dependent associations and decentralize them to some degree in order to meet the challenge of other groups; but continued support for the communal groups helps to keep the polity at some distance from pure associationalism. Groups are therefore important politically not only in terms of demands or inputs or even specific outputs; they also contribute to shaping the over-all structural configuration of the political system. We begin to see how they contribute directly to the establishment and development of many political parties, to which we are now turning. They also play a part in the development of other structures as well by helping political systems to maintain themselves, as with many of the broader groups, while others often rely on governmental structures to increase their own scope and influence, as with dependent associations.

6

Political Parties

With political parties, we turn to a structure which plays a crucial and direct, though varied, part in the life of most countries in the contemporary world. It was fashionable in the past to attack political parties as factions out to divide the polity. This view is rarely held at present: Many have recognized that politics is too complex to be organized smoothly without parties, and the structure, aims, and configuration of parties are so varied that almost any leader can find a party system to suit his convenience. Parties are not always divisive since many countries (indeed one-third of the countries of the world) have one-party systems; parties can be appropriately used to promote right-wing or left-wing policies, to defend liberalism, or to sustain an authoritarian and even a dictatorial government. For the observer, the problem is therefore to try to introduce some order and to suggest underlying similarities in a structure that has shown considerable flexibility.

Definitions of political parties are numerous. One of the most frequently adopted holds that they are groups that aim at taking power. Other groups and groupings are very often on the sidelines of politics; even if their political role is large, they do not try, by themselves, to run the government. Parties do so, or seek to. But perhaps a definition that takes into account the substantive ways in which parties differ from other groups would be more valuable. Associational groups, as we saw, can be divided into protective and promotional bodies, the former being fairly broad in their interests but open only to some, while the latter are open to all but tend to have narrow interests. Political parties can be viewed as the only associational groups that both are open to all and have very wide interests. They have wide interests because they concern themselves with problems of government and cannot concentrate on specific matters. They are open to all because they try to enlist the support of as many members of the polity as possible, though not necessarily through an electoral process. It is true that some parties defend minorities and that a few tend to concern themselves with a specific problem. But if a minority party becomes concerned with creating nationalistic pressure in order to achieve self-government or independence for the minority it defends, as that issue is resolved it becomes a party like any other. Similarly, single-cause parties broaden their appeal as they come nearer to power, or else they disappear from the political scene once the goal is achieved or abandoned. Indeed, parties based narrowly on a religious group or on a class can be viewed as minority or single-cause parties that gradually become more open and acquire broader interest. The wish to hold power and a concern with general matters affecting the population as a whole are two parts of the same question. Parties are thus a "limit-case" of both protective and promotional groupings.

Social Bases and Goals of Political Parties

How do parties originate, and how do they maintain themselves either in power or as important contenders for power? In order to answer these questions we need to examine the bases of parties in various types of political systems and to relate these bases to the goals they uphold. Parties are "associational" groups; they are located near the associational end of the dimension of communalism-associationalism described in the previous chapter. They have aims or goals, which are part of the basis for their support. But their strength also comes from the support of the communal groups in the polity, which may have created a party to protect themselves or to expand their influence. Bases and goals both help to describe the very essence and characteristics of parties. They also help to account for structure.

Legitimate, Legitimizing, and Imposed Parties. Like any other body, a party is legitimate if it has direct support. Its support need not come from the population as a whole; moveover, the support can be passive, merely the absence of opposition, as it can be for any other group. Some parties are relatively old, but many more are quite recent, and even the oldest are more recent than the communal groups that exist in societies. This is why in many polities parties are not legitimate and must either rely on a broad group for support or attempt to impose themselves on the members of the polity. They are undergoing a process of legitimization, which may be protracted and may not be successful in the end.

If parties follow a natural process of development, they will emerge slowly from the interplay of broad groupings in the society. As long as the polity is closely knit and one broad group prevails, for instance a tribe or a number of related families, parties will not emerge in a formal fashion, though some factions are likely to develop. Gradually, however, disunity and opposition will lead to the formation of the rudiments of a political party around some tribe, family, or clan. The implantation may be regional, if the tribe or clan is geographically circumscribed. This is true of some traditional Latin American parties and of many parties in Europe in the nineteenth century. In general, it is common for individuals and families to have a hold on a small area and to play an important part in the election process, for instance.

A similar point can be made in relation to the other broad groups from which political parties have often originated. Ethnic, religious, and class-based groups have created political parties in the past and continue to do so. The ethnic bases of American parties are well-known, the Democrats having characteristically represented the Southern and East European immigrants, while the Republicans tended to represent those of North and West European extraction. One finds religious parties not only in practically all continental countries of Western Europe (largely, but not exclusively, based on the Roman Catholic Church) but also in Israel and some Muslim countries. One finds class-based parties where social class has tended to be a major cleavage as a result of the Industrial Revolution, particularly in Europe, both East and West, where Socialist and Communist parties are strong and in places dominant.

Some parties, for instance the American parties and most West European parties, have become legitimate with the passage of time; that is, they have direct support from the population. But many parties are only half-legitimate, in that their support from the population is still in part transferred from a communal group. The consequences are important. If the support is direct, the group from which the party was originally drawn can no longer credibly threaten to withdraw its support. If the party is in the process of legitimization, when followers still support the group rather than the party, the party still depends on the support of the group and has therefore to follow the policies favored by the group. This also has an impact on the party's unity. When the party is legitimate, disagreements between prominent personalities or subgroups will not normally endanger the very life of the party. If it is not legitimate, divisions among communal subsections will cause the party to splinter. This has happened frequently in Western Europe and Latin America in the past, but in West European parties that are legitimate division or withdrawal of support (even by churches or trade unions) typically has had very limited impact by comparison with the over-all strength of the party.

It is not possible to examine here in detail the reasons for the development of a political party on the basis of a broad group. Over all, tribal, family, or ethnic divisions tended to produce some of the earlier political parties, whereas religious and class-based parties have tended to emerge when two conditions obtained. In the first instance the supporters of the group had to be numerous enough. A Roman Catholic party is unlikely to emerge in a country that is overwhelmingly Protestant, and a socialist party is unlikely to have any significance in a country with a very small percentage of industrial workers (imposition may change the matter somewhat, but only somewhat). Secondly, there had to be a gap which the older parties could not fill. If at the time when the challenge developed existing political parties were truly legitimate, these parties will have slowly modified themselves and come to represent the new groups. American parties developed at the time when the main cleavage was ethnic because of new immigrants. The challenge of industrialization was somewhat related to the ethnic cleavage for a long period; the parties slowly became legitimate and the class cleavage was later absorbed by the parties. No new parties were able to acquire enough support to change the party system. In Western Europe, on the contrary, parties were often still closely dependent on the groups from which they stemmed, and their legitimacy was consequently limited. A decrease in the strength of these older groups (of a family or regional kind) made it easier for new parties to emerge, whether church parties, which often replaced the traditional parties based on local leaders, or socialist parties based on class allegiance.

Many parties do not emerge in such a 'natural' fashion. Leaders of a new regime, in order to maintain themselves in power, may create a political party to spread among the population the goals they uphold. The maintenance of such parties does not depend principally on the size and strength of their social base but depends on the extent to which the political system is able to impose the party during the period when support is being built and on the rate at which this support is built. The building of the party will clearly be difficult if there is no support for the leaders among the population and among groups. Imposed parties that are eventually successful tend to rely on a nucleus of group support—a small tribe, a small working-class section, an institutional body, such as the army or the bureaucracy. But the long-term development of the party depends on an educational campaign among the population and on changes in the social structure leading to the gradual decline of the bodies opposed to the party's goals. It also depends on broadening support, for which the party is likely to change its goals somewhat and to meet the demands of the population half-way. In many cases, radical parties that started in violent opposition to traditional groups became more moderate in their goals. Eastern Communist parties, including the Communist party of the Soviet Union, fall into this category.

The Goals of Political Parties. The goals of political parties relate to their social bases. Obviously, a party closely dependent on a broad grouping that is in the early stages of legitimization will tend to have goals and a program that are acceptable to the broad grouping that sustains it. An imposed party that attempts to change the norms of the polity is much freer in the goals it can pursue, but it will have to be authoritarian in its means in order, as we just saw, to reduce the distance between its own norms and those of the population and of the broad groupings prevailing in the polity.

The analysis of the norms of political systems in Chapter 3 can be applied to the study of the goals of political parties, and the difficulties that beset the analysis of norms in the context of political systems are also inherent in the study of the norms of political parties. However, a somewhat crude examination of the parties of the contemporary world shows that, as with political systems, five types of normative configurations tend to prevail among political parties. These can be related to the major geographical areas of the world.

1. In the Atlantic area, which comprises Western Europe, North America, and, because of the marked influence of Western Europe there, Australasia, parties tend to be of the *liberal democratic* type, with some variations and a few exceptions. Exceptions are Communist parties, which are strong in only a few countries (France, Italy, Iceland, Finland), as well as some remnants of authoritarian parties of the Right (which were fairly numerous before World War II, under the influence of developments in Germany and Italy at the time). Conservative or Christian parties constitute variations, being somewhat more conservative than socialist parties in their policy goals. The differences are small, however, not only in practice (as the experience of socialism in power in Sweden, Britain, Germany, and Austria shows) but also in theory (since many socialist parties have abandoned the idea of a radical change in society). Thus parties tend to be liberal in

relation to means, relatively democratic in terms of participation norms, and "centrist" in terms of policy goals.

2. In the Communist area, which comprises the whole of Eastern Europe and much of North Asia, as well as Cuba, parties are not allowed to compete, though in some countries coalitions of a number of parties exist under the aegis of the Communist party (East Germany, Poland, Czechoslovakia). Communist parties are of the *radical authoritarian* type, with some variations. The League of Communists of Yugoslavia is more liberal in its means of government and probably also more democratic in terms of participation than the East German Socialist Unity party. But these variations are small: The experiences of Hungary in the mid-1950's and of Czechoslovakia in the late 1960's showed the extent to which liberal means are allowed to prevail.

3. In the rest of the world, there are many more variations in the pattern of parties. In Latin America one finds, sometimes in the same country, liberal democratic parties (prominent in Chile and Costa Rica, as well as possibly Uruguay), traditional conservative parties (Colombia in particular, or even Brazil), authoritarian parties of the right (for instance in Paraguay), and "populist" parties, which uphold relatively democratic views on participation, somewhat authoritarian means, and a policy of the "center" (Venezuela). Communist parties are weak or proscribed (except in Cuba, of course, and Chile and Venezuela), and socialist parties are almost nonexistent (even in Chile the Socialist Party is weak). The lack or relatively low level of industrialization tends to account for the absence of such class-based parties; indeed, the Communist party in Cuba was quite weak until Castro decided to use it as the main basis for his rule.

4. The same variety of parties can be found in South and Southeast Asia. Liberal-democratic parties prevail in Japan and India, while various forms of relatively traditional, authoritarian conservative, or populist parties can be found in the other countries. Where the political system is relatively liberal, as in Malaysia, South Korea, or the Philippines, parties tend to be of the traditional conservative (particularly Malaysia and the Philippines) or of the somewhat authoritarian

variety (South Korea). Populist parties are influential in Singapore and Ceylon, though in Ceylon they are in part associated with traditional Marxist views, at least in theory.

5. and 6. In the Middle East and most of Africa, parties are less firmly implanted, in part because the countries themselves are newer. These are the areas where one finds most of the truly traditional nonparty and preparty regimes (as in Saudi Arabia), though their number is on the decline (Libya, for instance, was subjected to a left-wing coup in 1970). They are also the areas where one finds the most nonparty military regimes, though the development of a party often follows fairly quickly, as we shall see in more detail in Chapter 8 (and military regimes may exist elsewhere, whether in the Third World or even in the Atlantic area, specifically in Greece after the coup in 1966). Where parties occur, they tend to belong mainly to single-party systems and contain a strong dose of populism. Only in a few countries, such as Turkey, Israel, Lebanon, and for a time in post-Nkrumah Ghana, are systems of more than one party prevalent. The parties in these countries are rarely of the liberal democratic variety (except in Israel) and tend to be more frequently of the traditional conservative or populist type.

Thus, the examination of the goals of political parties suggests that, where countries are new or developing, parties tend to be traditional, authoritarian conservative, or populist, whereas they are liberal democratic or radical authoritarian in industrialized polities. There are some important exceptions, mainly in Latin America and in Commonwealth countries, but the majority of Latin American and Commonwealth countries follow the pattern of other countries of the Third World. In many cases, particularly in the newest countries of Africa, the party system is still in the early stages of legitimization, and it is not surprising that parties are often weak and unable to maintain the political system for long. A party can be strong in such circumstances if it has wide implantation and popular leadership. The latter often does occur in new countries, but the former is often lacking and slow to develop. The study of party structures follows logically from the study of bases and goals.

Party Structures and the Implantation of
Parties in the Population

The implantation of a party is a critical variable in determining the extent to which that party will be able to sustain itself and achieve its goals. But this implantation can take a number of forms, which can reinforce or supplement each other. Technically, we need to distinguish between the internal structures, or the "tentacles," of the party proper across the country and the external structure that links these "tentacles" to the population as a whole; however, these links need also to be distinguished in terms of bonds between individuals and bonds between groups, which can be either the groups on which the party depends or the groups it has created. The party leadership occupies a special position, both because of its intrinsic importance and because it helps to link the internal and the external structures.

Internal Structure. Let us first consider briefly the problems of internal structure. A party may be very *extensive* if it has branches all over the country, with regional committees, town committees, district committees, many members who discuss party policy and do the daily work of propaganda. It is truly *inextensive* if it has an organization only at the top or at best at regional levels. It might seem unreasonable for a party to be inextensive, as its chances of defeating its opponents or educating the population will be small. But to be extensive may be wholly unnecessary, and it is of course costly in time, money, and other resources to build a large organization. A party need not be extensive if it can rely on the support of a broad group (a tribe, a set of families, regional loyalties). Extensiveness will tend to increase if population and challenge between groups (even tribal groups) take place within a given area and/or if "education" is one of the stresses of the party. A party that wants simply to maintain the norms that exist in the country and relies on existing social relationships for support will be much less likely to be extensive than a "populist" or radical authoritarian party that must combat the norms or policy goals of many groups and, indeed, seeks to change values. We can therefore expect parties of the Left (or parties that challenge the group structure) to be more extensive than parties of the Right and parties of an authoritarian center (populist) or radical kind to be more extensive than liberal parties. Of course, as one party develops its branches and builds its organization, other parties are gradually obliged to do the same.

Parties seeking to change the norms of the polity are likely to be extensive because they must ensure that the party "line" is adhered to at lower levels in the country. Here again we encounter the problem of centralization, which we discovered in Chapter 5 in relation to groups. Parties that aim at changing norms are likely to be much more centralized than parties maintaining the *status quo*, irrespective of the norms being upheld. However, their technical need for centralization might conflict with some of the party's norms. A party that upholds liberal or democratic values may experience difficulty as a result. In practice, parties with liberal norms are usually rather decentralized, though there are variations. Parties that uphold the norm of democratic participation often have to rely on an ideological rationalization for their centralization. The most convenient rationalization is to invoke "democratic centralism," which is propounded by Communist parties and according to which policies may be discussed before the adoption of the party line but must be actively supported once adopted. Parties concerned with changing policy goals are confronted with this problem to varying degrees, and periodic difficulties (including expulsions) arise as a result.

External Links. We have already encountered the question of links between the party and the rest of the polity, particularly in relation to the role of supporting groups. The problem has two aspects: the links between party and individual citizens and, complementary to these, the links between party and groups. The nature of the links between party and individuals has been the subject of long controversies among political scientists. It has sometimes been viewed as the main basis for the classification of parties, following a distinction introduced by Duverger between "parties of notables" and "mass parties."[1] According to this distinction, mass parties would be composed of "members," in the same way as formal associations, while parties of notables or "cadres" would be based on small committees and would not

---

[1] Maurice Duverger, *Political Parties: Their Organisation and Activity in the Modern State* (London: Methuen, 1955), pp. 62–90 (2d rev. ed., New York: Barnes and Noble, 1964).

have a rank-and-file. This distinction holds up in the matter of "extensiveness" since a mass party would have to have many branches and thus be extensive, while a party of notables or of local leaders would be inextensive.

The concept of the mass party goes further, however, and embraces the party's ability to enlist the support of large sections of the population as opposed to being merely passively accepted. That is why the criterion in general use is overlegalistic: The distinction between parties with members and parties without members has the drawback of excluding from the "mass" category a number of organizations, particularly American parties, where the notion of membership is loose or almost nonexistent. Duverger's distinction is based on the theory, which Socialist and Communist parties in Europe have tended to promote, that the party is somehow the "property" of its members, which leads to the corollary that the members must be fairly active. In practice, the situation is not much different from that in a joint-stock company, where shareholders, though theoretically owners of the company, participate scarcely at all in decision-making. Members of most European socialist parties do not exercise their rights as members. Membership is essentially a means of contributing to the party funds or, for some, a motivation for involvement in propaganda activities, particularly at election times. There are parties that do not have members in the same sense (e.g., in the United States), but to which large numbers of citizens contribute funds and many give electioneering help, hence the relationship of party to individual is in practice essentially similar. On the other hand, Duverger's distinction might lead to the inclusion of tiny parties that simply happen to observe a rule of "legal membership" among the "mass" parties. This does not mean the distinction has no value; it means simply that the grounds for distinguishing the relationship between parties and individuals cannot be just the presence or absence of a legal right to membership.

What the distinction was in fact aiming at (as the word "mass" suggests) is the recognition that some parties have a direct and positive appeal to the population as a whole, or to large segments of it, while others must be content with at best a passive acceptance. The true basis for the distinction is therefore the extent to which large numbers of citizens identify with the party (the party is *their* party) and the extent to which they are prepared to follow its policies, thereby implying their general approval of its norms and goals. Party identification assumes a fairly close linkage between the supporters' idea of the "good society" and the view the party holds, or at least professes. It entails that the party is "legitimate" in the eyes of its supporters. Obviously, legitimate mass parties have a better chance of maintaining their strength for a long period than do legitimate parties relying on passive acceptance. The norms of supporters are unlikely to change quickly, as we know, and a two-way relationship operates by which the party changes its policy objectives from time to time and the attitudes of supporters also change under the party's influence.

Legitimate mass parties are fully "in orbit." They do not need groups to maintain them, nor do they need, in principle, to create dependent organizations for extending their support among the population. But a fully legitimate mass party is a limit-case, and real-world situations give rise to a variety of linkages between groups and parties. Here, too, the question has been somewhat obscured by the existence of legal links between certain groups and political parties, for instance, between Socialist or labor parties and trade unions in the Atlantic area. Because these socialist parties have needed financial help on a large scale to maintain their organization, and also because they have claimed to be the "political representation of the working class," the trade unions in some countries, particularly the United Kingdom and some Commonwealth and Scandinavian countries, are corporate "members" of the socialist or labor parties. This type of legal linkage led Duverger to term them "indirect" parties, as opposed to "direct" parties, which had only individual membership. But this distinction again is almost wholly juridical.[2]

A party linked legally to a trade union is not for that reason necessarily more dependent on the trade union for its maintenance and strength. It has been considered "normal," in West European countries, for a trade union openly to finance a party, but church and business groups have always had linkages with parties that are not necessarily weaker for being hidden. The

[2] *Ibid.*, pp. 5–17.

real distinction is the party's ability to hold a policy line distinct from that of the parent group while keeping the loyalty of its supporters. Financial or other formal ties are only one aspect of the situation. If the party is not legitimate and has to rely on the group for its maintenance, the importance of financial arrangements is dwarfed by that of personal ties. If the party has become legitimate, the financial help given by the parent group will not prevent the party from following an autonomous course of action; legitimacy means the supporters will follow the party, and the parent group is not in a position to blackmail it.

The relationship between party and groups is also important when the roles are reversed. The party may find it useful to create and control dependent associations to help increase its support among the population. We noted in Chapter 5 that a Communist party, in particular, tends to control trade unions and other groups on the grounds that the party, as the "vanguard of the proletariat" is presumably entitled to lead all working-class organizations. In practice, such a party will try to influence indirectly trade unionists who are not party members, and it may do likewise in relation to other sections of the population, for instance, young people, women, farmers, and so forth. A network of ancillary groups will thus be built around the party.

It is not surprising that such a development should occur particularly among Communist parties, which attempt to change drastically the norms and goals of political systems. The trend is similar wherever an effort is made to change the goals of the population or when the challenge of traditional groups must be opposed if a party is to maintain its influence. This is why "associated" or "dependent" groups are created in close parallel with party; party extensiveness and dependent associations are parts of the same idea. Thus both characteristics can be found in radical parties and, in decreasing order, among populist, liberal democratic, and authoritarian conservative parties.

If we summarize the different ways in which parties and groups can be associated, we find situations that range from, at one extreme, the full dependence of the party on a broad group to, at the other, the party's creation of a number of groups, which it controls while being itself dependent on none. The first type of party is necessarily very inextensive; it may be in the very early

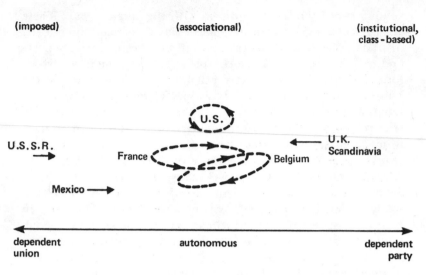

Diagram 5 Changes in union-party relationships.

stages of a natural process of legitimization and may slowly become less dependent on the group from which it originates. The
second type is typically highly imposed and has to fight the
norms that prevail among groups and in the population as a
whole through extensive tentacles. At the midpoint between the
two extremes, one finds parties that are in equilibrium with respect to groups. This can be achieved in one of two ways: (1)
Either the party is truly independent from groups, being neither
dependent on any organization nor in control of any organization, or (2) the situation is in equilibrium in the strict sense, for
dependence on one group is balanced by control of others. The
first of these two cases—an ideal-type situation, of course—corresponds to the legitimate mass party examined earlier and is only
in part approximated by American parties and certain other liberal democratic parties of the Atlantic area. The second situation
may not seem very common, yet in practice the creation of "com-
pensating" dependent associations is one way by which a party can
attempt to disengage itself from the domination of the group or
groups from which it proceeds. Indeed, the party may try to de-

velop a two-way relationship even with the parent group. These arrangements exist frequently, particularly among church-based or trade union–based parties. The links between a socialist party and trade unions are often a complex maze of committees, which formally embody the two-way relationship, for instance in the United Kingdom. In a church-based party, the women's, youth, or labor organizations of the party are the means by which the party tries to counterbalance the influence of the church. An attempt is made to attract support among the very sections that the church itself is trying to influence directly (the West German Christian Democratic Union has many instances of this type of arrangement). Thus, dependent organizations are by no means solely confined to "imposed" parties whose legitimacy is low. In fact, few parties are fully legitimate mass organizations, though a large number approximate the model in the Atlantic area. The relationship between parties and groups is thus a good indicator of the character of a party in any type of party system.

Patterns of Leadership. Leaders are the main link between parties and the rest of the polity. In many cases, parties are almost wholly maintained by the popularity of a leader. Thus questions of leadership, for instance, the selection and tenure of leaders, cannot be considered only within the party or on the basis of the legal mechanisms, democratic or otherwise, that the party constitution devises.

Max Weber divided leaders into traditional, bureaucratic-legalistic, and charismatic. *Traditional* leadership is likely to be found among parties that are in the early stages of legitimization. Indeed, at the beginning of this process, it can be scarcely said that leaders stem from the party as such. They stem from a group, and the group controls the party. In Western Europe in the nineteenth century (and sometimes even now) and in some traditional parties in Latin America at present, a few important families constituted the party leadership. This leadership was truly external; its position within the party depended more on social status and on occasional rivalries among leaders than on developments within the party. As the legitimacy of the party increases—and in particular if the party acquires a legitimate mass character—the very extensiveness of the party leads to a decline in the strength of the traditional families and to a slow build-up of procedures by which the leaders emerge from within. Some make a political career in the party and owe their positions to the support of other party men. At this point, the leadership has become *bureaucratic-legalistic.* The procedure is not necessarily democratic. An observer of the life of socialist parties, Michels, suggested that an "iron law of oligarchy" prevented the rank and file from having much say in either leadership selection or decision-making, even in extensive parties with large memberships.[3] However exaggerated this description may have been, the manipulation of votes at party conventions on the basis of patronage, compromises in the drafting of so-called composite resolutions, and the role of parliamentary leaders and of the party "bureaucracy" contribute to a decrease in the influence of rank-and-file members, as can be seen for instance in social democratic parties in Western Europe.

One further reason for the relatively small influence of members is that party supporters extend beyond the membership in the legal sense, and leaders must take both supporters and members into account. That is why, even in parties that are highly structured and old, leaders are never fully bureaucratic. Some of their strength comes from their personal appeal among the population. To a limited extent, they have *charisma,* which means their displacement may have some consequences for the party, for instance at the polls. But personal appeal is a much greater factor in many new countries. Where a leader creates a party or is prominent in its build-up, the transfer of support examined in Chapter 4 tends to operate. When such a leader is present, the amount of imposition required is reduced. In Communist countries, where personalization is often very low (though not always, as the cases of Yugoslavia and Cuba show, not to mention the Soviet Union under Lenin and, in a bizarre way, Stalin), the degree of imposition is, on the contrary, higher. Where *charismatic* leadership is pronounced, the party may be weak and likely to face problems upon the disappearance of the leader, since his successor typically will not have as much personal appeal. Yet it

[3] See in particular M. Ostrogorski, *Democracy and the Organization of Political Parties,* 2 vols. (1902; reprint, New York: Haskell House, 1970), and Robert Michels, *Political Parties* (1914; reprint, Gloucester, Mass.: Peter Smith, 1960).

is not surprising that new countries and new parties systems should rely markedly on popular leaders in order to create governmental structures. In a system where legitimacy levels are low, patterns of leadership are perhaps more important in accounting for the existence, or at least for the rapid development, of a party system than the social bases of parties.

Party Systems

A party system is the configuration that exists in a given country as a result of legal requirements and the long-term influence one party has on the others. It is a considerable oversimplification to define party systems exclusively in terms of the number of parties in a polity, particularly in terms of the dichotomy between one-party systems and systems of more than one party. Along with the number of parties, four other variables must enter into any comprehensive description of a party system. The first is the relative strength of parties: A system in which two parties are almost equal is different from one where (as in Singapore, Mexico, or Madagascar) one party receives 90 per cent of the votes or more. Second, the goals of the parties are critical: It remains to be seen how far parties with widely differing norms and policy goals can coexist. Third, the basis of support and the extent of legitimacy or imposition must be taken into account: As we noted, legitimate mass parties are likely to maintain themselves more easily when confronted with the challenge of a group. Fourth, competition for popular support may cause variations in party structures that are otherwise similar. These four variables have not been examined systematically for all party systems of the contemporary world. Studies have tended to concentrate on the number of parties, but some broad distinctions can be made that help at least to give an impression of the variations.

Let us first note, however, that about thirty polities—one-fourth of the countries of the world—have no parties. These fall into two categories of about equal size. The category of traditional dynastic regimes is shrinking as different regimes replace them or as parties are slowly allowed to form. In these countries, most of them in the Middle East and Western Asia, the traditional groupings, in particular the tribal or ethnic groupings, tend to hold the polity together without a need for political parties. The other category is composed of a fluctuating number of military regimes. In many of these cases, a party system existed in the past and is likely to reemerge in the future. Greece had a developed party system before the military coup of 1966. The same is true of Latin American countries like Argentina, which is prone to military rule. Most of the African countries that experienced military coups in the middle or late 1960's had previously had one-party systems. Military regimes are not normally long-lasting, as we shall see in Chapter 8. Therefore, only a small and shrinking number of countries can be said to be wholly outside the influence of parties, and it is quite plausible that this category will eventually disappear.

Table 1—Party Systems at the End of the 1960's

	Nonparty	One-Party	More than One Party	Total
Number of countries	35	48	55	138
Per cent	25	35	40	100

One-Party Systems. One basic distinction is the contrast between one-party systems and systems of more than one party. One-party systems increased in number and in percentage during the postwar period. Almost fifty countries, or one-third of the polities, now belong to this group. Communist countries form only a small minority among them, though many countries, in particular new countries, have imitated the Communist model of the single-party system, at least in structure, if not in norms and policy goals.

The precise borders between single-party systems and no-party systems, on the one hand, and between single-party systems and systems of more than one party, on the other, are difficult to draw. In some countries (the Soviet Union, other Communist states, and some African states), only one party is allowed by law (though other Communist states have compulsory coalitions of parties, as East Germany and Poland). But in other countries, the single-party system is simply the result of harassment of the opposition or the result of a group structure that, *de facto,* makes the emergence of other parties difficult or impossible. Some countries have more than one party, but one of them is so dominant that in effect it alone controls the polity (as in Mexico, Singapore, or Madagascar). Finally, there are one-party polities where the party is so weak and so inextensive, and thus so unimportant in the decision and communication processes, as to make them very nearly no-party systems. This seems to be the case in some African countries and, less so, in Portugal. Single-party systems therefore cover a broad spectrum and are best defined behaviorally as those systems in which decision-making processes are dominated by one party, irrespective of legal differences and even if a small opposition is allowed to exist.

Differences are more marked if we consider the goals, basis, or structure of the party in a single-party system. Norms and policy goals range from traditional conservative to radical authoritarian but, admittedly, are rarely liberal democratic. Yet not all single-party systems are dictatorial or even markedly authoritarian; nor are policy goals always radical. The variations in norms echo marked differences in the bases of support of these parties. Single-party systems are often the main vehicles through which imposed systems, whether radical, as in Communist states, or conservative —in reaction to Communism, for instance, as in Nazi Germany, Fascist Italy, or Falangist Spain—develop in a polity, but they are also, at the other extreme, characteristic of the early stage in the natural development of a traditional system. Pre-1966 Nigeria or pre-1930 Brazil were characterized, to a large extent, by a number of single-party systems territorially juxtaposed. When a communal group is overwhelmingly strong in an area, it may create a party if national policies are determined at the center by compromises among representatives of a number of areas, as happens precisely in such large countries as Nigeria and Brazil. These single-party systems emerge therefore in the early period of legitimization under a parent group and not as a result of imposition or in order to press for new norms or new goals. Between these extremes of natural and imposed development, there are a variety of situations of relative impostion, where the personal influence of a leader (as in many contemporary African states) combines the role of communal groups (mainly in the rural areas) with a more modern extensive party (mainly in the towns). The party has this character in Tunisia and Kenya, for instance, where populist goals of a relatively conservative kind tend to prevail.

The structure of the party also varies markedly in single-party systems. In the Soviet Union and many Communist states, the party is a very large organization (more than 10 million members in the Soviet Union), buttressed by a number of dependent associations of young people, women, professional and cultural groups, sports, clubs, and so forth. The party, deemed to be the spearhead of progress, must be everywhere in order to ensure that the aims of the leadership are implemented and to coordinate efforts wherever necessary. This does not describe many of the other single-party systems, even where, particularly in Africa, efforts are made in the same direction. The Tanzanian single party (TANU), which is remarkably open since the law states that there shall be two candidates of the party in each constituency at the general elections, may aim at mobilizing or educating the population. Yet the party's control over the polity is much weaker than in Communist states. It is weaker still in most other African single-party states where the party is populist. It is of course weakest where the party is dependent upon a communal group; at the limit, the party is almost nonexistent, and effective control is wielded through the group system.

Despite these variations, all single-party systems alike experience difficulty when faced with demands for greater openness or liberalization. In traditional systems the problem is less acute, for demands will be few. In more "progressive" systems the pressure of demands often accounts for a large amount of the imposition that occurs, particularly where the leaders do not have a wide popular appeal. To alleviate the problem temporarily, devices have been used, such as electoral contests between party members, as in Tanzania and, to a lesser degree, some East European Communist states (in particular Hungary) since the late 1960's. In the long run, however, single-party systems have to come to grips in a much more general and comprehensive fashion with the question of open discussion and opposition, as difficulties in Mexico, let alone in Czechoslovakia in 1968, have shown. Yet it would be an exaggeration to conclude that change can come about rapidly or that single-party systems are necessarily doomed in the long run. They have shown considerable resilience and have enabled polities to develop economically. In some countries, including Yugoslavia, efforts are being made to increase the levels of effective participation substantially. Whatever the ultimate outcome, it is clear that, by allowing some forms of dissent and by maintaining a general pressure in favor of the over-all goals of the polity, the more extensive and mobilizing single-party systems have been able to control many states of the contemporary world for very long periods.

Systems of More than One Party. Two-fifths of the countries of the world are ruled by systems of more than one party, but variations in the structure, basis of support, and goals of these parties are almost as numerous as the parties. Just as single-party systems cannot be equated with imposed radical parties, systems of more than one party cannot all be lumped in the liberal democratic category. It seems possible to distinguish at least in principle between two broad types of situations. In some countries, the system of parties is truly a "system," in that developments affecting or taking place in one party will affect the other or others. In other cases, parties appear to be juxtaposed or to "coexist." The distinction is due in part to the age of the party system, as parties are more likely to react to each other after a long period. But it is perhaps due more profoundly to the extent to which the parties are of a legitimate, in particular a legitimate mass, character. If two parties are closely dependent on a communal body, such as a tribe or racial group, they will not react to each other. They will be juxtaposed. If one party represents traditional groups in the rural areas while another is essentially based on urban elements, they too will be juxtaposed. Their coexistence may be unstable, but as long as it lasts, the parties are likely to differ far more in character, structure, goals, and norms than do parties that form a system through competition for the same electorate, in which the criss-crossing of associational loyalties is large.

When parties are juxtaposed or coexist, their number and strength are much more random than those of parties that form a system. If a party represents a tribe or racial group, its strength will depend on the size of that tribe or race. If parties form a system by competing for the same electors and aiming at increasing their support where they are relatively small, the party system is likely to tend toward an equilibrium position. In countries having legitimate mass parties, the party systems cluster around one of four positions, which can be labeled the two-party system, the two-and-a-half-party system, the multiparty system with a dominant party, and the multiparty system without a dominant party. In two-party systems (the United States, the United Kingdom, New Zealand, Australia, and Austria), two parties receive approximately the same percentage of votes (about 45 per cent each), and there is usually (but not in the United States) a small third party, which has little impact on the polity (the Liberal party in the United Kingdom). In two-and-a-half-party systems (West Germany, Canada, Luxembourg, Eire, and, in the past, Belgium), one party receives about 45 per cent of the votes, the second somewhat less than 40 per cent and the third around 15 per cent. The system is not balanced as is the two-party system. Nor is the multiparty system with a dominant party (Sweden, Norway, Denmark, Iceland, Italy, post-1958 France), where one large party also receives about 45 per cent of the votes, but where the rest of the electorate distributes its votes fairly evenly among three and sometimes four other parties, which receive 15 to 20 per cent each. Finally, in multiparty systems without a dominant party (Switzerland, Finland, pre-1958 France, Belgium, and the Netherlands since the late 1960's), the votes are fairly evenly distributed, with two or three parties receiving about a quarter of the votes each and two or more parties sharing the rest. In Atlantic countries and certain other countries where the party system has developed naturally for a fairly long period (Israel, India, Chile, and Commonwealth countries in the West Indies), the distribution among the parties is either very stable or has changed only as a result of a major reshuffle, which almost everywhere can be attributed to profound upheavals (Germany, France, Italy) or ethnic difficulties (Belgium). After such a change, the party system stabilizes itself once more at one of the four cluster points. Since these cluster points are not based on equality between parties, it follows that a system need not be balanced to be in equilibrium. Two-and-a-half party systems and multiparty systems with a dominant party have an

imbalance seemingly resulting from the existence of segments of
the population, mainly agrarians or Communists, who do not
coalesce with the rest of the Right or Left, respectively. But it
also seems empirically true that only systems at the first three
cluster points produce political stability when the polity is fairly
large. Germany, Italy, and France, among Atlantic systems, and
Brazil, Argentina, Indonesia, Zaïre—previously Congo (Kinshasa),
—Chile, and elsewhere, were each characterized at one time or another by a multiparty system without a dominant party. None
of these countries has such a system now. Many of them have experienced serious political difficulties and even periods of dictatorship.

When parties form a system in the true sense, they are more
likely to have similar structures and similar bases of support
than coexisting parties. Even the norms of the parties are not
likely to vary markedly where parties form a system. This, too, is
the consequence of their competition for electors and their ability
to maintain themselves in isolation from each other. It is true
that some parties form "subcultures" of their own (as was often
said of European socialist parties in the early twentieth century,
notably the German Socialist party before World War I). Communist parties in Western Europe are a present-day example.
But even these tend to come closer to other parties in the non-
Communist countries where the Communist party is strong (Italy,
France, Iceland, Finland, or Chile, though not India).

On the other hand, in countries where the party system is less
well-established the bases, structure, and norms are dissimilar,
and the configurations of parties do not cluster so neatly into
four groups. Perhaps because of their apparent instability, multiparty systems without a dominant party are particularly rare.
Lebanon, Panama, and possibly Ecuador are the only instances,
and even there the parties are "diluted" as numerous indepen-
dents emerge alongside tiny parties. These systems are almost
without parties. On the contrary, juxtaposed systems tend to have
a dominant party, and sometimes the dominance is overwhelming. This is true both where there are three main parties and
where there are only two. One thus finds in the Third World a
large number of unbalanced two-party systems where one of the

parties is much stronger than the other, which does not occur in any of the Atlantic states. This occurs either in very new countries (Gambia, Cameroon, Mauritius, for instance) or where the party system has been interfered with (in Brazil, a two-party system was imposed by law in the mid-1960's). This suggests that the parties are indeed juxtaposed rather than related to each other in a system. The same appears to occur in newly established systems that approximate the two-and-a-half-party cluster (Japan is one, though there have been numerous realignments in that country), but it is interesting to note that no country appears to have had a durable three-party system in the strict sense, with all three parties approximately equal; the only country to have such a system at all, Peru, quickly found itself under military rule, which suggests that the coalitions that might have formed between parties would have been too unstable to govern (a situation that parallels to some extent the multiparty system without a dominant party).

When parties do not form a system in the strict sense, they may be quite dissimilar, but there are limits to the possible differences in structure and even more in norms, for parties that are in profound disagreement over policy goals will be tempted to destroy each other. The maintenance of a system of more than one party of a juxtaposed character thus depends on the presence of one of two conditions. Either the norms should not be too divergent—for instance, a traditional conservative party may tolerate an authoritarian conservative party, a populist party, or a liberal democratic party (as in Colombia, with limitations) —or the imbalance between the parties must be so pronounced that the larger or largest party can "afford" to be tolerant. This is probably why a number of unbalanced two-party systems remain in existence and why, when the imbalance is reduced, difficulties sometimes occur, as in Lesotho or Sierra Leone, as a result of an opposition victory. In practice, the system is most likely to be maintained if both conditions prevail at the same time. If the system, particularly a two-party system, moves toward greater equality between parties, difficulties are likely to occur. As supporters of less authoritarian standpoints (e.g., traditional conservative or even liberal democratic) are made to choose between relatively liberal means and their own policy goals, they may choose authoritarian means rather than risk the coming to power of a radical party.

The importance of the differences arising out of the social bases and the goals of the parties suggests that electoral systems have perhaps less of an impact than has sometimes been suggested and may not deserve the extensive analysis they have received.[4] We cannot attempt here to describe the many types of electoral systems and their mechanics. But it may be sufficient to note that the debate has centered on an alleged correspondence between majority systems, specifically the U.S. and British systems of one ballot within single-seat constituencies, and the two-party system, while other electoral arrangements are said to lead to systems of more than two parties. Proportional representation and the two-ballot majority system, which has been in use in France at most times particularly since 1958 (and in many American primaries, especially in the South, under the name runoff primaries), are two examples of the latter. It is sometimes thought that the two-party system proceeds from the majority system for the simple reason that votes for third and fourth parties are wasted. This argument is valid only at the *constituency* or district level. Nothing in such an electoral system would prevent a party from commanding negligible strength in one constituency and a plurality in another. There can therefore be three or more parties at the national level. This was the case in Denmark before the introduction of proportional representation, and even in the United Kingdom before Eire became independent and Irish nationalists won most of the seats in that part of the country. The reason for concentration on two parties at the national level is much more closely related to cultural characteristics, and it is interesting to note that Anglo-Saxon and Commonwealth countries tend to be ruled by two-party systems. Two-party systems, single-seat, one-ballot majority systems, and the Anglo-Saxon culture are related, but it is not at all obvious that the causal relationship is in one direction only.

4 See Duverger, *Political Parties;* among the numerous analyses and criticisms of the "law" of relationship between electoral systems and party systems, the most comprehensive is Douglas W. Rae, *The Political Consequences of Electoral Laws* (New Haven, Conn.: Yale University Press, 1967).

The point is not to deny some apparent relationship between electoral systems and party systems. It is first to recognize that countries are very likely to choose the kinds of electoral system that correspond to their prevalent and enduring cleavages. Scandinavian countries moved to proportional representation not in order to maintain a multiparty system, let alone to create one, but in order to bring about more justice in an existing multiparty system. The controversy over the causal relation between party systems and electoral systems arose in large part because some felt that multiparty systems led to governmental and regime instability (apparently on the evidence of Germany's Weimar Republic). We have found that this may be true of multiparty systems without a dominant party but not of other systems. The idea that there might be a relationship between some types of electoral system and certain systems of parties therefore seems almost incidental. The consequences are certainly far less important than are the implications of other aspects of the electoral process, which often are not studied, such as literacy requirements, the secret ballot, equality of party propaganda, and general conditions of pressure and influence, which are frequent in rural areas where one group is dominant and are of course very marked where one party dominates a country, whether by legal fiat or through various manipulations. This in turn relates to the over-all questions of the extent of juxtaposition of parties and of the norms that prevail in various sections. These may result in a situation of low toleration, meaning either an outright single-party system or the sanctioning of token opposition. This is why, in the last analysis, a system of more than one party is not a recipe for liberalism or freedom, any more than a system of one party is proof of authoritarianism.

We have often stressed differences in the goals of the parties and in their relationship with the various groups of the polity. It is logical that the functions of parties as well should vary appreciably—indeed, almost diametrically—from one type of system to another. Parties can play a major part at the input side and can help to select and combine demands. They can also help to make sure that outputs are implemented, after having in many cases contributed to the determination of the general rules on which these outputs are based. Naturally enough, we would expect imposed parties to be more concerned with outputs and naturally developed parties to be more concerned with inputs. But our examination of the structure of parties, in particular their extensiveness and degree of centralization, suggests that the measurement of the role of parties in relation to inputs and outputs depends also on what might be termed the *weight* of political parties: This measures the extent to which decisions in the polity and the inputs into the system pass through the political parties rather than being processed by other means. If the party is a mere façade and has very few branches, its weight is likely to be small. If, as in the Soviet Union, it is highly organized and extends deep down in the polity, its weight will be large.

When parties emerge from communal groups in a natural fashion, their weight is likely to increase and the party becomes more legitimate, since groups will need to use the parties to achieve success. Originally, the system probably did not have any party at all, and party weight would therefore have been nil. Conversely, a strongly imposed party is likely to have a large weight, which, however, will in fact decrease as the party becomes more legitimate, because the groups created around the party to pursue its efforts will slowly become more independent. Youth and women's organizations will start suggesting or implementing policies at variance with those of the party. Within the broad context, it is also possible to say that the input functions— and the "aggregation" function in particular—of the party will also increase as the party moves either from a group basis or from strong imposition toward mass legitimacy. Demands will increase, and the party will find itself less and less able to stop them; it will have to compromise, in effect to aggregate.

The output, mobilizing, or educative functions of the party follow a different course. They are quite limited when the party is a close dependent of a group and increase as the party becomes a more legitimate mass (in order to compete successfully with other parties). But they are much stronger still in imposed parties, since these parties must endeavor to change the norms of the population, as we saw. It is unfortunately not possible to measure adequately either the weight of parties or the precise ratio of aggregation to education in each case. But one can see that, on the

whole, weight increases from group-based parties through legitimate mass parties to imposed parties (the presence of highly personalized leaders tending to decrease the weight). One can also
see that the ratio of aggregation to education is highest in favor
of aggregation at the group-based end, and lowest at the imposed
end (but, with a much greater weight, some aggregation may in
fact occur), and that legitimate mass parties are located in the
middle, with educative functions being far from unimportant. Of
all the structures of government, the political party is perhaps
the most flexible in its internal arrangements and tends to reflect
best the characteristics of the political system. They have been
far less subject to the influence of "constitutionalism" and of
"myths" of government than have executives and legislatures, to
which we shall now turn. It is not surprising that parties should
have attracted the attention of so many empirically-inclined
political scientists and should have given rise to what is perhaps
the most developed body of behavioral analysis that exists in
comparative government.

7

The Structure of
Central Governments

The structure of central governments, more than any other part of the political system, raises the question of the role of constitutions in shaping the character of political life. Of course, institutions of central government have to exist, whether or not the country has a formal constitution. But the idea of constitution-making has played a very large part in the development of these institutions in the last 150 years; it probably came to prevail almost too rapidly. While constitution-making was a liberal idea, introduced primarily in order to restrain governments, the existence of a constitution became a symbol of "modern" government. Leaders adopted constitutions even when they did not wish to apply them or could not do so. When the norms of the government are primarily focused on policy goals and not on liberalism, the constitution serves little purpose and is by-passed, though not necessarily set aside. This has in turn been possible largely because constitutional arrangements are based on a theory of political behavior that is at best very imprecise and often wrong. A set of arrangements is prescribed by a constitution on the assumption that the introduction of these arrangements will have a specific behavioral effect, but that assumption often does not correspond to a "proven" empirical relationship. This is not to say that constitutions fulfill no purpose: they do, alongside other arrangements, help to restrain government. But the limits of their effectiveness have to be recognized.

Constitutionalism has therefore fallen into some disrepute even as constitutions have spread through almost the entire world, with the effect that a divergence between theory and reality, law and practice, has become widespread in the institutions of government. Analysis of the organization of the central government becomes difficult as a result. There is a need for more empirical studies in a large number of countries, some of which have scarcely been examined, before it will be possible to know the reality of structures, the extent of their "grip" over society, and the true importance of constitutions in shaping behavior.

To examine structures of government, we must first relate constitutional arrangements to the problems a particular structure raises to see to what extent and under what circumstances the arrangements can be expected to meet the problems. We shall do so for each of the three problems that the analysis of structures raises, and must raise, in every polity. The first problem is the relationship between the center and the periphery. No executive can decide on everything by itself; there has to be an element of decentralization, however limited. The second problem is the internal structure of the executive. It is impossible for all powers to be concentrated in one man in a complex system; ministers will have to be appointed and dismissed, and these ministers will have some influence, however small. Third, there will be some two-way traffic between the executive and the polity at large through what might be called the "organized political public," some of whose members will be in a close personal or formal relationship with the executive. Advice may not be sought, but some certainly will be given. Admittedly, the constitutional form the advice takes may vary from a formal assembly to the holding of referendums, and some countries may have neither. But it is impossible for a polity to be run without councils or advisory bodies of some kind. These may be more or less representative, and their freedom of action may be more or less restricted by the executive, but they will be found everywhere. In the question of the role and powers of assemblies, as well as in decentralization and the organization of the executive, we must therefore try to see how constitutions modify the nature of the problem and how far they may as a result give a particular character to the polity.

Centralization and Decentralization: The Constitutional Blueprint of Federalism

By centralization or decentralization, we refer to the proportion of the decision-making process of the political system at large that takes place at the level of the central executive (including its bureaucracy, which we shall examine in the next chapter) as against what takes place at the level of other public agencies, such as local authorities, public corporations, and so forth. Although we are concentrating here on the activities of the central government, it is clearly important to know how widely political systems are likely to differ in the extent to which decisions originate with the central government or with other authorities. Ideally, a precise measurement would consider all the decisions of a political system (weighted according to importance) before attributing a "ratio" of centralization to a particular country. In practice, we shall have to be satisfied with far less, but it remains possible to advance somewhat in the direction of determining the relative amounts of decisions taken by the center and the periphery.

The problem is complicated—and the analysis of centralization consequently made more imperative—by the many constitutions that aim at protecting decentralization through various institutional arrangements. One of these, federalism, is held to be particularly in favor of decentralization. Can countries whose constitutional blueprints are federal be said to be more decentralized than other countries? If that is the case, it becomes valid to say that the constitutional arrangements of federalism are instrumental in achieving decentralization. If it is not the case, the practical effect of constitutional arrangements will come into question.

The problem has not as yet been systematically examined by political scientists. We cannot hope to give here more than a partial answer. The solution depends in reality on five requirements that decentralization raises if one examines it logically:

(1) An authority must be chosen to decide on the allocation of decision-making powers between the center and the periphery. Otherwise there will be chaos. (2) The fields of decision-making must be determined in advance, or the extent to which each authority is to be involved in these fields of decision-making must be determined. (3) A decision must be made on the way in which the various authorities are to be created and on the number of levels (for instance central, regional, local) that are to exist. (4) Decisions must be made about who appoints the executive, or decision-makers, at each level. (5) Decisions must also be taken about the nature of the bureaucracy (and judiciary) in each of the authorities—whether they are to be common, independent, or otherwise.

Clearly, the more the central government is responsible for deciding each of these five questions, the more centralized the system will be. To give two examples: If the central government can decide on the allocation of powers between authorities, it can in fact wipe out at will and wholly reconstruct the local authorities and the regional authorities. Similarly, if the central government is responsible for the appointment of a bureaucracy common to both central and local authorities, it is likely to be very influential in the way in which decisions will be implemented, and the extent of decentralization will be reduced. Conversely, if decisions on these matters are left to the local authorities, giving the central government no say at all, one can see that, at the limit, there would be no longer one polity but a number of polities. In particular, if local authorities or regional authorities alone are to decide on the allocation of decision-making powers to themselves and the central government, or if they are to decide which fields of decision-making are to be theirs and which the central government's, it is possible to reduce the central government to inactivity. This is in fact what tends to happen in alliances or organizations that are loose, where the center can be said to have little power, such as the United Nations, the Organization of American States, or the Organization of African Unity. In the past such organizations were often known as confederacies, the Holy Roman Empire being an example. The West European states of the 1960's and 1970's have organized, with difficulty, a somewhat more powerful center in the form of "supranational-

ism" in specific fields—coal and steel, trade and customs, and to
some extent the regulation of the economy.

Federalism is said to constitute a "halfway house" between
confederated arrangements, in which only local or regional
bodies can decide, and unitary states, in which the central government bodies determine the existence and the powers of regional and local bodies. It has indeed bred a number of devices
designed to maintain some form of equilibrium between center
and periphery, but their effectiveness has been limited and no
agreement exists on the nature of the "over-all package." So
many variations in devices exist that even specialists disagree as to
what constitutes "true" federalism. In fact, unless one considers
that there are variations in the degree of decentralization provided
by different types of arrangements and avoids such expressions as
"quasi-federalism," one will soon find that only the United States
and, possibly, Australia and Switzerland qualify as federal countries.

Let us consider, then, the variations in devices that exist
among the seventeen countries (slightly more than 10 per cent of
the world's polities, comprising one-third of the world's population) that are organized as federal countries. In the first instance,
a number of arrangements attempt to establish equilibrium between central and regional governments in the power to allocate
powers. These are the arrangements that are most studied, and
they vary appreciably. Typically, the existence of states (regions,
provinces, cantons) is recognized in the constitution, which normally can be amended only by the approval of the states or by
referendum. Their existence in some cases is protected by a supreme court, which adjudicates between states and central government. In a number of countries a second legislative chamber
is established to "represent" the states, and it occasionally gives
equal membership to each of the states (United States, Switzerland, Australia), but not in most countries. It must be appreciated that these three arrangements are not always found (they
scarcely exist in the Soviet Union and in West Germany), nor
do they, in the last analysis, protect the component units against
the determined encroachment of a majority, even if a qualified
majority, of the populations and of the components. In fact, the
federal system cannot strictly both protect the component units

and give the central government "independence" from them. It is ultimately a compromise of a somewhat makeshift character.

The other devices are even less satisfactory. Granted, most federal countries are organized on a principle of division between two types of "equal" authorities—the federal authorities and the state or provincial authorities. In general the appointment of the decision-makers in each of these authorities is decided freely by the authority, but there are sometimes emergency situations that allow for federal intervention, as in India or Mexico. A profound divergence exists between the American or Swiss model of federalism and the West German model, which is based on one common bureaucracy, admittedly appointed by the state governments, but under some control of the federal government, to administer both federal and state laws. The parallel bureaucracies of America or Switzerland are said to be wasteful of resources and somewhat divisive in character. But the most important problem relates to the question of the determination of the fields of government: In reality, federalism never had a full answer to the question that is probably the most crucial if real content is to be given to decentralization. Unless regional authorities are given powers to intervene in fields of major moment for the citizens, it is quite possible to organize perfect independence of state authorities on paper and leave them with so little to decide that the system can remain very centralized. It is true that federalism is sometimes organized on the basis of what is known as "residualism," by which the constitution lists the powers of the central government and states that all other powers, not mentioned, go to the states. But not all federal states are organized in this way; more important, there is no principle by which to decide the amount of powers required for federalism to be "real." It might once have been suggested that the "proper" central government functions related to foreign affairs, and therefore defense, currency, customs. In practice, all federal systems have gone beyond this, if only because, as in the United States, the question of "interstate" activities has to be decided by federal authorities.

It can easily be seen that, if the federal blueprint is silent or vague about the number of fields to be allocated to the center and to the periphery, the decentralization-content of federalism

may be very small indeed. This is why it has often seemed that
the content of federalism was low in countries such as the four
Latin American federal countries, where central government intervention in many fields has been very common. This is also
why it has sometimes been asserted that federalism is slowly de-
clining and that central governments are taking increasingly
more powers: as new powers or new questions have arisen (in
the World Wars, of course, but also as a result of demands for
greater economic protection, greater social equality, and so forth),
the central government has gradually increased its powers and, it
seems, centralization has gained in federal systems to such an extent that the difference between unitary and federal states no
longer exists.

The over-all evidence does not support such a general view.
The question has to be examined in relation to two other problems, the growth of powers of government in general, whether
central or local and regional, and the development of a trend
toward centralization in *both* unitary and federal states. It is
true that the powers of government have increased and that,
whether in capitalist or Communist states, the amount of regulation and of direct intervention by government has become very
large: A quarter to a third of the GNP of the industrial states of
Western Europe is in government hands or government-con-
trolled. It is therefore not surprising that the central government
should have increased its share; but it is also the case that local
and regional governments have become involved everywhere in
new forms of expenditure. It therefore becomes necessary to take
into account indirect forms of influence on states and provinces,
which often develop through circulars, model laws and regulations, and conferences of chief officers and, in particular, technical officers. These have unquestionably reduced the autonomy of
states and regions, with the result that one must regard the
powers of the center and the periphery as shared, and no longer
independent—in contradistinction to the theory of federalism, at
least American or Swiss federalism—but not necessarily with the
result that decentralization disappears.

The other problem—the comparative extent of decentralization as between unitary and federal states—cannot yet be given
a precise general answer. It seems empirically true that some

unitary states are more decentralized than some federal states. In the United Kingdom, the Scandinavian countries, and the Low Countries, traditions of municipal government have hitherto allowed for sizable powers over appointment and the bureaucracy, as well as the fields (housing, education, planning) that are mainly in the hands of local authorities. In federal states such as Argentina, Mexico, and Venezuela, the powers of the states are not very pronounced, and in Communist countries (particularly the Soviet Union and Czechoslovakia, but not Yugoslavia) the indirect or direct influence of the central government is very large over the economy and many social services. But the federal states that have been historically more decentralized (the United States, Switzerland, Canada) are still more decentralized than the most decentralized unitary states. This may not be only the result of federalism. Many federal states are quite large, and the component units of federal states, being much less numerous than the component units of unitary states, are therefore more powerful. Over all, though the question of decentralization requires the elaboration of more effective and more precise instruments to provide a rigorous ranking of the countries of the world, and thereby a definitive assessment of the role of federalism in maintaining or promoting decentralization, it seems possible to suggest that, in part because of federalism and, probably to a greater extent, because of the structure of the countries that have become federal, the degree of decentralization is still larger in federal states, though the federal blueprint is clearly not a foolproof way of dividing powers between the center and the periphery.

Executives

Executives are the nerve centers of the governmental process, and yet their effective structure has remained relatively unstudied. The activities of executives are sometimes difficult to analyze because they are carried on in secrecy. It is usually (but not always) possible to know what has been decided, at least in a number of fields, by cabinets meeting regularly; some of the decisions of ruling monarchs or presidents are far more difficult to know, and in all cases it is almost impossible to know the details of preparation for decisions and the discussions and oppositions that preceded them. Yet this knowledge is required if we are to be able to examine precisely the structure and powers of all executives. In all central governments, the head of state is surrounded by a number of ministers and advisers. If we are to be able to compare executives from the point of view of their real structure, to say, for instance, whether a president or a whole cabinet rules, we must know whether the decisions arrived at reflect essentially one man's views or the collective thinking of a small group. The constitution may specify the legal arrangements in this question, but only the practice of decision-making (which often we do not know) tells us about the organization. Structure is thus one of the problems that have to be raised when executives are examined. The constitution may provide an answer, but it may not be the correct one.

There are four further problems that executives raise. The first is the question of succession, or how executives begin and end. It must always be answered, even if the answer is bloody assassination or a bloodless coup. Because of the chaos that can arise as a result of succession, it is perhaps on this point that constitutions are most important, though often not followed. Second, duration or tenure relates both to succession and to the empirical question of a polity's capacity to sustain numerous changes of government or, at the other extreme, very few changes. Third, the social origins of the members of the executive are of considerable importance in assessing the extent to which a system is "representative" and whether the norms of members of a political system can be expected to be implemented by the executive. Finally, fields of executive intervention relate to the size of the domain in which the executive has the ability to intervene—and thus can be expected to act—on its own, whether or not an assembly, an advisory council, or any other body is close to the executive and is empowered to regulate public decision-making.

Structure. It can be seen, at least in theory, that an executive at one extreme can be wholly "pyramidal," with one man at the top in charge of decision-making, and at the other extreme wholly "collegial" or "collective," with the whole of the executive (in effect the ministers) in charge of the nation's decisions. The constitutional blueprints that exist cover both the one-man model (presidential systems on the American pattern) and the collective model (systems of "cabinet" government on the British pattern). The British pattern is not, strictly speaking, fully collective, as it grants special powers to a Prime Minister (appointing and dismissing ministers, or advising the Monarch to dissolve the Chamber, in particular). There are systems that in theory or in fact are more collective, the archetype being the Swiss model, where a body of seven equal men chooses a president by rotation every year and truly comes together to make decisions. In systems known as "convention" systems, which have tended to be incorporated in the constitutions of many Communist states, collective cabinet decision-making is also the professed rule. But this blueprint of a collective executive, also fully responsible to an assembly, has in fact been more a myth (except in Switzerland) than a reality.

The fact that a fully collective structure constitutes a myth almost everywhere and that the exception is a country such as Switzerland (along with, for a fairly long period, Uruguay, which was known until the 1950's as the "Switzerland of Latin America" for its stability) is far from insignificant. Whatever the constitutional arrangements, some technical and political constraints operate that tend to push many governments toward a pyramidal or hierarchical arrangement and away from the strict equality of ministers. It can easily be perceived that the greater and the more pressing the problems confronting a polity, the more the executive will need leadership and even strong leadership. Collective executives tend therefore to emerge where difficulties are relatively less pressing and where compromise is the key to problem-solving. Hence the collective character of the Swiss cabinet; hence, *a contrario*, the fact that, as long as French cabinets (before De Gaulle) were composed of equals under a weak prime minister they were unable to solve major problems. Hence also the fact that in developing and particularly mobilizing countries, strong leadership has been the norm. It is not surprising that these countries should have, in the main, turned presidential in the structure of their executives. This is true not only in Latin America but also in many countries of Africa, where either the French form of presidentialism has been extended and sharpened or, very often, the British model of cabinet government has been twisted in favor of some form of presidential structure (Zambia,

Kenya, and Tanzania, for instance). All that can be said is that the British system of prime minister and cabinet is very flexible and has allowed for both very weak and very strong prime ministers, in the United Kingdom and elsewhere.

Succession. The succession of governments can be said to be smooth if recognized and formalized means exist by which a new executive is created when the previous executive ceases to rule. Smooth succession, of course, is not a universal phenomenon. Coups occur every year in five to ten countries, either to install a military regime or to "restore" liberalism and democracy. Elsewhere, there are situations in which opposition to the system of succession is so strong that an important part of the state's activity is devoted to the maintenance of orderly succession and protection of the rulers. In fact, succession will be smooth only if one or both of two principles prevail in a country: (1) the *manifest destiny* of an individual or group and (2) rotation after a fixed period. The point is that potential opponents or contenders must be restrained, and the two principles are likely to be effective in so doing.

Manifest destiny is the oldest and most widespread form of succession. In its traditional form it regulates the succession of monarchs, as from father to son. But it covers many other types of situations, for instance the selection of a leader from within the major party or from the appointees of such groups as the church or the military, and so forth. This principle means that executives are chosen from among people who occupy a particular position or have certain characteristics, which has the effect of excluding all others from the contest for power. And if the principle is manifest, and therefore carries authority, those who do not have the requisite characteristics either will be prepared to agree or will have no supporters if they disagree. In highly complex countries, the principle applies at successive levels. There is a recognized pattern first for choosing the leadership of the party and second for choosing the chief executive from the parties. Without the manifest destiny principle, it is unlikely that a polity can have smooth succession, as contenders would be legion.

The principle of rotation can be substituted for manifest destiny. Some presidential constitutions state that the president is elected for a fixed period of years. Some add that the president may not be re-elected (as in many Latin American states) or may be re-elected only once (as in the United States). This leads of course to some circulation at the top. But without manifest destiny, rotation alone would not be effective because some principle must regulate the selection of the leaders even if they are to rotate. Clearly, rotation will not always be obeyed on its own (and there is evidence from many countries, including nineteenth-century France, where Napoleon III maintained himself in office in 1851 after having been elected only for a term in 1848). And if manifest destiny is not added to the constitutional requirement of rotation, various individuals or groups will begin to contest the constitutional executive for power, particularly in new states or with new regimes, which are both cases where the principle of manifest destiny is unlikely to be agreed to by the whole population.

Duration in Office. While rotation is written into the constitution, duration is also affected by *de facto* arrangements. The two elements are connected: constitution-makers who find that the duration of previous governments was too long will try to use constitutional devices to reduce it (the Twenty-second Amendment to the U.S. Constitution, for example, forbade presidents to serve more than two terms, after Franklin D. Roosevelt had been elected to a fourth). Pressure for change is likely to increase if the duration of executives is very long. In fact, it is interesting to note that the duration of executives appears to decrease as the society becomes more complex and as, therefore, the number of contenders for power can be expected to increase. Both traditional monarchies and societies in early stages of development are led by executives who last ten or twenty years, or even longer. In West European and other Atlantic liberal democracies, on the other hand, the typical duration of chief executives is in the vicinity of three to five years. Some of the well-known exceptions (Mackenzie King in Canada, Menzies in Australia, Adenauer in Germany) were followed by much briefer successors. Two types of political systems appear to constitute exceptions to the rule: In military regimes, the turnover is often very high, mainly, however, when the regime remains fully military, despite the fact that these regimes occur mostly in developing countries; and, conversely, in Communist states, though they are mostly highly developed societies, the general secretary of the Communist party appears typically to be the "true" executive, and the same man has often remained very long in this post, though not as long as the monarchs in traditional states. But it is perhaps questionable that a party general secretary can in all cases be considered the chief executive.

Given the difference in length of executive tenure between traditional and developing polities, on the one hand, and industrial liberal democracies, on the other, the problem of governmental instability in liberal democracies is perhaps less important than is sometimes alleged. We noted in Chapter 6 that proportional representation is often identified as the cause of difficulties in systems of more than one party, because it encourages an increase in the number of parties and thereby, allegedly, leads to coalition governments (which it does, to some extent), which are weaker governments (their heads have to compromise and cannot lead). A correspondence between proportional representation, coalition government, and shorter duration indeed exists, but it is not strong. A number of countries with proportional representation do not have coalition governments, and some coalitions last several years. It is wrong to generalize for all West European governments from the experience of France before 1958, where governments averaged about two a year. The system there was multiparty without a dominant party, and not merely of a coalition type. In fact, differences in duration between the United Kingdom and most West European countries are very small, perhaps a few months to a year for governments lasting three to four years. At a technical level and for the countries concerned —France before 1958, Italy, and Finland—the question is probably of importance, but globally, the real difference is between liberal democracies on the one hand and mobilizing and traditional systems on the other, and it appears to be accounted for by the socio-economic characteristics of the polities.

Origins and Representativeness of Executives. Comprehensive surveys of the origin of all members of all executives are lacking, but an examination of chief executives shows clearly that executives, rarely drawn at random from the population as a whole, come disproportionately from the more educated middle classes. This is true even in Communist systems, where the proportion of industrial workers is relatively large. It is even more often the case in developing societies, whether traditional or progressive and populist. In Western liberal democracies, businessmen and lawyers usually hold a large share of the positions, while in populist systems, teachers and civil servants, as well as military men, are more often prominent.

It is clear that the development of left-wing parties, even of the radical type, let alone the reformist social democratic type, has not led to parity or even near-parity of representation in the leadership for manual workers and agricultural workers in the overwhelming majority of political systems. It is more difficult to know to what extent this unrepresentativeness extends to the views and attitudes of the population. Studies of the parties in power in the Atlantic area, where the system is liberal and is based on the rotation of political parties, have shown that, except for some Scandinavian countries, left-wing parties are at a considerable disadvantage, even if one takes in the whole of the postwar period. It would seem to be the case that *a fortiori* where rotation of parties is not accepted and merely comes about by accident (through a coup, for instance) if at all, the representativeness of views is even lower. We have noticed the existence of imposed systems that emerge for a variety of reasons. The world shows a great variety of systems, and almost any views will be represented in power somewhere! But the relationship between the views of given leaders and those of the population is sometimes—indeed, in most cases—haphazard.

Fields and the Extent of Executive Activity. The question of the fields and extent of executive activity comes close to the problem of the role of assemblies or other councils that may exist to limit and restrain executive action (to which we are coming in the next section). But it is best to look at the question first from the angle of the executive, where it has one general aspect, namely, the extent to which public authorities can intervene in the affairs of the nation and, in particular, can regulate private activities. We saw in the previous section, in relation to decentralization, that the involvement of both the central government and the local or regional authorities in public affairs may increase at the same time. Similarly, the involvement of the executive is—perhaps sometimes mistakenly—conceived as automatically entailing a decrease in the powers of assemblies, parliaments, congresses, or other bodies placed alongside the executive. The truth is that the executive has always been given powers in certain matters deemed of prime importance for the nation. At the height of European and American liberalism, foreign affairs was in a special position, as can be seen by the role of the American President in this field, both on his own and with the consent of the Senate alone. The area of executive leadership has increased since then. For many countries, economic and social development is of greater moment than foreign affairs, or at least there is more that the executive can do in these fields. It is therefore recognized almost everywhere that the function of the executive is to lead in those fields which are important for the well-being of the citizens. The priorities have simply become somewhat different from what they were at the time liberal constitutions were drawn up.

More efforts have been made recently to enable the executive to by-pass the legislature through a number of procedural devices. Various forms of "enabling legislation," "decree-laws," and "outline laws" have come into use in many liberal democracies, either under the aegis of the constitution itself (the French 1958 constitution restricts the scope of the law and thereby increases the scope for executive action) or by customary arrangement (laws in the United Kingdom and the United States often allow considerable scope in executive intervention). But this is neither entirely new nor as dangerous as is sometimes alleged. The core of the discussion in these matters relates to the role given to assemblies in the field of rule-making and hinges on the extent to which it is felt that such a role can indeed be implemented in the reality of modern government. We must therefore turn to assemblies and consider both the constitutional functions given to them and the changes that have resulted from the widening scope of intervention by public authorities.

Assemblies

Legislative assemblies are perhaps the constitutional bodies *par excellence,* through which one sees best both the limitations on the influence of constitutions and their role as a symbol. A comprehensive study of the councils (councils of elders, royal councils, revolutionary councils, and so forth) in existence across the world would show that they are present everywhere and have, of course, varying composition and varying powers. Yet it is first and foremost to give formal existence and a series of broad powers to representative assemblies that most constitutions have been introduced. "No taxation without representation" was the cry that led logically to the introduction of constitutions and of formal assemblies. This cry has been followed, at least on paper, in the vast majority of countries: In the 1970's, about 110 of the 140 countries or so that exist have representative assemblies.

Unfortunately, perhaps, assemblies were considered so central to the idea of liberal government that they were given powers and a role they did not and could not fulfill, particularly because the evolution of societies since the eighteenth century increased the importance of social and economic management by government on a scale that could not be anticipated. The result has been that assemblies have been decried by both supporters and opponents alike, on the grounds that they are either mere "talking shops" unable to come to a decision, or so streamlined that they are mere "rubber stamps." Ever since the nineteenth century, it has become fashionable to talk about the "decline of assemblies"—perhaps the most encouraging sign in the situation, since bodies that have been in decline for so long and survived may not, after all, be too unhealthy!

The problem that assemblies raise stems from the liberal theory of government on which constitutions, at least in most countries, are based, namely, that assemblies are sovereign under the constitution and therefore are entrusted in particular with the elaboration and approval of the major rules of the polity as well as, in many cases, the control of the executive and the power to dismiss it. This theory has been translated into two types of provisions. First, the assembly alone will pass "laws," which are defined technically as the most general rules under the constitution. Second, the relationship between assembly and executive will be regulated by one of two, or possibly three, main series of arrangements. The first, known as the separation of powers, or *presidential* system, leaves assembly and executive independent from each other, neither being able to dismiss the other (though there are usually, as in the United States, various reciprocal powers, such as the veto of legislation, the right of the assembly to pass on appointments, or the power to try members of the executive for certain high crimes through the impeachment procedure. The second type of system organizes a reciprocal power to dismiss; the executive must resign if it loses the confidence of the chamber as expressed by a vote, but the executive can retaliate by dissolving the assembly. This *parliamentary* system evolved slowly in the United Kingdom and has been adopted in various forms in most European and Commonwealth countries, while the presidential system has spread through Latin America and has tended to be adopted, with various modifications, in many African countries. Finally, a system known as *convention* government places the executive at the disposal of the assembly. The assembly can dismiss the executive but cannot be dissolved by it. In theory convention government is the rule in nearly all Communist countries, particularly the Soviet Union. The Swiss case has some similarities, but the executive is elected for a fixed period and is somewhat more independent. The convention system theoretically gives by far the most power to the assembly. The fact that the power is not exercised where it exists suggests, however, that there is something exaggerated or purely mythical in the granting of such powers to an assembly. The same can be said of the parliamentary system, for in most countries the power to overthrow the government is seldom used (where it has been used, as in France before 1958, critics have constantly complained about the resulting impotence of the political system). Perhaps most important, and less obvious, the same mythical quality can be found in the power of an assembly to decide the major rules of the country.

The power of the assembly to make laws appears in principle normal. The representatives of the people should be the ones to make decisions relating to the basic rules of the country. But we begin to wonder about the validity of this standpoint when we recognize that, in all the countries of the contemporary world, almost all important laws are prepared by the executive and the bureaucracy. Even in the United States, where the Congress is held to be powerful, the President's and the bureaucracy's roles in major legislation are essential, even if it often takes time for the executive's views to prevail. This is true in West European countries. Although the systems of government are liberal, the laws are almost exclusively prepared by the executive, admittedly after receiving considerable advice from a whole series of bodies. The suggestion that assemblies themselves originate laws if there is to be liberal government is clearly not warranted. But then it must be asked whether a principle so commonly violated is indeed realistic and whether it corresponds to the true role of representative assemblies in a society.

If we begin to reflect on the reasons why laws are prepared by the executive and the bureaucracy rather than by the assemblies, and if we look at the reasons why eighteenth- and nineteenth-century constitution-makers suggested that assemblies should make laws, we find first of all that the early drafters of constitutions viewed the law primarily as a means of regulating private relationships. Laws pertained to contracts, family relationships, and possibly tariffs. They were not concerned with social security administration, levels of welfare benefits, housing development and urban renewal, transport coordination, and so forth. Indeed, even many laws on personal relations passed in the contemporary world have wide social and economic implications. A civil rights law will concern itself with segregation in public housing (there was no public housing in the eighteenth century) and discrimination in various types of jobs (which were much less complex and varied at the time). It follows that the conception of the process of rule-making is, and logically so, quite different in the two situations. For the supporters of the role of assemblies in the eighteenth century, the law was a once-and-for-all statement, on which men could deliberate at length beforehand and for the enunciation of which the assembly representatives were particularly competent, since they were themselves, in many cases, lawyers. But laws of the contemporary period tend to be part of an on-going policy process, which implies considerable knowledge about technical and economic feasibility as well as consequences. There is no point in decreeing that there shall be full employment or a minimum wage unless there are also means of ensuring that there is a bureaucracy able to oversee the implementation of the law. In fact, much of rule-making tends to be increasingly what foreign policy was in the eighteenth century, namely, dealing on a daily basis with urgent questions that cannot be left aside for the next meeting of the assembly. In the same way that it was suggested in the eighteenth century that foreign affairs be treated differently from other forms of rule-making, and should be controlled more closely by the executive, much of public rule-making in the internal field today needs to be controlled closely by the executive.

It does not follow from this development that assemblies have no part to play; but it does mean that the most "glorified" parts of assembly work may not be the most important. The concentration of interest on lawmaking and (where applicable) on the making or unmaking of governments has tended to conceal the real role of assemblies. The role of assemblies should be measured in terms of their over-all influence in a dynamic process during which policies are elaborated, discussed, modified, and eventually adopted. Moreover, concentration on lawmaking has obscured the fact that assemblies and their members can be, and indeed are, concerned (like advisers and councilors, or even courtiers in the past) not only with large questions and rule-making but also with less important matters and with rule-implementation or control of implementation. It is normal that the member of an assembly should be asked by electors or others about problems of a very limited and even personal kind in order to bring pressure to bear on the executive or the bureaucracy. From this it follows generally that we should perceive assemblies and their members as engaged in a variety of operations of influence and pressure ranging from the most particular to the most general and covering inputs as well as outputs. If the effective role of a particular assembly is to be assessed, it should be in relation to the extent to which its members are active, and if active, effective, in relation to inputs and outputs from the most particular and individual to the most general. But it should be also recognized that the more general the question at stake, the more likely it is that the executive will be involved and the more time will have to pass before the matter is settled, as colleagues, groups, parties, the bureaucracy, and public opinion will have to be convinced, even in the freest of systems, about a matter of general importance.

It is in this light that one should consider the problem of the powers of assemblies, specifically the relationship between assembly and executive. It is true that, ever since constitutions were introduced giving powers of lawmaking to assemblies, devices have also been invented, on behalf of executives, to reduce the power of assemblies in this field. But it is also true that this is not, by itself, an unliberal move; as we have noted, the characteristics of policy-making, and thus of lawmaking, in modern government make it truly impossible for an assembly to "really" make the laws. Hence it is not surprising that we should find either that the sovereign powers of the assembly are maintained in theory but are in effect curtailed by the "real" powers of the executive, or that the powers of the assembly are in fact curtailed by various procedural devices introduced in the constitution itself. Indeed, except in the few traditional systems where the monarch can still rule without an assembly, systems that dispense with an assembly altogether tend to be military or military-backed regimes that would perhaps be unable to control the assembly were one in existence. Besides, the abolition of the assembly tends to be of a temporary nature: Very few countries have in fact been without an assembly for ten years or more, Cuba being the main example, where Fidel Castro presents his regime as one that goes beyond representative institutions and directly toward popular participation.

An executive that has fewer informal instruments of power may have to rely on various procedural devices in attempting to maintain its position. The paradox is that the need for procedural devices increases as the executive becomes weaker, but the procedural devices cannot in fact be used if the behavioral strength of the executive is limited. French executives before 1958 were quite weak, and procedural devices invented after World War II (for instance, those making the question of confidence less dangerous for the executive) were of no avail. Since 1958, the strength of the executive has stemmed much more from De Gaulle's popular support in the country than from the new and even more drastic devices introduced with the Fifth Republic. It will be interesting to see how far the strength of the executive will survive De Gaulle in the long run. The same can be said about the German Federal Republic, where complicated devices were introduced to avoid repetition of the weakness of

executives under Weimar (deemed to have helped Hitler to come
to power), but these devices were scarcely used, and the strength of
the regime was due first to Adenauer's building of a strong Christian Democratic party and to the maintenance of this party after
him. The same may indeed happen in France, as the Gaullist
party has replaced the very loose coalitions that used to exist on
the Right and at the Center. Over all, it is therefore essential, if
procedural devices are to be used at all, that some behavioral
strength exist in the executive. Typically, this strength comes
from a strong and disciplined party (which is why multiparty
systems without a dominant party can lead to instability) or
from a strong president elected by popular suffrage, who therefore looks for his support not to the assembly but beyond it. This
is not to say that procedural devices are of no value. They may
streamline the debate and indeed help the assembly to concentrate on key issues as well as help the executives to see its program through. But they can only be of somewhat marginal importance in what is ultimately a trial of the relative strength of the
support that the assembly and the executive have in the country.

To assess the influence of assemblies, one must consider two
levels of activities: those taking place overtly on the floor of the
chamber or, perhaps more important, in the committees and
those carried on more informally either by individual members
or in small groups. Of course, much more information is available on the activities on the floor, though it is remarkable how
little is known about most assemblies, in particular those of the
Third World. The bulk of activities in the full house are related
to debates on laws and finance (a legal function of assemblies);
but in many countries, other types of debate—question periods,
points of order, brief interpellations or motions—enable members to raise individual issues or to initiate pressure in matters
whose resolution will take a long time. Clearly, assemblies that
meet very infrequently appear to have a much smaller potential
for influence. The U.S. Congress and the British Parliament
meet for 200 days or so every year and West European parliaments meet somewhat less, while most assemblies of the Communist world meet only for a few days—perhaps eight to ten—in one
or two yearly sessions (and Third World assemblies tend to fall
somewhere between). The control or pressure that can be ex-

erted is clearly much smaller when the assembly meets infrequently.

Activities in committees often enable an assembly to follow the policies of the executive much more closely, in part because committee members are more specialized in their interests and in part because of the semisecrecy of committee proceedings. It is in the United States that committee investigations have been most developed and have perhaps most harassed the executive. The British executive has often argued against the development of specialized committees in the United Kingdom precisely in order to avoid such harassment. Investigations of executive activities have also some important part to play in the Soviet Union and other Communist countries, particularly since the second half of the 1960's, when the number of committees was markedly increased.

Seen in this light, the problem of second chambers, which have led to much controversy and numerous analyses in political science literature, is of far less importance than has been traditionally suggested. About half the countries of the world have second chambers, among them almost all the federal countries (for the sake of representing the states as such, as we said in the first section of this chapter) as well as most of the larger countries and a majority of Atlantic and Latin American countries. Second chambers have been attacked as undemocratic, and their powers have often been curtailed or their mode of representation has to some extent been democratized. But, if lawmaking tends everywhere to be under strong executive influence, and if the role of representative assemblies is to apply pressure, supervise administrative decisions, and try to modify the policy of the executive in the long run in larger matters and more quickly in smaller matters, the problem of second chambers is reduced to secondary importance.

We should therefore consider very closely the informal activities of members, individually or in groups, in order to measure the precise effectiveness of assemblies. It is in this context that the members' origins, their views, and the extent to which they can devote their activities full time to assembly business are of importance. As with members of executives, we find that legislators tend to be drawn disproportionately from middle-class elements, although Communist states and left-wing parties have attempted deliberately to increase the representation of workers (and sometimes farmers). Where lawyers predominate in the assembly, as in the United States and Canada, the idea of "brokerage" between constituents and government will figure largely in the legislator's activities. Where workers are present in large numbers, consideration to the needs of the working class is likely to be greater, though other attitudes have also to be taken into account. Measurement of the pressure these men, with their backgrounds and their views, are able to achieve is difficult, however, even in countries where the processes are most open.

It is known that, in all countries (including those where the assembly meets infrequently, as in the Soviet Union), representatives acting on behalf of constituents often achieve change through amendments to legislation and through the reports made by committees on administrative action. However, the results obtained in these ways are less significant in Communist and many African assemblies than in Atlantic, Latin American, and the more active Commonwealth assemblies. It also seems that long-term changes based on ideas originated by members of assemblies (on civil rights, the environment, consumer control, various forms of liberalization of the status of individuals) occur essentially in Atlantic countries and perhaps a few Latin American and Commonwealth assemblies. This is a process that requires "education" of the assembly itself, dedication on the part of some members, and a willingness of the executive to respond to pressure. It is perhaps not surprising that many new assemblies have not achieved much in these fields. Meanwhile, executives everywhere tend to have their way on economic and "mainstream" social problems in the same way as they did traditionally in foreign affairs, assembly influence being indirect and slow and being closely related to the evolution of public opinion. It is no disgrace for assemblies that this should be the case, nor should it be inferred that assemblies as a result are of no significance.

The study of the structures of the central government suffered for a long time from the overlegalistic fashion in which it was conducted, with the result that more efforts have tended recently to be placed on the examination of party structures or on bureaucratic or military organizations than on the real scope of the central government's work, its internal arrangements, or the effectiveness of the pressure of assemblies. Slowly the emphasis is changing, and a comprehensive picture can begin to be drawn. This will enable the study of institutions to be more realistic and to produce a truly cross-national analysis, taking into account countries that have and do not have constitutions as well as countries in which the constitution may or may not be applied. It will also enable political scientists to answer one of the key questions of the study of government, that is, to what extent norms can be changed and practices modified by means of a legal device such as a constitution. As we saw in this chapter, all countries have problems of organization that need to be solved, but constitutional devices have often been based on oversimple views of the relationships among structures or on liberal norms rather than on policy goals. The study of governmental structures should lead to greater modesty about the effectiveness of constitutional devices based on liberal norms as against arrangements based on other norms, while it should enable us slowly to discover the constraints that exist within any configuration of institutions.

8

Administrative Organizations: Bureaucracy, Military, and Judiciary

All governments, however small, have at their disposal administrative structures whose main function is to help to implement public decisions, sometimes through the use of force. And all governments have created a judiciary to ensure peace among quarreling citizens and to give the people an opportunity to complain about decisions that affect them. The growth of the modern industrial state and the general demand for social and economic development have given administrative structures such importance, size, and technical know-how, as well as, in many cases, such a feeling of intellectual superiority over "rank amateur" politicians that the question of the role of the administration and of the military has taken on a new, more clearly "political" flavor. In many countries, some people feel that the influence of administrators is so great as to pose the danger of a "technocracy." Also, discontent among members of the government's civil and military forces is sometimes enough to raise possibilities of a takeover. Indeed, in a number of polities the military has displaced civilian and party government, and it continues to do so regularly in several parts of the world. In such cases, it can no longer be claimed that administrative bodies and the military merely implement decisions of the central government. Is it likely that this trend will increase and that representative government based on party, which replaced traditional absolutist governments in the nineteenth and twentieth centuries, will in turn be replaced by a combination of technocracy and military rule?

The relationship of bureaucracy, the military, and even the judiciary does indeed raise problems of a different nature with the growth of these organizations in most polities. But the problems are not entirely new and stem from the organizational characteristics of these bodies. The danger of "technocracy" has existed in various forms in the past. As far back as Imperial Rome and the Inca Empire, the role of the bureaucracy at times was quite large; it was large in the government of absolutist France and the enlightened despotism of the eighteenth century in Central Europe. The military played a part in the politics of Rome and of certain Renaissance Italian cities. To some extent the liberal and constitutional theory of the nineteenth century assumed too easily that, once it was so "stated" or "declared," the civilian government would rule, representatives of the people would give orders to administrators, and judges would simply "apply the law." These expectations were unrealistic from the start, and it is not surprising that they have been largely disappointed.

Yet all administrative organizations of the state tend to lack one fundamental characteristic that is critical if regimes are to be maintained: sufficient support to give them legitimacy. The military's recourse to force may give it considerable potential for overthrowing a regime and displacing it for a period, at least under some circumstances. But regimes based on the military or on any other administrative organizations need some support if they are to maintain themselves and achieve their goals. Their lack of support or their inability to increase their support appreciably without transforming themselves suggests that, though they may threaten to take command in many societies, they can hold the full burden of government only in certain peculiar circumstances.

Bureaucracies and Their Role in the Political Process

The theory of representative government apparently assumes that the sole function of bureaucracies is to implement the rules made by the central core of the governmental machine. Rule-implementation, as conceived in this theory, is a seemingly mechanical and quasi-automatic process. This view is obviously oversimplified. First, it is quite clear that administrators are asked, and have always been asked, to prepare the decisions of the rule-makers. Ministers themselves cannot draft all the rules and regulations; they ask administrators to do so. As rules grow in complexity, the preparation stage becomes longer. For instance, administrators are involved, in industrial societies as well as increasingly in developing states, in the preparation of economic plans and social policies, which require long-term thinking and discussions with countless individuals and groups. As a result, the demands of groups are often made to administrators, who thus become involved in the input and selection part of the machinery as well as the output side. Relations begin to develop between lobbies and the administration in many countries; elsewhere, individual representatives or persons with influence generally will discuss matters with civil servants. So the concept of the "implementing" administrator is mythical, and with the growth of the state apparatus it is increasingly *seen* to be mythical.

Even the process of implementation itself should not be seen as "automatic" and "mechanical." A choice must always be made among various alternatives, an intellectual operation not greatly different in nature from the determination of laws and of the most general rules. It is fair to say that there is less scope for maneuver as we go down the chain of rule-implementation, but twists to the rules and differences between letter and spirit can always leave open possibilities of intervention for administrators. Moreover, and perhaps more important, implementation is too facilely conceived in terms of the juridical effort by which rules are found to apply, or not to apply, to particular cases. A large part of administrative work is of a different character and should be described as "management" and technical achievement. This has always existed, but it is becoming increasingly important. Management occurs when a social or economic service is being created, for instance a health or social security service. Technical achievement is involved when roads or ports are built and administered. Rule-implementation in these cases means efficiency in the job and the best use of the resources available, including manpower, and therefore includes the possibility of confronting labor discontent. For managers, the notion of implementation has none of the characteristics of the more juridical types of administrative activity. Indeed, the attitudes involved in management are profoundly different from those—real or imaginary—which administrators are often said to have.

Management implies a belief in the particular activity for which managers and technicians have been trained, whether they build bridges, run a transport system, organize a health service, or develop agriculture. Technicians are specialists, and their aim is the growth of the service and its achievements. The purpose of the managerial organization is to develop the service, not to apply rules. Pressure is automatically brought to bear to obtain the means to achieve the purpose. It is true that not all state bureaucracies have, or have to the same degree, specialist civil servants involved in and eager to develop a particular service. The French civil service and its counterparts on the Continent of Europe have traditionally been more involved in technical development than the British and even the American bureaucracies. But the growth of the public sector has led to a greater emphasis on technicians everywhere. Even if, as in the United Kingdom, managers and technicians remain somewhat on the sidelines—and indeed complain about this—their role in the civil service has grown large, as it has in Communist states and increasingly in developing nations.

Because of the development of managerial demands and the consequent increase in the numbers of specialists in positions of considerable importance, the relationship between bureaucracy and government has taken a form quite different from that which the theory of representative government anticipated. Admittedly, even in the most restricted notion of rule-implementation, the control of civil servants raises problems. First, implementation levels are not merely a question of supervision; they are affected by a number of variables, in particular the skills of the civil servants and the size of the bureaucracy. For the skills of the bureaucracy to increase, education and training must expand, which may not be possible if the civil service is increasing quickly in size at the same time (hence the value of schemes by which a developed country lends technicians to the civil service of a developing country). For the size of the bureaucracy not to affect implementation levels adversely, or at least not too strongly, some decentralization of decision-making is required (whatever the centralized goals of the system), as there comes a point where the central bureaucratic machine is clogged by the numerical bulk of decisions. Moreover, controls can be effective only if the executive can rely on inspectors who are ready and able to control the civil servants, but the proximity of many inspectors to the civil servants sometimes makes them unwilling to investigate and castigate the men they control. With administrative structures, as with any other structures, a paradoxical law operates: If the inspectors are near those whom they control, they will know what is going on but may be unwilling to act, while if they are distant, they are unlikely to be as competent to spot and correct irregularities, even though they are willing to do so.

With management and the growth of specialists, the question of obedience to the government takes on a much more general character. Specialists are likely to be primarily concerned with the development of the services they run, which limits their horizons somewhat. They do not normally take into account the general development of the country or the economy (except for economists, who are not, in this sense, true specialists, but generalists with a special skill). They are concerned exclusively with the health service, the school system, the transport system, or agriculture. Their goal is therefore the development of that service, often irrespective of any other. The notion of "control" therefore pertains to integrating the specialists within the general framework of the purpose of the government. More social and political pressures have to be applied to specialists than to administrators whose main function is to elaborate the particular rules for implementing the law. If specialist civil servants are not convinced that the government wishes to develop their service, they become frustrated. Unless some ideological or social pressure exists—for instance, through a party or through the socialization provided by education or membership in other groups—technicians are likely to oppose the government and the regime and to consider alternative leaders.

Managers and technicians are thus likely to constitute the nuclei of institutional groupings. Even in political systems where the emphasis is not on development, such groupings may gradually become influential, as public works, education, and other social and economic services are created and as specialist civil servants increase in numbers as a result (foreigners will be employed on a temporary basis even where they constitute a sizable group, and hence will not constitute a force or a counterforce in the host country). A demand for a change in the goals of the government may become irresistible. Indeed, since services can be almost indefinitely expanded, the demands of specialists are "insatiable." Thus pressure is likely to arise even in political systems that emphasize development. This is why technicians have had to be "controlled" in all contemporary societies. Communist systems in particular have taken considerable pains to ensure the loyalty of technicians; the supremacy accorded to the Communist party can be explained partly in this way. In developing countries, one important role of a single party is to ensure that specialists do not grow isolated from the rest of the community and constitute a potential opposition. This requires strength and party extensiveness, which often are insufficient to the task, in part because time is required to build the party and in part because the political "class" is ordinarily not very large in developing countries, so that many populist parties have of necessity been created around the urban middle class, of which civil servants, and specifically technicians, form an important segment.

The absence of the required social pressures and the presence of enough specialists for the idea of development to prevail in a bureaucracy may well become instrumental in the overthrow of a political system. From this analysis the idea of the "technocratic state" or the "administrative state" has emerged and has aroused apprehensions in contemporary societies. It can be seen that the danger will be greatest where the political system is at an early stage of development. If the polity is quite traditional, technicians will not be very numerous; if it is very advanced, the mere fact that the society has been maintained for long will be proof that the social and political controls (through parties in particular, as well as through more general forms of socialization) have been sufficient to keep technicians under general control. But when the polity is at an early stage of development, the expectations of specialists are likely to be very large while the means at their disposal are small. Besides, the norms of the leaders of the political system and, indeed, of much of the population may well be quite alien to their own. Tension may therefore increase markedly and lead to a breakup.

Yet, while technicians can constitute a potential for change in the political system, the technocratic state is in fact very difficult to bring about, for technicians are caught in the contradictions of their own sectional interests. We noted that each group of specialists or managers is interested in the development of its own service. They will therefore agree more easily about the defects of a particular political system than about the way of organizing a polity on a new basis. They are not primarily concerned with the resources needed for the developments they aim for; they are unaware of the costs, in resources and manpower, necessary for the over-all parallel development of the services that they call for. Therefore, if they are to come to power, they are constrained to agree to the arbitration of some element, which, by definition, cannot be their own.

This arbitration may come from other civil servants, in particular from administrators who are concerned more with the implementation of rules than with management. But such administrators may not be acceptable to the technicians, since their decisions about priorities are likely to be unacceptable to many technicians, and since they are no more likely to be development-orientated than the leaders of the political class. Moreover, even if administrators and technicians were to unite to control the government and to decide on rules, only in very special circumstances will they have support in the country. By origin, administrators and technicians are from groups (the urban middle class in particular) with relatively few links with the population at large. They are likely to start believing in socio-economic development before the rest of the population does, and this is precisely why they constitute the nucleus of a "progressive" opposition against traditional groups. The only kind of political system they could help to promote is therefore one that will require considerable imposition, and yet they lack on their own the means of imposing it, either in the short term (as they lack force and may often be concentrated in the capital and a few other centers) or in the long term (as they cannot easily educate the population, having no training in the building of a party and of a propaganda machine). Technicians and administrators therefore find themselves obliged to ally with and, to a large extent, depend on other groups in the polity. They may achieve considerable influence in the types of authoritarian system where, as under the enlightened despotisms in Central Europe in the eighteenth century, the leader of the political system wishes to change the bases of his political support or to increase the prestige of the country abroad. They may also play a major part in regimes that have emerged through a coup and that have better means for maintaining themselves than do the technicians and administrators. Hence the very common situation in which the military and the administrators join forces to constitute the core of the government.

The Role of the Military and the Conditions for Military Rule

The principle of subordination of the bureaucracy to the government under which most political systems are organized has traditionally been applied to the military as well. The armed forces can be viewed as part of the same group of government servants whose function is to obey orders and implement rules. This is why the participation of the military in politics in the contemporary world is still regarded by some as an aberration to be found only in countries whose institutions are weak or whose political culture is "militaristic." In reality, the analysis of military intervention shows that military men everywhere have a propensity to intervene, and that the conditions that fostered the predominance of the theory of civilian control, particularly in nineteenth-century Europe, were highly exceptional. But an examination of the conditions favoring military intervention also indicates that there are degrees in the probability of intervention, as well as in the massiveness of the impact the army will make. The examination of military regimes that result from some types of intervention shows also that the army, if it wishes to hold power, is no more favored than the rest of the government bureaucracy.

The reasons for the role of the military in politics have been well documented and systematically analyzed by Finer and by Huntington.[1] They stem generally from what might be called the basic dissatisfaction or pessimism the military tends to entertain about civilian society and the high value it necessarily places on order and discipline. For military men, particularly for the more traditional corps of the army, both the external dangers the country may face and the sense of pride the country should have in itself call for as much order as possible in the country and require that the political, social, and economic systems function as smoothly as possible. It is not so much that the military as such wants war (many of the largest wars have in fact been started by civilians). What it does want is to keep the country in a state of preparedness, which dissension and defeatism about the future make difficult. If one adds the fact that the army can contrast its own discipline and alleged sense of duty to the selfishness and lack of effort they often see in civilian life—particularly among politicians—and the critical fact that the army has the necessary weapons to overthrow a regime and silence opposition, one can understand why members of the armed forces have the "mood," to use Finer's expression, to intervene in politics on a much broader plane than technicians and managers of the public sector may have.[2] Not only do they have the means of intervention, but their antagonism is more deep-rooted, because the contrast between their own discipline and the "anarchy" of the rest of the country is much more marked. Indeed, they may even consider that the lack of discipline of the civil service and its laziness are a further reason for intervention.

Yet, whatever this general mood, which exists everywhere and will be found, if only in a latent form, even in political systems where the civilian government is best entrenched, four variables

[1] S. E. Finer, *The Man on Horseback: The Role of the Military in Politics* (New York: Praeger Publishers, 1962), and Samuel P. Huntington, *The Soldier and the State: The Theory and Politics of Civil Military Relations* (Cambridge, Mass.: Harvard University Press, 1957), esp. pp. 7–97.

[2] Finer, *Man on Horseback*, pp. 61–71.

help to increase or decrease the propensity to intervene, and it is from their combination that the chances of overt replacement of the government may arise. First, the military's aversion to the characteristics of civilian life will increase if the military is isolated socially from the rest of the nation. Before the French Revolution, the armies of the European kings tended to be led by officers who belonged to the aristocracy and were therefore personally related to many leaders of the polity. With the advent of new regimes in Europe the military has tended still to be staffed by members of the aristocracy, but in many countries they have no other links with the polity. The military is more isolated, and its propensity to intervene increases. It will increase similarly wherever the military tends to be highly "professional" and very inbred.

Second, the military will tend to intervene where the legitimacy of the regime is low. "Anarchy" and discontent will be high in a country where legitimacy is low, and the military will therefore conclude that the system is unable to run the country as it should be run. The military tends to prefer a stable political system. Third, the military is likely to object more to some types of norms than to others. Because of the part played by discipline in their own life, military men are unlikely to be positively disposed toward liberal means and democratic participation, while they may have fewer objections to radical norms, at least as long as they do not lead to major upheavals in the polity. Liberal and democratic goals are likely to reinforce the cleavage between the military and the rest of the nation, in part because the political forces are likely to be suspicious of, and indeed to despise, the disciplined character of the military. Thus it is important for liberal or democratic regimes to be legitimate if the military is to be prepared, on the whole, to maintain or support them. In nineteenth-century Europe (as was not sufficiently perceived), many regimes slowly became more liberal and democratic on the basis of the maintenance of a monarchy to which the military remained loyal, rather than to the new values. These regimes rested on what might be termed "dual legitimacy" (e.g., the German Empire after 1871), in which links between the military and the rest of the political system were limited and tended to pass through the monarch.

Fourth, the probability of military intervention tends to decrease with the complexity of the political, social, and economic system. The vision of military men does not extend much beyond the possible overthrow of the regime and its immediate reorganization. As the bureaucracy of the country increases to cope with more complex problems, the military finds itself increasingly tied first to the bureaucracy, which it cannot replace because no other skilled personnel exist, and more generally to a maze of groups and organizations that it will have to tolerate, even if it must control them. The probability of a successful takeover becomes more remote as the number of centers that have to be "taken" at the same time grows, and the probability of attempts at a takeover decreases as a result.

Since these conditions alter the probability of military intervention, it is not surprising that the forms of military intervention should also vary markedly. As we noted, all military men have some mood to intervene, and as we cannot expect none of the four variables just analyzed to play any part at all, some form of intervention by the military must be expected to take place everywhere. It is not because some countries have a militaristic culture that the military intervenes more in them, as was sometimes suggested about Japan or Germany. Conversely, the absence of a militaristic culture will not lead to zero military intervention, though members of the armed forces will be involved in more limited or less frequent actions and will have to narrow down the goals they can expect to achieve.

Military intervention in politics can range from the mildest forms of pressure on the government to obtain a specific result to the most naked and overt replacement of the whole executive.[3] Pressure itself can range somewhat, from perfectly legal and commonplace advocacy (as when generals solicit a large budget from the executive or the parliamentary assembly) to forms of "blackmail" (as when officers threaten to resign unless some policy is changed), though it is difficult to see exactly at what point protests turn into true blackmail. At the other extreme the military may either "supplant" the old regime and install itself in power or participate in an operation that replaces one group of political leaders with another, occupying the sidelines

[3] *Ibid.*, pp. 86 ff.

and playing a general role of arbiter. Here, too, it is difficult to draw a precise line, as the military may back a group that is otherwise very weak and create what might be termed a "puppet" military regime. In practice, a number of contemporary political regimes are difficult to classify because they are on the borderline between military and military-backed regimes. Algeria since 1966 and Brazil since 1964 are instances. The movement from one type of situation to another is in reality continuous and corresponds to variation in the extent to which the military exercises its influence over the structure and decisions of the political system.

The more the conditions favoring military intervention are present, the more the military will tend to supplant or at least depose the leaders of the political system. When these conditions are less pronounced, the action will tend to take the form of blackmail or pressure. This is why military intervention tends, on the whole, to be most marked in regimes that are at the "take-off stage" of socio-economic development, and least marked either in industrial liberal democracies or in very traditional regimes. Industrial liberal democracies tend to be organizationally too complex and generally endowed with a legitimate political system; since the nineteenth century, the professionalism and isolation of the military have markedly declined. In traditional societies, the political system is typically legitimate and based on unchallenged communal groups, and the professionalism of the military is low. Moreover (unlike in liberal democracies) the ideology of the regime tends to be of an "oligarchical" and mildly authoritarian type, which fits the army's general norms. In intermediate positions of socio-economic development, on the contrary, the break-up of legitimacy, changes in ideology, and the professional character of the army, which becomes isolated from the communal groups and tends to form an institutional group, contribute to the propensity of the army to intervene and indeed to replace or supplant the political leaders.

Yet the military's efforts at supplantation or its backing of such efforts by a set of political leaders does not ensure the stability that the military typically seeks to introduce. This is true whether the role of the military can be called a basically "conservative" attempt to maintain traditional norms, and the groups that upheld these norms, or whether it is "progressive" or "radical," seeking, for instance, to bring about greater equality through socio-economic development (to enable the country, perhaps, to take pride in itself and cease to be a colony or dependency of one or several foreign powers). The army has the means to take over the system. But it is impeded both by its lack of technical expertise in the running of the administration and the preparation of policy-making and by its inability to give a new legitimacy base and new legitimate structures to the political system it upholds. Because of its relative limitations in the field of administration and policy-making, as we have noted, the probability of military intervention tends to decrease as the political and socio-economic system becomes more complex; it is also because of their need for administrative and managerial support that the military tend to associate frequently with the bureaucracy. From a practical point of view, the military clearly needs the bureaucracy if it is to make a serious attempt at remaining in power.

Even with the backing of the bureaucracy, the military's long-term maintenance in power has a low probability—as empirical evidence shows in the contemporary world—because the armed forces have few or no means of enlisting the support of the population. Either the regime is basically conservative and must rely on traditional groups to maintain its predominance (and these groups will probably attempt to restore their direct influence), or the regime is radical or populist and will need instruments other than force to build groups designed to change the norms of the population and to combat the traditional groups. The military often eschews political parties when it comes to power by a coup, abolishing by force the existing political associations. Yet typically it is constrained either to surrender power through another coup or to buttress its position in the long run by building a political party. Moreover, the leader of the government, after having come to power as leader of a military junta or of a revolutionary council, slowly takes postures more akin to those of a political leader. If he acquires personal support among the population, his regime comes to be based as much on his own "charisma" as on the military, if not more. This "civilianization" process, which characterized Mexico in the 1920's and 1930's and

Egypt under Nasser in the 1950's and 1960's, is unavoidable. Supplantment brings military men power, but the need for legitimacy means a return to civilian rule, at least in part, which no regime can escape. Hence, paradoxically, the military creates a system as unstable as those it aims at replacing, unless it takes on the very characteristics of a "party-imposed" regime. While the intervention of the military is a constant and recurrent problem in all polities, fully military regimes can never be more than transitional.

The Judiciary and Rule-Adjudication

The role of judges in politics is less flamboyant than that of the military and the bureaucracy. Indeed, like assemblies or other institutions and procedures developed by constitutionalists, the judiciary is buttressed by liberal reforms, one of the main demands being that judges be independent from the executive. Yet the question of the role of judges is much more complex and ambivalent than traditional liberal theory suggests.

First, it is not easy to see exactly how to ensure the full independence of judges or indeed what, in the last analysis, such an expression really means. It is practical (and it may be useful) to observe that the rules by which judges are appointed and dismissed are different from those relating to other servants of the state. They may have full inviolability, for instance, and be appointed for life. But someone must appoint these judges, in particular the chief judges of the supreme courts or supreme tribunals that exist in every country. Whether these appointments are left to the executive or chief executive (as in the United States and many other countries), to the executive and assembly, or even to popular election, the judges will be to some extent dependent on the opinions of those who appointed them. More profoundly, it has often been noted that judges, who are primarily drawn from middle-class groups and from the legal profession, tend to be somewhat conservative in attitude and, in the absence of pressure to the contrary, somewhat more lenient to those whose views are more in the conservative than in the radical direction. Indeed, it may be suggested that the duty of judges is to defend the norms of the system, since their function is to implement the laws. But in so doing, they tend to be relatively dependent on, or responsive to, the social attitudes of the polity at large, if not necessarily the political objectives of the executive.

It is not easy to see either how much influence it is rational to give judges in the process of decision-making. In a first approximation, it might seem valid to suggest that judges be concerned with the supervision of all the decisions taken on the basis of pre-existing legislation, or even on the basis of the constitution. But experience showed fairly quickly, as analysis could have demonstrated, that if this power is given fully to judges, they are in reality in a position to "make the law." We noted in the first section of this chapter that "implementation" never means the mere mechanical application of general rules to particular cases. There is always an element of choice between existing rules, even when there is no management content in the operation. What is true of bureaucracies is also true for judges: If judges are required to see, *ex post facto,* if a rule has been correctly applied in a particular case, there is a tendency to ask judges for a second interpretation of the way in which the rule should be implemented. Their involvement will then be no more mechanical than that of administrators. This is particularly so since it is unlikely that the opinion of judges will be asked in relation to simple problems. They will be involved where there is real conflict between two rules, where the rules are silent or obscure, and so forth. Judges are therefore very likely to be frequently involved in "making the law." Logically, the deeper judges are involved in decisions, and, specifically, if they are asked to rule on the constitutionality of the laws themselves, the more likely they are to be involved in rule-making and, indeed, in lawmaking.

While the problem of the independence of judges has led to the introduction of procedures designed to reduce the pressure that the executive can exert on them, the problem of the judges' role in relation to lawmaking and the guardianship of constitutions has never been solved satisfactorily in theory, either in liberal countries or elsewhere. In liberal countries, marked variations exist. In the United States and other countries, the Supreme Court is entitled (or in fact took upon itself the authority, since the Constitution was mute in this respect—a cogent example of judges' "making" the law or the constitution) to quash legislation on the grounds that it is unconstitutional. In the United Kingdom and Scandinavian countries, statutes are supreme and judges must apply them. Indeed, in those countries where constitutional control exists, judges have tended, in the long run, to take a rather restrictive view of their powers: They have been quick to intervene against the action of local authorities or regional governments (for instance against state governments in the United States) but have felt increasingly uneasy about overturning statutes passed by the national parliament. The battle that took place in the 1930's in the United States over the quashing of New Deal legislation showed the problems entailed in this type of action (as well as the limits of the independence of the judiciary). It also made judges increasingly aware of the fact that to a large extent they were pitting their judgement against that of others (the others being the elected representatives). On balance, Supreme Court justices have since taken the view that the benefit of the doubt should be left to the legislature and executive and that only cases of gross unconstitutionality warrant sanctions (a view which was upheld in 1970 when the U.S. Congress passed the law lowering the voting age to 18 for federal elections). Outside of the United States, many countries, including some Continental European countries, have adopted some form of constitutional control, but it is often somewhat inoperative in practice (as in Latin America) or restricted in theory (as in France).

The growth of the public sector and of state intervention in social and economic life has caused another type of involvement of judges in the life of the polity to increase, and this in turn has led to a growing number of confrontations between the judiciary and the bureaucracy. For liberal theorists of the eighteenth century, the judiciary was concerned either with private litigations between citizens or with matters pertaining to the freedom of citizens, specifically in relation to criminal proceedings. The aim of the changes then introduced was to ensure that trials were fair and that the state did not use the judiciary as another form of police force or bureaucracy. The relationship between state and citizen was viewed as one in which the state was prevented from acting unless forms and "due process" were applied and seen to be applied. Although this problem is still of considerable importance, and can have vital implications in dictatorships and other authoritarian regimes, a further type of encroachment has followed the increasing role of the state in the social and economic sectors. The bureaucracy has acquired greater powers to constrain citizens, individually or in groups, in a variety of fields. Limitations on property rights for planning and other purposes, rules placed on business and commercial activities for a variety of reasons, the regulation of social welfare benefits, and the protection of the health of citizens entail the consequence that administrative bodies are enabled to act, with or without notice, on individuals or groups, in ways totally different from the rightful actions of private bodies, and in ways that may, even if not due to malice, have very serious consequences for particular people.

Thus, while it was possible at the turn of the century to suggest that the law of the state (or the principles of the law applicable to the state) should be the same as that of any other person (a principle that, according to the English lawyer Dicey, made British law superior to much Continental European law), it has become increasingly difficult to deny the existence of a body of *administrative law* with special rules, and, accordingly, to refuse to agree to the creation of special courts, known as administrative courts, designed to supervise the actions of the bureaucracy and to ensure that no inconvenience, or at least a minimum of inconvenience, falls to the citizens. Without such courts, the administration is in fact typically stronger, for it can claim in its own defense special conditions and special legislation. Only if bodies applying somewhat different rules and accustomed to administrative procedures consider the cases brought by the citizens is there effective protection of rights and a limitation of hardships.

These courts have taken a variety of forms, but their number and scope have been on the increase, even in countries that do not otherwise rank as liberal. The French network of administration courts, led by the almost two-centuries-old *Conseil d'Etat,* has long been a model, in view of the generality of the problems it can handle and the ease and low cost for the claimant (though the slowness of the procedure has often been a handicap). On the Continent of Europe, in Latin America, and in parts of Africa, a similar type of structure has been created, often with much less success, though it should be noted that it took about a century for the French *Conseil d'Etat* to establish its influence. Elsewhere the piecemeal development of *ad hoc* tribunals for specific problems (as in most Anglo-Saxon and Commonwealth countries) has been paralleled in the 1960's by the spread of the institution of the *ombudsman,* a commissioner who is empowered to look at individual cases as they are presented by claimants from the public at large. The idea of the ombudsman appears to be gaining support even in Communist countries, where, on the other hand, institutions of administrative justice or "double-checking" have long existed as part of the machinery of state.

The role of the judiciary has thus tended to change, in part because of the new types of problems modern societies have raised, in part because experience has shown that a potential for rule-making existed in the very development of rule-adjudication procedures. Differences among the areas of the judiciary, inquiry, supervision, control of the bureaucracy, and, at the limit, inputs by citizens as feedback from previous administrative decisions are perhaps no longer as marked as in the past. In this respect, empirical analyses are too few to allow more than tentative generalizations. It would be most enlightening to know whether, in day-to-day life and in relation to the problems that link citizens to the bureaucracy, the judiciary plays a larger part in liberal countries than in authoritarian countries, or in newer countries than in older polities. Little is known about the number of decisions that go against the government or the administration in the majority of countries; even less is known about the extent to which the citizen relies on judges, whether "ordinary" or "administrative," in his difficulties vis-à-vis the executive. It would seem that his reliance on this channel is limited, but it is permissible to suggest that it increases with the development of education and therefore with socio-economic development. It is therefore not unreasonable to assume also that the role of judges—at the level of administration, not for high-level grievances—will be on the increase in future generations.

It is surely fitting that we end this brief survey of the structures of government with the institutions that the new "technocratic state" has tended to develop and on which, it is often felt, the future lives, freedom, and well-being of citizens depends. As our interest is naturally drawn toward the immediate and most apparent, much more emphasis is placed on the military than on the judiciary and, perhaps, the administrative bodies. Yet, in the long run, the military will probably have less impact on social and political life than the bureaucracy and the courts, at least those courts or tribunals that, like the ombudsman, can have some direct effect on administrative redress. Involved as it is, in many cases, with groups, parties, and governmental structures, the bureaucracy has such a complex and varied series of functions, and its technical competence is required in so many fields of government, that it is difficult to imagine how polities can be maintained in the future without further administrative structures, involving themselves ever more deeply with ever more areas of society, as well as with their own problems of coordination. The judiciary, the administrative judiciary in particular, therefore has the crucial task of helping to counterbalance the role of administrators. The boundaries of groups, parties, and assemblies in the input and feedback processes are much less precise than is often suggested—and they may, in future, be even less precise.

PART THREE

The Political Systems
of the Contemporary World

9

Traditional Conservative Systems

In this chapter and the next four, we shall describe the characteristics of the systems in the contemporary world, examining both the interrelationships between structures and the kinds of evolution these systems are undergoing or are likely to undergo. This panorama is not in the strict sense a typology. We know that each system can be characterized by a particular position in relation to three dimensions of norms: the dimensions of means (liberalism-authoritarianism), participation (democracy-autocracy), and policy goals (conservatism-radicalism). To produce an exact typology, a comprehensive analysis would have to examine each system and determine its exact position in the three-dimensional space, see to what extent systems cluster around particular points, and determine precisely the characteristics of each cluster. However, as was pointed out in Chapter 3, the precise location of systems in the three-dimensional space cannot yet be determined with the empirical indicators at our disposal. We shall therefore analyze only a number of "ideal cases" that appear to correspond broadly to the way in which political systems of the world tend to divide. We shall note to what extent certain actual systems appear to diverge from these ideal positions in the three-dimensional space and suggest also which ones seem to be moving slowly from one position to another. In Chapter 3 we identified five such ideal cases, which we called traditional conservative, liberal democratic, radical authoritarian, populist, and authoritarian conservative. These are the distinctions on which we shall base our description of political systems in this and the coming chapters.

Traditional conservative polities are probably the only type to have markedly declined in number in the last century, and the type from which many, if not all, of the older polities of the contemporary world have emerged. However, it would be wrong to consider that traditional systems constitute a "stage" of development and that every polity undergoes a traditional phase. Many new countries began as populist regimes; some started with conservative authoritarian or liberal democratic governments. Traditional conservative systems can be found only in polities in which the state developed very slowly, often through processes of annexation of tribes or ethnic groups. If the process took long enough, some of the divisions stemming from these annexations may have died out to give the polity an "integrated" appearance. But more recently, under the impact of the development of liberalism in the Western countries and the idea of socio-economic development in Communist and Third World countries, new divisions often revamped from some of the older ones, have emerged. The "reservoir" of traditional conservative countries has shrunk, and the ways in which one type of system changes into another vary markedly. In the early 1970's, about twenty countries can be classified as traditional conservative, most of them monarchies located in the Middle East and in South and Southeast Asia, with a few Latin American countries being borderline cases. Libya, which had been one example, was taken out of the group by a military coup in 1970, while the change of regime in Somalia in the same year removed that country from a position fairly close to that of a traditional conservative system. But some monarchies of the Middle East appear relatively stable (larger countries, as well as the smaller Sheikdoms), and it is therefore unlikely that the group will become wholly extinct in the near future.

The Configuration of Structures in Traditional Conservative Systems

Traditional conservative systems are conservative and not very authoritarian, and they have a low level of popular participation. This is because the main structures on which they are based are the communal groups—tribal, ethnic, and religious—that have existed in the region for long periods. In the most extreme form, these structures are not confronted by challenges, that is, they are accepted without question by the whole population. Demands are those traditionally put forward by the groups; ideas for other demands are likely to emerge, if at all, only among marginal elements, mainly those in towns, with whom the groups have lost, or have never had, complete legitimacy. Almost certainly, each individual is represented by and belongs to only one group. If several tribes or ethnic groups make up the polity, there will be a marked separation, often reinforced by geographical partition, between those belonging to different tribes or ethnic groups. Such a polity is a *de facto* "confederacy" of tribes or ethnic groups; the absence of criss-crossing cleavages makes more complex arrangements unnecessary.

Personal loyalties play a part in the system and personalities have influence, but their influence is institutionalized. The leaders of tribes or ethnic groups are accepted because the principle of "manifest destiny" makes their claim to leadership clear, at least in theory. If it is not clear—if, for instance, two heirs come into contention for leadership—the traditional character of the political system may indeed be shaken, just as problems may arise when the legitimacy of the groups comes into question. But in normal circumstances there is no call for such divisions, and traditional leaders are among the most "accepted" in all the political systems. It follows that they are relatively free to act and take decisions, although they are not personalized or "charismatic." Their freedom of action comes from, and is limited by, the origin of their position. They are free to act because the system is based on limited participation, and the legitimacy of the group is high among the population as a whole. The limitations on their freedom relates to the structure of the groups and to their norms. Leaders who have a free hand in matters that do not concern the life of the group (e.g., foreign affairs) may well have little freedom internally, because customs organize relations among the members. Limitations may also stem from some degree of oligarchical participation in the group (advice given by elders, for instance), established by traditional rights that cannot be infringed without a decrease in the legitimacy of the group as a whole, as well as a decline of the authority of the leaders.

Given that the groups produce the national leaders, are wholly legitimate, and constitute the main channel through which demands are made, it is not surprising that outputs should also typically be implemented through the groups and that the system as a whole should be relatively decentralized. We stated earlier that the system has some characteristics of a confederacy of groups: If there are several tribal or ethnic groups, most decisions will have to be accepted by the group leaders; it is impossible to see how the decision would be implemented if these leaders were bypassed. It is well known that the more traditional areas of a polity that is otherwise industrialized and modern in socio-economic terms are also more closed and less receptive to new concepts. Thus decisions taken above or outside of the groups will be implemented sporadically, very slowly, or simply not at all. The leaders of the political system may be free to decide matters not affecting the communal groups, but they have very little scope for maneuver within the groups.

The same freedoms and limitations may extend to the level of subgroups within the broad communal groups, but not everywhere. The system within the tribe may be rather centralized or, at the limit, it is likely to be centralized within the smaller family (which, of course, is more extensive than a family in the strict Western sense). If there is a pyramidal decentralization, like the feudal organization in medieval Europe, the position of tribal leaders with respect to the subgroups is again independent in matters that do not affect the internal life of subgroups and highly restricted in matters that do. Clearly, however, if the pyramid has many levels, with numerous semi-independent cells in the political system as a whole, there is a danger of a break-up for the whole polity. Each group may be legitimate, but only indirectly, depending on the legitimacy of the subgroups, so that any break in the chain may have serious consequences for the polity. Even if only statistically, the more elements there are, the greater the chances of discord.

In traditional conservative systems, the structure *par excellence* is thus the communal group. Other political structures are appendages of the communal group, and the support they obtain is indirect and dependent on maintenance of the support of the group and its leaders. As we noted in Chapter 6, moreover, these are the political systems where parties may not emerge at all. Seven of the nine Middle Eastern traditional systems do not have parties, and in the other two (Iran and Morocco), the parties are somewhat inchoate; indeed, as we shall see in the next section, these two countries are far from being wholly traditional. Five of the six traditional countries of Southeast Asia are also without parties, and the sixth, Malaysia, provides the best example of the reason for the early emergence of parties in polities of this type, namely, the need to organize diverse ethnic (tribal, geographical) groups when their strength in the political system is approximately balanced and their interests are widely divergent. (Nigeria before 1966 and Brazil before 1930 were similarly organized; Colombia is a roughly similar case in that the distinctions between Conservatives and Liberals, as well as between the factions within both parties, have partly regional and almost feudal characteristics). If one group is predominant, however, or if the divisions between the groups are not very marked, a traditional system will not have parties. Precisely because of the confederal character of the polity, decisions will tend to be consensual or unanimous.

In the traditional systems of the Middle East and Asia, then, parties are rare. Where they exist, as in Malaysia, they respond to the need of groups for a political organization to ensure compromises. In Africa, however, the few polities that can be defined as traditional tend to have party systems. In some cases, notably in Commonwealth countries (Lesotho, Swaziland), there are two-party systems. Elsewhere, there are single-party systems, except in Ethiopia, where the structural arrangements resemble those of Middle Eastern and Asian states. The best traditional conservative example of a single-party system is probably Liberia, where the True Whig party has lasted a long time and is the object of

very little challenge. But some of the French-speaking countries,
in particular the smaller ones, can probably also be defined as
traditional, though the border between traditional and populist
systems is sometimes thin. Gabon and possibly Chad and Rwanda
might be included in this group, though they lean toward populism or authoritarian conservatism; some elements of the traditional system are also present in other polities.

The reason for the difference between African or some Latin
American states (such as El Salvador and possibly other Central
American polities) and Middle Eastern and Asian traditional
systems can probably be inferred from the fact that the former
are both new states (even if they were created in the nineteenth
century) and republics, while the latter tend to be long-estab-
lished polities (though they might have been protectorates of a
European country for a time, the structure of the polity continued
unbroken) and monarchies. No nonparty republic can be classified as traditional conservative, as all such republics have been
military regimes of a populist or sometimes authoritarian conservative character. A few monarchies have party systems, either
fairly well organized (Lesotho, Swaziland) or inchoate and subject to periodic purges and other difficulties (Iran, Morocco). But
the very existence of a monarchy of a traditional character (and
not just the monarch as such) marks the system as traditional
and helps to maintain the legitimacy of groups, as well as establishes a manifest destiny principle of succession in the polity.

Traditional systems typically are organized on the basis of
customs arising from the group structures. As a result, the governmental structures have a customary character, and written
constitutional arrangements are meaningful only to the extent
that they conform to the customs. The apex of the structure is
the executive, though with the reservations already made about
the decentralized character of these systems and on the basis of a
leadership which is institutionalized and not strongly personal.
In the majority of these states, which are monarchies, loyalties
can be secured as long as, and to the extent that, the system is
traditional. The choice of ministers and the policies followed by
them depend on the king's acceptance, hence the structure is
fully pyramidal. Where the system is a republic, the organization
of succession may create problems, which the party (single or

dominant) may not altogether remove. There may therefore be a somewhat more collegial organization of the executive, unless, as sometimes occurs, the president succeeds in building some loyalty around himself, making the regime populist as well as traditional (as was the case in Liberia under Tubman). But the very conditions of organization and support of the system make for some type of compromise at the top in nonmonarchical systems, and it is not accidental that in Colombia the parties should have come to an agreement to split the spoils of office. The same type of compromise occurs in Lebanon, where tribal, ethnic, and religious arrangements are at the root of the political system, which, however, is not wholly traditional and has a number of features that appear to place it nearer to the liberal democratic polities. This suggests that the methods for resolving conflicts found in many liberal democracies, which we shall consider in Chapter 10, probably have their origins in the procedures of those traditional systems where custom does not provide for obvious succession arrangements between tribal and ethnic groups (one might possibly extend this analysis, for instance, to some of the characteristics of the Swiss system).

The structure and role of assemblies should be related to customary groupings in the same way as the structure of the executive. A number of traditional conservative polities do not have assemblies, but many do (about two-thirds to three-quarters). Those with no assemblies constitute the hard core of the truly absolutist states remaining in the second half of the twentieth century; they are all located around the Persian Gulf and are very small in population. In fact, all traditional polities are slowly acquiring assemblies. But the difference between the traditional states with assemblies and those without is not necessarily very large, for such assemblies tend to be emanations of the group structure and thus a formalization of the advice that elders and leaders of the tribes and ethnic groups customarily give to monarchs (republics have assemblies; the absence of a traditional system of government implies the drafting of a constitution, and no constitution so far has failed to include an assembly, though this is of course not the only reason for the assembly's existence). Thus the function of representatives is to convey more formally and publicly the desires of the groups and their leaders as well as to involve them in the policy processes that might affect the groups. Individual grievances are also presented, though even these are channeled through the group leadership.

Given the existence of strong legitimacy ties, such a system can maintain an assembly—and sometimes one with powers to overthrow the government—without a party system. The likelihood of the overthrow of the government by the assembly is remote. Governments fall when they incur the displeasure of the monarch, though the latter may have to engage in manipulations of the assembly reminiscent of the activities of British kings in the eighteenth century. Retrospectively, one can therefore understand why the instability of governments, a cause of considerable concern among some contemporary West European parliamentary systems, was not anticipated by those who drafted constitutions in Europe in the early part of the nineteenth century. One can equally understand why the development of a party system was not conceived of at the time as necessary or even useful. A no-party system with an assembly informally controlled by the pressure of communal groups and by some manipulation by the monarch's followers could easily present itself as the natural consequence of the parliamentary system. The distaste the founders of the American polity had for such a system was perfectly logical in this context.

The restricted role of the central government, consciously hoped for or simply unavoidable because of the importance of the group structure, accounts also for the limited development of the bureaucracy and the dependence of the courts. Even the military is scarcely more independent: The tradition of the aristocratic classes is to serve in the army, and as a result the king's army is in many ways also the tribal chief's army. The growth of technical services in the military does lead slowly to the development of a more specifically "royal" army, which, at the same time, is more independent from the whole of the structures that the king represents (but this growth is slow because of the cost of airplanes, tanks, and artillery). Thus the danger of military coups is directly related to the development of a professional military and consequently, as we noted in the previous chapter, is much less likely than in most other systems. Yet it is probably the military and the bureaucracy that are responsible for the first true challenge any traditional system will have to face, which can ultimately lead to the appearance of a populist or authoritarian conservative system. Sooner or later, these institutional bodies become groupings with their own communal loyalties. The sheer growth in size and the repeated frustrations arising from the opposition of the tribes seem to lead unavoidably to a clash, in which traditional systems might fall. The configuration of structures of traditional systems therefore seems both extremely solid and extremely fragile. Unchallenged, tribes or ethnic groups have sizable reserves of legitimacy, but once the challenge occurs, the system may not have the means to resist successfully.

Variations Among Traditional Conservative Systems and the Future of These Regimes

These seemingly doomed systems do not disappear at a strikingly rapid rate, and some seem even to have succeeded in forestalling the apparently inevitable trend toward their disappearance, though they may have changed their character somewhat in the process. As we noted, wholly traditional states—those with no party, no assembly, a very simple group structure, and little apparent danger of challenge—are very few, constituting a handful of states around the Persian Gulf, to which a few polities in the Himalayas (Nepal, Bhutan) might be added, even though they have a constitution and an assembly. The location of these states is of importance: They have remained isolated, and Persian Gulf states often go to considerable lengths to maintain their isolation (by barring entry to foreigners, for instance). They are also very small, among the smallest in the world. Over all, Malaysia, Iran, Ethiopia, and Morocco are the only states of any size in the Middle Eastern and South Asian group, and only Colombia can qualify as a traditional political system (with reservations) in Latin America. All together, these twenty or so states (about 14 per cent of the world's polities) comprise less than 4 per cent of the total population of the world. This probably accounts for the resilience of many of the traditional systems.

164   *Political Systems of the Contemporary World*

Isolated from world currents by geography, either mountains or
deserts, in the large majority of cases, with small populations and
therefore few concentrations in urban areas, which in turn would
engender a large bureaucracy and a large military which might
become professional, these political systems can be expected to
survive for a long time, unless the accidents of war or perhaps
annexation by larger neighbors (some of the Persian Gulf states
are rich and thus tempting targets) change the conditions of
political life, in particular by breaking the legitimacy links between people and leaders.

This explanation is valid for the majority but not for all of
these states. A few polities have remained largely traditional in
character, both ostensibly in terms of institutional structures and
profoundly in terms of the type and level of legitimacy, even
though they lack most of the characteristics just enumerated.
These states—Iran, Morocco, Malaysia, Ethiopia, and Colombia
—are relatively large both in geographical size and in population;
their locations (except, perhaps that of Ethiopia) make them
easily accessible; and still, despite some accidents and indeed
some danger—as an attempted coup in Morocco in 1971 showed—
they seem to offer at least some resistance to the changes they
might have been expected to undergo.

It could perhaps be suggested that the persistence of a handful
of such states can be discounted as random occurrences or explained by the individual characteristics of each case. In three
cases, for instance, the monarchs appear unusually strong and in
fact have benefited from special circumstances that have enhanced their personal prestige (conflict between major powers or
liberation from a colonial power). In Malaysia, the divisions between the ethnic groups, Malay and Chinese, are so deep that
paradoxically they help to keep the communal groups strong. But
the conflict appears capable of turning (as in Nigeria) into civil
war, causing the traditional system to give way to a more authoritarian system. (Riots in 1970 in Malaysia indicated that this
might be occurring; then again, no armed effort was made to retain Singapore when it seceded from the federation.) Colombia is
perhaps the most difficult case to explain, for its traditional two-
party system of Conservatives and Liberals, based as it is on local
groups and regional loyalties, has survived vicissitudes of various

kinds and indeed has provided the world with what seems to be the only case of return to a traditional conservative system after a period of authoritarian conservatism under a dictator. Other South American states either never had such an organized party system or have become liberal democracies, populist regimes, or authoritarian conservative systems. El Salvador, in Central America, is too small in area and population to present an analogy.

The fact that these exceptions exist suggests that, given a number of favorable circumstances, traditional conservative states may be able to maintain themselves, though possibly always on a razor's edge. The key appears to be a combination of *controlled* socio-economic development (as zero development in relatively large states is difficult to imagine) and the existence of *controlling agents* able to counteract the groups that might naturally be expected to grow strong enough to overthrow the system. In the complicated configuration of groups that exists, the legitimacy of the communal groups must not be so overwhelming among supporters as to render wholly ineffective the leadership of the center. Rather than mere "confederacies," in the sense suggested above, these larger polities are more "federal"—by which we do not mean federations in the legal sense (only one of these states, Malaysia, is a federation, while the others are legally unitary), but are referring merely to the type of loyalty that links the people and the group leaders to the center. The monarch must have some, but only some, personal appeal (for with purely personal appeal he probably would be tempted to overthrow the groups altogether, as Norodom Sihanouk tried to do, without notable success, in Cambodia). The bureaucracy and the army must be drawn from the communal groups in sufficiently large numbers to retain some of the traditional loyalties, and the opposition of educated classes to these groups must not be so strong as to create an unbridgeable chasm between new institutional groups and old communal groups. Over all, there probably must be some measure of toleration, which may seem a bizarre expression to apply to a country like Colombia, which has known *la violencia* for years and even decades, but where toleration none the less does seem to exist, for the leaders of the political system do not seem to push their strength to its limit, nor are opponents ready to widen the cleavages to the point of no return.

Traditional conservative systems are somewhat exceptional in the contemporary world, but no less interesting for that. Much of their interest lies in what they show about the origins of many modern polities, which, in Europe or elsewhere (e.g., Japan), developed into liberal democracies through a slow process of change and, in a less natural and more brutal fashion, into some of the populist and authoritarian conservative (and radical) systems. It is helpful to see how modern political parties slowly emerge from communal groups, if one is seeking to measure the strength and legitimacy of political parties, and the existence of traditional conservative polities in the contemporary world gives a more immediate understanding of this emergence than study of the history of European polities can provide. But traditional conservative polities have more than merely value for an antiquarian. Precisely because some of them have resisted the changes that were to be naturally expected, they enable us to understand better the roles of a number of variables that, singly or in combination, such as the presence of a legitimate monarch bent on reform, the presence of legitimate communal groups from which the military or bureaucracy are drawn, etc., can help political systems to maintain themselves. Because they exist, they must be described and examined. Because they exist, they induce students of comparative politics to inquire more carefully into the relative strength of a number of elements that, in our search for generalizations, we might otherwise be tempted to overlook.

10

Liberal Democratic Systems

Somewhat less than one-third of the countries of the world—about forty—can be labeled liberal democracies. In these polities, the norms of the regime are liberal, relatively democratic, and center from the standpoint of policy goals. Emphasis is placed on liberal means, and constitutions, which in general play a large part, normally include bills of rights, which are intended to embody the priority given to liberalism. The origin of these regimes can be traced to a revolt against authoritarianism in parts of eighteenth-century Europe, but their development through the nineteenth and twentieth centuries proved far less easy than had originally been expected and in many ways different. At the time of the French and American revolutions, it was assumed that, once the main problem of "lifting the curtain" was solved, despotisms would easily be replaced by liberal regimes. It was assumed also that the idea would then spread smoothly and naturally from Western Europe throughout the whole world. But despotisms proved able to maintain themselves in many polities, and the aftermath of the French Revolution was a major blow to the early vision of a simple linear development. Indeed, throughout the nineteenth century, France itself was characterized by a succession of regimes that oscillated abruptly between strong autocracies and attempts at liberal achievement. By the opening of the twentieth century, it seemed that liberalism was at last gradually gaining ground in much of Europe, but World War I and its consequences showed this development to have strict limits. After two world wars, the liberal democratic system has indeed been maintained, but it has failed to take hold in much of the Third World, while Communist systems have constituted a major challenge, which liberal democracies have slowly been compelled to recognize as permanent.

While the notion of liberal democracy was slowly spreading, its characteristics began to change. The founders of the system—Locke, Montesquieu, Madison, and the leaders of the American Revolution—had thought in terms of constitutions, rights, representative assemblies, a restrained executive, and a network of courts. They had not discovered groups; they tended to see "factions" as an unhealthy occurrence and thus deprecated parties as well as other groups.[1] The role of an opposition and its current association with liberal democracy was not visualized and would not have been approved had it been anticipated. The weight of bureaucracy was scarcely noted. Thus, in the course of two centuries, liberal democracies developed structures and to some extent adopted norms (the role of popular participation, and even a trend toward equality in terms of policy goals) that gave these systems the aspect not of products of human constitutional engineering but of slow-changing and adaptive systems, groping for new techniques and new institutions. This has made liberal democracies more alive and probably more varied than they would otherwise have been, and it explains why the study of constitutionalism, though important, is only one aspect of the study of liberal democratic systems. But it probably also explains why these systems did not, after all, spread universally: Engineering alone was too rudimentary to be able to adjust to all social situations.

The Spread of Liberal Democratic Systems in the Contemporary World

Liberalism originated in Western Europe and North America as an idea of government. Gradually, popular participation was

[1] See *The Federalist Papers*, Number 10.

linked to liberalism in the Atlantic area, though not without major difficulties. It is therefore not surprising that liberal democracies should include in particular the twenty or so countries of the Atlantic area. This means that about half the liberal democracies in the contemporary world are within the area, while the rest are scattered across the world, mainly in Latin America and the British Commonwealth. Liberal democracy can therefore be described as a West European product, in fact almost as a British product, which expanded somewhat haphazardly to countries where West European countries, Britain in particular, had major influence (it did not take significant root in former French, Belgian, or Dutch territories). For instance, Japan, India, Chile, Jamaica, Israel, and Malta are liberal democracies. Leaving aside certain limitations and upheavals, Turkey and Ceylon, Costa Rica and Venezuela, South Korea and the Philippines, Gambia and Sierra Leone are also liberal democracies, and a number of other countries are at the borderline, such as Guyana, Madagascar, and Colombia, where the system has strong characteristics of either a populist or a traditional regime.

The influence of Western Europe is clear; that of Britain is perhaps even more patent. Yet it is also remarkable that, on the whole, liberal democracies have tended to take root more easily in the economically richer parts of the world than in its poorer parts, particularly if we exclude countries of the Commonwealth. It is true that East European Communist countries are richer than most countries, but they are poorer than West European countries. Several Latin American countries have a somewhat higher per capita income than African and Asian countries; and in Asia, while India and Ceylon are marked exceptions to the tendency for poorer countries not to be liberal democracies, the presence of Japan and, to a lesser extent, South Korea among liberal democratic countries could have been expected on grounds of their wealth. Over all, as political scientists have shown in various instances, there is indeed a correlation between liberal democracy and socio-economic development, in that the richest polities are most inclined to be stable liberal democracies, while Latin American polities and other Third World countries can be expected to shift periodically between liberal democracy and some other form of regime.[2] Latin American political instability (as well as that of many other countries, such as Turkey, Sudan, and Greece) is thus no longer merely a consequence of a lack of socio-economic development, as is commonly suggested, but instead is almost the logical outcome of the fact that, if these countries are to be liberal democracies, they will be unstable liberal democracies, in the same way as France, Germany, Italy, and Austria were unstable liberal democracies in the nineteenth century and the first half of this century.

There appear to be both a socio-economic and a cultural basis for the spread of liberal democracy, however. The various characteristics of liberal democracy we are about to examine imply the acceptance of a certain slowness in the pace of the decision process as well as a toleration of other people's views and behavior. These may be engrained by a socialization process, and probably must also be buttressed by a standard of living that is high enough to be accepted by the population as tolerable while not raising vast questions of injustice about the distribution of wealth among a large radical segment. It is not accidental that early proponents of liberalism, Locke in particular, considered property to be one of the main correlates of liberalism: The self-sufficient farmer is able to respect the freedom of others whose property he need neither covet nor call into question. Liberal democracies have spread around the world, and, more than any other country, Britain has clearly played a large part in hastening this spread; but in the contemporary world, as well as in the past, liberalism, with or without democracy, seems to be an advantage that the leaders of many countries feel should not be acquired at the expense of other gains.

The Role of Constitutions and Declarations of Rights in Liberal Democracies

As distinct from traditional conservative systems, constitutionalism plays a major role in the normative configuration on which

2 See Seymour M. Lipset, *Political Man: The Social Bases of Politics* (Garden City, N.Y.: Doubleday, Anchor Books, 1959), pp. 45–76, and P. Cutright, "National Political Development," in Nelson W. Polsby, Robert A. Dentler, and Paul A. Smith, *Politics and Social Life: An Introduction to Political Behavior* (Boston: Houghton Mifflin, 1963), pp. 569–82.

liberal democracies are based. It is a liberal axiom that the first measure with which a political system should be concerned is its constitution, the foundation of all other legislation. Priority is thereby given to procedures, on the grounds that procedures distinguish the political life of liberal countries from that of despotisms. The constitution is perceived both as a once-and-for-all affair and as "neutral" regarding the content of future political activities. The theory is that any policy goal can eventually fit within the framework provided for by the constitution. It is of course not true that West European supporters of liberalism always considered the advent of liberalism to be the final goal of their efforts. Many in the past felt that liberalism would gradually encourage the development of political democracy, which in turn would lead to greater equality or "social democracy" (or, in the terminology we have been using, radical policy goals). But as long as the problem is seen not in terms of a choice between alternatives but in terms of a natural sequence, liberal means of government could still be given priority.

Given this emphasis on constitutionalist approaches to government, two main purposes were to be achieved. The first was summarized in the formula of "restraint," particularly restraint of the executive. As a result the word *constitution* itself came to have different meanings: it can be a purely descriptive term (any basic law of the state); it can also mean a law that sets the boundaries of state action, allowing the executive to take only certain decisions in a certain way and after having followed certain procedures. A "constitutional government" in this sense is one that is limited; indeed a country that has no formal written constitution, like the United Kingdom, can only be said to have "constitutional government" in this sense. (Though of course there are many written documents which, together, can be said to form constitutional laws and arrangements in the U.K., there is no single document which has the title of constitution, and many customs and unwritten rules and conventions are added to these written laws in practice.) Legalism, or the "rule of law" followed from this emphasis on restraint as the means to ensure that governments would not overreach their constitutional powers. In practice, restraint and legalism have been markedly eroded. Moreover, constitutionalists failed to see—or at any rate to solve—the problem of laws that, though legal, would be highly repressive (discriminatory laws in a state such as South Africa technically conform to the rule of law). But, clearly, legalism has constituted and still constitutes one of the main tenets of liberal democracies, both in theory and in practice.

The second constitutionalist purpose is reflected in an emphasis on the rights of individuals and their protection. While the constitution is expected to achieve restraint in government, further guarantees must be introduced to ensure that limitations imposed on the freedoms of expression and movement of citizens are kept to a minimum and will affect freedoms only insofar as their exercise will have serious consequences for other citizens of the whole polity. Thus constitutions of liberal democracies (and countries that wish to pass for liberal democracies) include "declarations of rights," which, on the model of the U.S. Bill of Rights or the French 1789 Declaration of Rights, state that citizens have a number of inalienable rights, in particular freedom of movement, freedom of expression (including of the press), freedom of peaceful assembly, and freedom of religion. At the time they were "expounded," these rights were thought to need only to be declared and protected against encroachments, particularly by the state, through independent courts. That is why courts played a large part in the state envisioned by early constitution-makers. Hence written constitutions tend to have a section, sometimes a long section, on the organization of the judiciary. This, more than the question of the constitutionality of laws, which we examined in Chapter 8, was felt everywhere to be fundamental if a constitutional state was to be established. To the present day, constitutions of liberal democracies state the existence of these rights, and proponents of liberalism consider them one of its characteristic marks.

Difficulties arose gradually, however, as liberal countries slowly became liberal *democracies* and emphasis shifted to popular participation and some equality of opportunity, if not radical goals. From the end of the nineteenth century in many European countries, the traditional rights came to be questioned for their formalism. Merely to expound them was not enough, for economic advantage often allowed undue exercise of these rights by some at the expense of others. When the newspaper industry becomes big business, the question of freedom of the press takes a different turn: No one may be forbidden to start a newspaper and to print what he wishes, but it may simply be impossible to do so without large amounts of capital. Guarantees of individual rights also began to appear insufficient because the mass of the population seemed increasingly to require various kinds of opportunities, from full employment to education and social security, without which large numbers would find the right to demonstrate or the right to express critical opinions meaningless. And such new rights cannot be merely expounded; they require large expenditures and large administrative organizations. The courts cannot merely "grant" them. Indeed, even a borderline case like civil rights, as the U.S. experience, among others, shows, involves large public expenditures as well as changes in the attitudes of many. This may be one reason why liberal democracy tends to be restricted to richer countries, where it is possible to give to citizens a modicum of both types of rights, and not merely the principle of liberal rights.

The appearance of new rights is one of the ways in which the practice of liberal democratic systems came to be changed and emphasis on formal legalism decreased. Increasingly, or so it seems, liberal democratic systems have come to stress the role of practices and *de facto* situations against the strict definition of institutions and procedures. Moreover, the development of bureaucracies and of the public sector in general led to a reduction of the part played by "restraint" as the basis for the organization of government. Hence a basic ambiguity in the nature of contemporary liberal democracies, which we shall find in the characteristics of the structures these systems have evolved, more through custom, as we said at the outset in this chapter, than as a direct consequence of the constitutional blueprint.

The Configuration of Structures of Government

For the early supporters of liberalism, and even of liberal democracy (except proponents of "direct democracy," in which the whole populace met and made decisions, which was considered impractical by almost every theorist, particularly in large states, as Rousseau noted), the basic structure of government was to be a representative assembly; the people would participate through the election of the assembly members, who made the laws; and the people could also be involved in the selection of the executive, though it was also deemed quite natural for the assembly to be involved in the process. Rights of minorities were to be preserved, particularly the rights of assembly members who did not agree with the decisions taken. But no other institutions or structures were suggested. Problems would presumably "emerge" and be solved as they appeared.

This description no longer corresponds to the characteristics of modern liberal democracies. Admittedly, elections and electoral systems play a large part, but most of the problems which these raise relate to the effect electoral systems may have on party systems, along with party cleavages in the electorates. Moreover, considerable stress has come to be placed on the recognition that, in reality, liberal democracies are more *polyarchies* than strictly *democracies;* a large dose of pluralism allows groups to emerge and express themselves.[3] Liberal democracies may then be more liberal, in that they allow for a variety of views, than democratic, as the participation of the mass of citizens is quite limited, occurring perhaps only once every few years in national, regional or state, and local elections and usually as a "passive" choice between alternatives or candidates presented to them.

In contrast with traditional conservative systems, however, the groups that exist are very often associational groups with relatively narrow aims. Consequently, their area of legitimacy is small and their leaders have to take into account the attitudes of the rank and file, which might not follow the group leaders if they extend their aims too widely or too quickly, as we saw in Chapter 5. But, though associational groupings spring up frequently in liberal democracies, no liberal democracy can be said to be wholly associational in character. For associationalism to be full, no communal group can exist in the polity, while each demand must lead automatically and instantaneously to the creation of an association. Even if there is in principle no legal bar to the creation of new groups (a consequence of the notion of

3 See Robert A. Dahl, *A Preface to Democratic Theory* (Chicago: University of Chicago Press, 1956), pp. 63–81, and *idem, Polyarchy: Participation and Opposition* (New Haven, Conn.: Yale University Press, 1971).

individual rights) and although counter-groups often express positions opposite to those prevailing, nowhere is the proliferation of groups wholly without limits. Even in the United States (which was noted by Tocqueville in the 1830's to be already a country of marked associationalism), *de facto* restrictions prevent groups or counter-groups from emerging. Financial costs, milder forms of repression, and lack of opportunity limit group development. The socialization process, mentioned in Chapter 2, has the effect of increasing the viscosity of the group configuration. Participation in groups can also be very low in promotional as well as protective associations, although the latter tend to have larger memberships because of their function as "insurance," for instance to enable workers to obtain higher wages, employers to press for laws and regulations that are to their advantage, and generally citizens threatened by new developments, for instance urban, road, or airport developments, not to be wholly without recourse. Though liberal democracies are located on the associational side of the associational-communal dimension, they are at some distance from the associational end and do not appear to move markedly farther toward it.

This is in part because, as we noted in Chapter 5, all groups have an inherent propensity to create patterns of social relationships, and this tendency exists in liberal democracies as in other political systems. Workers' and farmers' organizations have always been a long way from being associations with narrow aims, whether in the United States or elsewhere. Moreover, as one cleavage ceases to have a strong communal pull (as perhaps class in some European countries), other cleavages emerge, in particular those of ethnic groups, which not only aim at an improvement of their economic conditions but also make cultural demands, thus forming subcultures with a communal base.

The predominance of associational over communal groups that characterizes liberal democracies is one further indication of the fact that liberal democracies are to be found mainly among richer industrial polities, since, as we saw in Chapter 5, communal ties tend to be broken as mobility increases, either geographically or educationally, and this mobility increases with socio-economic development. The two movements are not accidentally linked, however, although there are considerable variations among liberal democracies; communal ties are more widespread in India or Costa Rica than in the United States or West Germany. Indeed, the paradox of the maintenance of a caste system in India within the framework of liberal democracy has often been noted as one of the potential dangers for that country's political system. Conversely, the degree of urbanization that has characterized Continental European countries since the nineteenth century has led to the break-up of communal ties. Where the level of urbanization is lower, as initially in France, communalism has been stronger and liberal democracy weaker; the rapid urbanization that characterized France in the 1950's, and even more in the 1960's, has indeed been accompanied by a growth of associationalism and, despite some authoritarian executive action in the early De Gaulle period, a basic strengthening of liberal democracy. Over all, associationalism appears to give greater legitimacy to a liberal democratic system, for groups transmit demands, thereby allowing greater participation and a less selective mechanism, and the party system can more easily acquire a legitimate mass character as a result.

Although traditional conservative systems can function without political parties because of the legitimacy of the communal groups and, in general, the "natural" leadership structure, an associational or near-associational polity could not function without a party system. This system prepares the framework of policy by coordinating the sectional demands of the groups and looks after the implementation of difficult decisions. It also provides a means by which new leaders emerge and rotate. The more associational the polity, the more a party system is required.

But an associational or near-associational polity cannot "produce" a party system, because associational groupings do not have the broad capital of legitimacy needed to build parties. Hence the paradox of the development and maintenance of liberal democratic polities: Communal groups must have been sufficiently influential to lead to the creation of a legitimate party system before themselves slowly giving way or losing influence to associational groups. Theorists of constitutional government neither recognized this requirement nor realized how difficult the process of legitimacy transfer would be likely to be. It is therefore not surprising that the party configurations found among liberal democracies vary around the four types of party systems we described in Chapter 6. Nor is it surprising that there have been many "accidents," particularly where the process was speeded up exaggeratedly through the desire of constitutionalists to implement liberal democracy almost by imposition. If communal cleavages are too complex or too numerous, the emergent party system will not be one of the stable types; the regime itself may in turn be unstable, as in France, Italy, or Weimar Germany. If cleavages are too few and one group is overwhelmingly strong, opponents might feel frustrated, and leaders might not obey the canons of the liberal democratic system. The party system was able to develop very slowly in Britain in part because of the absence of any "better" model with which the system could be compared unfavorably; such a slow pace is probably needed for a party system to become legitimate naturally. But even in Britain the two-party system went through a phase of one-party dominance in the eighteenth century before the parties settled first around regional, personal, and to some extent religious communal loyalties, and later around the class cleavage.

Party systems are not of the legitimate mass type in most parts of the world, as we noted, and the absence of a time sequence during which communal groups slowly decrease in strength makes such legitimate mass parties a short-term impossibility; admittedly, imitation has helped in many cases—particularly in the Commonwealth—to create a party system that, though still not fully legitimate, appears sufficiently stable, and sufficiently distinct from the groups, to display some of the characteristics and fulfill the functions of a network of legitimate mass parties. But it follows that the process is likely to occur only in a portion of the world's polities and to be particularly rare among new countries. In some of the intermediate cases, where the party system is still legitimizing (as in Turkey or Venezuela), "accidents" are likely to occur, and the party system is bound to remain in question.

Yet the existence of a party system is essential. With a party system, liberal democracies appeared to solve some of the social and economic demands that emerged in Western Europe at the turn of the twentieth century. By becoming more democratic and moving toward less conservative policies, liberal democracies in fact abandoned somewhat the truly liberal creed, which calls for the priority of means. This development led to a different view of the role of government, which included the promotion of new services and a better distribution of social benefits. When this ran up against the idea of "restraint" it undermined the over-all premise of a weak executive. Thus a system had to be found by which the tenets of liberalism could be generally maintained but somewhat transformed: From a system of checks and balances, which was the epitome of constitutionalism (at least in its more realistic form), liberal democratic systems were gradually changed, through the party system, into a system of government and opposition, where limitations on action are due more to time and custom than to law and procedures.

We noted in Chapter 7 that theorists of constitutional government devised two and possibly three systems: the presidential or separation-of-powers system, the parliamentary system, and the "convention" system, in which most of the powers reside with the assembly. The third of these was rarely implemented, and in the one case when it was, under the 1792 French Convention, it led to dictatorship. Presidential systems still probably constitute the most elaborate means of restraining the executive. This perhaps stems from the fact that their (relatively limited) success has come despite the constitutional constraints rather than because of them. What started as a means of restraining the executive became in many countries (nineteenth-century France was one) a means by which a popular leader could install himself in power and never abandon it. In Latin American countries, presidentialism has generally been not an instrument of executive restraint but a technique by which forms of *caudillismo* could more easily establish themselves. For a very long time, only in the United States did the separation-of-powers system come to be a "halfway house" where the powers of Congress were strong enough to match (and at times more than match) presidential strength. But even there, the system came to be maintained because the President was recognized to have powers of leadership through popular election; elsewhere where presidential systems maintained liberal democracy, as in Chile, Costa Rica, and, at times, Venezuela, Argentina, Brazil, the Philippines, or South Korea, the popular legitimacy of the President had to be able to match and even override the power of Congress. In the end, it is the existence of this leadership that has given presidentialism its ability to develop within liberal democracy; more than checks and balances, the system has made it possible to organize government, though it has not done enough (as Americans have often noted) to organize an opposition able to counterbalance, coherently and systematically, the powers of the executive.[4]

The parliamentary system became better able to organize political life around government and opposition because it allowed for the influence of a cabinet and a prime minister, which was limited more by the political influence of the assembly than by judicial restraints on executive powers. Indeed, at the origin of constitutionalism, the parliamentary system was often viewed as a means for monarchs to continue ruling through manipulation of the assembly. This view of the British arrangements led to the more rigid separation of powers in the United States. The parliamentary system was never characterized by checks and balances, but it became acceptable to liberals because, while providing a means of gradually reducing the power of the monarch, it seemed to promise that the executive ultimately would be made and unmade by the assembly, wherein the question of confidence would become the key element. It could be said that the government was merely a committee of the assembly; the chief of state was a monarch with few and purely decorative powers; and the real leaders of the country were chosen by, and stemmed from, the legislature.

The growth of parties turned this view into a myth, as the power of the assembly to overthrow the government slowly became as decorative and unreal as the power of the monarch. But this transformation gave power to the cabinet, and even more to the Prime Minister, only if two conditions obtained. The first was that the number of parties be relatively small and, more important, that the largest party have a majority or a near-majority of the votes. We have seen that this is the case in three of the four types of party systems that exist in liberal democracies of the Atlantic area—the two-party system, the two-and-a-half party system, and the multiparty system with a dominant party. The

---

[4] For an analysis of the nature of the party system in Congress, see David B. Truman, *The Congressional Party* (New York: John Wiley, 1959).

multiparty system without a dominant party has become very rare, in part because, as we also have seen, the instability of regimes has often led to a change in the party system (as in Germany or France) or to the end of the liberal system. The second condition is that the parties be disciplined and that the mass of legislators be prepared to vote as the leadership suggests. This in fact came about as a consequence of the development of legitimate mass parties; since electors vote for the party as a whole—for what it represents or the image it projects—individual congressmen or deputies rarely owe their election to their own following (candidates for nomination by the party may do so more frequently, as primary elections suggest in the United States). It is therefore possible to threaten members of the party who vote against the party line on major issues with expulsion from the party or the loss of the party label. As such members are likely to lose their seats as a result, the threat is usually not without effect.

Parliamentary or, more aptly, cabinet systems were thus able to develop where parties were few and disciplined. The party system became truly a "system" in that the strength of the executive (which was little restrained since it could count on the loyalty of a majority of the deputies to pass legislation and to support it in office) led to the only alternative form of restraint, which was the development of an opposition aimed at replacing the party in power, meanwhile undertaking to examine and scrutinize the activities of the executive and make public opinion aware of the government's failures. It could thus be suggested that the function of the assembly was more to provide a forum for debate and to prepare the next general election than to take part in decisions over laws and other questions, since the laws were often prepared by the executive and were accepted by the majority.[5] This view is an exaggeration, for the long-term influence of the legislature in important matters and its short-term influence in many matters of lesser concern can be significant. But it remains broadly true that the restraint by constitutional procedures that the liberal system was originally meant to provide turned into a match between government and opposition,

---

[5] As suggested in Bernard R. Crick, *The Reform of Parliament* (London: Weidenfeld and Nicolson; Gloucester, Mass.: Peter Smith, 1964).

the protection of the population coming from the apparent equality of rights given to the two sides.

This form of the parliamentary system is of course better achieved with a balanced two-party system than with any other party system. But most liberal democracies are not balanced two-party systems, and the opposition is either much weaker (as in some of the new states) or much more divided. Scandinavia, for instance, is characterized by a multiparty system with a socialist party far larger than any other party, hence the opposition there seems weaker than in Britain or Australia. Yet even in countries having the multiparty system with a dominant party or a two-and-a-half-party system, the notion of an opposition prevails. Either the largest of the other parties is considered to have special rights, or all the opposition parties jointly constitute the opposition (and indeed sometimes unite to form the government, as in Norway or in Denmark in the second half of the 1960's). Although many more forms of coalition may occur, various alliances take place (in West Germany, with a two-and-a-half-party system, all three possible coalitions have occurred, and the same happened in Belgium when such a party system prevailed), and the concept of an opposition truly depends on the existence of a two-party system, the idea of government and opposition characterizes parliamentary systems and also seems to constitute the solution for all liberal democracies, for it has sometimes permeated into presidential systems, at least in theory.

Thus, liberal democratic systems have in fact permitted strong government (the growth of the bureaucracy has made it even stronger) while retaining scope for discussion and for change of the executive. The idea of restraint has not altogether disappeared, but it tends to be more marked at the periphery of the system than in the ability of the government to act. Some rules and customs lead to the maintenance of rights for the opposition either in the chamber or in the polity at large, particularly in the mass media. Freedom of the press (despite the limitations imposed by high costs) and the establishment of independent or neutral government-owned radio and TV networks also imply that the executive has to be restrained. Moreover, limitations on the bureaucracy, either informally through legislators or through the judiciary, in particular through the various administrative courts, tribunals, or ombudsmen examined in Chapter 8, suggest that the protection of rights still plays a part in these systems. But it is also true that these limitations do not appreciably affect the power of the executive and, under the executive, of the bureaucracy to act decisively and to further the development of a welfare state and a controlled or semicontrolled economy, which limit the freedom of individuals and cannot easily be reconciled with many of the original tenets of liberalism.

The Problems of Liberal Democracy

The development of the welfare state and the guidance of the economy, through the development, at least in European liberal democracies and even in North America, of a large public sector seemed possible because for a large part of the twentieth century the party system was characterized by a form of competition that pitted the supporters of the traditional system, conservatives under various labels (including Christian democrats), against the proponents of major change (social democrats, labor parties, and Communists). Even in the United States, where social democracy did not take root, the Democratic party seemed to become more radical and, at least under Franklin D. Roosevelt, engaged in a large program of left-wing reforms. Traditional liberal parties became less influential and, after losing ground electorally, often allied with conservatives, although occasionally (sometimes because of antichurch attitudes) they supported for a period governments of the left. Under this arrangement, it was possible to describe liberal democracies of the Atlantic area, as well as some liberal democracies across the world (Japan, Chile, Israel, and other liberal democracies under various labels) as states in which "competitive mobilization" occurred, with the normative standpoints in competition being sufficiently distinct to lead to the mobilization (or at least the apparent mobilization) of the electorate behind each of the two main labels.

Evolution through the 1950's and 1960's markedly decreased the extent of competitive mobilization in Western liberal democracies and others. It was argued at some point, on the basis of empirical evidence or logical deduction, that the parties in two-party systems necessarily converged in order to catch the crucial votes of the "center," which either party needed to obtain a majority.[6] Whether the theory is indeed empirically valid or not, the activities of the main political parties seemed to suggest that differences had decreased. This is why we stated that parties (possibly with the exception of the Communist parties) tended to have similar liberal democratic norms in all of these systems. Right-wing parties have become eager to appear "social" and to cater to the underdog, and socialist parties have introduced reforms with such caution that little change took place in the redistribution of social and economic power in the 1960's, for instance, when a number of socialist parties were in power or shared power (in Britain, Sweden, Germany, Austria, and Belgium, while socialists had long been strong in Norway and Denmark). Changes had taken place on a moderate or even large scale in the first half of the twentieth century, but the ability or will for reform seemed to have been exhausted, and socialist parties, when in power, seemed more constrained by problems of balance of payments or short-term economic difficulties than intent on major change, the idea of which had even been abandoned in the programs of these parties.

Thus competitive mobilization can scarcely be said any longer to constitute the main characteristic of Western liberal democracies. But while it seemed that the movement toward convergence was acceptable in the late 1950's and early 1960's, discontent arose in the later 1960's in a variety of forms, sometimes around truly serious problems, sometimes outside the ambit of a particular problem and seemingly as a diffuse form of protest against what to some appeared to be the inability to channel grievances, let alone to overthrow, peacefully or otherwise, the capitalist system. Criticisms of the "establishment" under its various forms (including the Communist party itself in such countries as France or Italy, where that party is strong and forms one of the most important, if not the most important, opposition force) have been voiced, somewhat anarchistically, especially by the young (but also by blacks and other ethnic minorities in several Western countries). In the liberal democracies of the Third World, except for a time in Chile when the hope for a radical

---

[6] See Anthony Downs, *An Economic Theory of Democracy* (New York: Harper and Row, 1957).

transformation was widespread among left-wing groups, the same feeling of discontent and impatience with established institutions and with the inability to find a new solution or to revive competitive mobilization is noticeable. As a result, liberal democracies appear to some as repressive as other systems, which they are not, for the appearance of repressiveness stems from the impatience of small minorities and from the absence of a practical model on which change might take place. But this impatience does create a problem, as does the type of inequality that these systems seem ready to retain and scarcely to challenge. Liberal democratic systems in Western countries and in the Third World have achieved major reforms in the direction of liberalism and some reform in the direction of political democracy and economic well-being. It would be serious if they proved unable to move further in the direction of reform.

Reform is difficult in liberal democracies, because the very pluralism of these systems leads increasingly to slowness in the process of advice and discussion these systems entail. Bureaucracies may be vast, and assemblies may often be prepared to rubber-stamp the proposals of executives. But often these proposals have been prepared and discussed for years among interested people, which of course include not all, but at least large sections, of the polity's leaders. The system becomes clogged, and reforms can be achieved quickly only if such techniques of advice are limited or brushed aside. This is unlikely to happen in the short run. In order to win over opponents, even at times extremist ones, committees, councils, or bureaus are created, which are often means of co-opting these opponents and enabling them to become "constructive" in their criticisms. It is difficult to oppose such a method in principle, but it becomes possible to wonder whether the very idea of government and opposition, which, as we saw, characterized liberal democracies for several decades, any longer constitutes a true picture. Liberal democracies are faced with a dilemma, and opponents, even extremist opponents, are often unready to choose within this dilemma. Long-term changes in the society require mobilization or education of the electorate, which is contradictory to the solution of many short-term problems. The pluralistic system based on associations is particularly well designed to solve short-term problems, although not all of them may be solved and the associational network may not be fully comprehensive. What liberal democratic systems seem unable to do, both in Atlantic countries and in the Third World, is to deal successfully with long-term problems, because their mechanisms and structures (and perhaps the attitudes of many of the leaders and much of the population) seem in fact to be better adapted to the solution of short-term problems than to the patient examination of cures for the long-term.

11

Communist Systems

Since the Russian Revolution and particularly in the post-1945 period, Communist systems have constituted the main ideological challenge to liberal democracies. In the interwar period, the challenge of Communism contributed to the emergence of a number of authoritarian conservative systems in Eastern and Central Europe. But these did not succeed in presenting a real alternative. In the contemporary world, as we shall see in Chapter 13, they constitute more of a challenge to populist Third World polities than to liberal democracies. Communist systems, on the contrary, have provided a radical authoritarian challenge that has appealed, though less so since the late 1960's, to a working-class and intellectual segment in liberal democratic polities. With fourteen polities in the world belonging to this group, two of which, China and the Soviet Union, are among the most populous countries of the world, Communism has succeeded in less than half a century of development in establishing itself as a form of government that is both truly different and viable (though it can be argued that the two world wars were instrumental in this development, to which Marxists would probably reply that the wars were an inevitable consequence of the difficulties of capitalism).

Yet the 1960's seemed to suggest that radical authoritarian polities based primarily on the rigid organization of the Communist party had passed their peak. Externally, the limited expansion of Communism must have disappointed and possibly surprised supporters of Communism. Outside the area of Eastern Europe and North Asia, including Vietnam, where Communism was implanted in the late 1940's, only Cuba came to join the group. Guinea seemed most likely to verge toward Communism after its independence in 1958, but it did not (although its policies in some areas are similar to those of Communist countries), nor did some of the African and Middle Eastern countries that showed signs of becoming radical at one point or other in 1960's. Internally, Communist countries became split, not merely through the rift between China and the Soviet Union but also through the increased influence of Yugoslav policies and of demands elsewhere for more liberal policies, greater participation, and less bureaucracy (which was clearly one of the reasons for the Chinese Cultural Revolution). The dislike for Soviet imperialism may have been in many cases a profound reason for discontent (though it is quite possible that Communism as a whole may not have survived and clearly would not have been so successful—in Eastern Europe, for example—if the Soviet Union had not been so "imperialistic"). But the dislike for imperialism is probably more the by-product of a general disappointment that the "millennium" that was to have come about with this new system of government did not in fact materialize. Communist systems appear radical in policy goals, many of which have been implemented, but participation is not really high, nor does the level of authoritarianism introduced by the system seem to many to be acceptable after such a long period of implantation. Thus, externally and internally, Communist systems have suffered from a low level of legitimacy, which in turn has heightened their need to protect themselves by further authoritarian measures and, indeed, by authoritarian interventions, such as in Czechoslovakia in 1968. Though an undisputed achievement, the Communist system or systems of government are no longer considered by many to foreshadow the obvious development of the future.

The Normative Base: Rights and the Role of Constitutions

It is sometimes argued that constitutions play no part in Communist systems. We have stated repeatedly that constitutionalism was the direct by-product of a liberal or liberal democratic viewpoint, but it would be wrong to infer that constitutional arrangements and, even more, constitutional myths are of little importance in Communist systems, not only in the more liberal systems (Yugoslavia) but also in the Soviet Union and most of the radical authoritarian polities. Of course, one reason why constitutional arrangements exist and are given apparent importance in Soviet literature, for instance, is that the Soviet and other Communist systems proceed from the model of the liberal democratic government, however much they distort it and profess to despise it. For a variety of reasons, it seemed politically useful in the prewar and the immediate postwar period to stress that Communist systems, unlike fascist and Nazi systems, were based on regular procedures and institutions that showed respect for the representative system of government. This is why constitutions play a much smaller part for some of the Asian Communist states (and for the Soviet Union in the very early period of its development); it is also why constitutional arrangements play scarcely any part in Cuba, the only Communist state that eschews the idea of representative government altogether and claims to achieve participation through direct communication between the leaders, specifically Fidel Castro, and the people, where the process of government has scarcely been formalized at all, except in relation to groups and the party.

Political expediency is not the only reason for the part played by constitutions in Communist systems, particularly in East European Communist systems. The constitution is in large part a symbol and is therefore one of the means by which the political system is impressed upon the citizens. It establishes principles of equality and participation—tempered, admittedly, by the role given to the Communist party as vanguard of the population. It establishes, in the Soviet Union, Yugoslavia, and more recently, Czechoslovakia, principles of freedom and equality for the various nationalities within these polities, as well as detailed arrangements of a federal character. It places a high premium, as is to be expected of documents inspired by Marxism, on determination of the economic conditions under which various freedoms can be expected to flourish. In particular, the celebrated article 125 of the Soviet Constitution specifies that freedom of the press is in fact established by giving printing presses to the working people, thereby granting them the means of expression. Whether the system allows opportunities for dissent in practice is another matter, but the fact that printing is transferred to "the people" is of considerable symbolic importance (and it does not *logically* entail that dissent is viewed with suspicion).

These constitutions have to be seen as symbols that help to make Communist systems acceptable to at least a section of the polity. The need for them is enhanced by the fact that, to a very large degree, these systems have always lived, so to speak, in the future. The existence of imposition is not denied altogether, though its extent and pervasiveness are denied. In the early years of the Soviet and of other East European Communist regimes, imposition was justified on the grounds that "imperialist" and "bourgeois" elements had to be unmasked and the mass of citizens protected. However exaggerated this claim might have been, opposition to these regimes was clearly large. With the legal means of action out of operation (namely, the electoral process, which, in Russia after World War I and in the East European states after World War II, had given the Communists neither a majority of assembly seats nor a majority in combination with allies), opponents had to be prevented from turning to other means. Moreover, Communism aims at changing the economic structure of society and the attitudes of men, neither of which is easily done and both of which require considerable imposition, if they can be achieved at all—and Communist experience has shown that it may not be possible to change the attitudes of men.

Thus imposition is justified in the short run to protect citizens not only against "enemies of the people" but also against themselves, to lead to the creation of a "new man" devoid of the bourgeois attitudes (presumably acquisitive and profit-oriented, as well as individualistic) that characterize capitalist states. More attention has been paid to eliminating bourgeois attitudes in China than in the Soviet Union, where the accent has been (in orthodox Marxist terms) on the economic transformation of society and the creation of a basis for plenty rather than the transformation of attitudes. Indeed, in Eastern Europe and even in the Soviet Union no serious effort has been made to change the characteristics of individuals. Imposition has taken the form of repression, propaganda, and advantages given to followers. But the need to transform the society, whether for psychological or for economic reasons, has led to an orientation toward the future in Communist states, which has always been of primary importance for understanding the policy outlook as well as the role of various symbols, including the constitution, in the structure of politics.

These attitudes have begun to change. In Yugoslavia, constitutional reforms in the 1960's and the early 1970's have shown a tendency to use constitutional arrangements for "constitutionalist" purposes, such as allowing greater popular participation in the organs of government and workers' participation in the management of firms. Changes are also taking place in other East European Communist states, including the Soviet Union, however slow the process may appear to be. Demands for "Socialist legality" to ensure that the excesses of Stalinism do not recur constitute one form in which liberalization takes place. In the Asian Communist states (and probably Cuba) radical authoritarian systems are keeping close to the old ideal of living for the future and the reconstruction of mankind. In Eastern Europe, those Communist systems which are still markedly authoritarian have to some extent shied away from the radical "justification" of imposition for future benefits, and constitutional rights correspondingly play a greater part.

The Structures of Communist Systems

Whatever the symbolic role of constitutions in radical authoritarian systems, the key structure responsible for the over-all maintenance and the detailed working of these systems is the single party. One crucial distinction is that between party and state, the party being the spur with which the state can be kept moving in the right direction. All state organizations are supervised or controlled by the party; all aspects of society, at least in theory, are infiltrated by the party, which can act as both an instrument to counteract or suppress potential opposition and an agent for mobilizing segments of the population that might otherwise be apathetic. It is no exaggeration to say that the major "invention" of Communist political systems is the party. In liberal democratic systems in the nineteenth century, parties emerged more haphazardly and with much less exalted functions, although by the time of the Russian Revolution, socialist parties in Germany and other West European countries had acquired considerable importance and status.

The Communist party is conceived as the vanguard of the proletariat; it is therefore not conceived anywhere as a "mere" representative of the people. It is an elite and is viewed as such. This is the ostensible reason why it is given a special position and why its position is recognized in the constitution. The Communist party is not everywhere the only party legally allowed, though this is so in the majority of the radical authoritarian polities. For various reasons, some polities have maintained the existence of other parties, or the Communist party has been merged into a broader organization of the working class. In East Germany, Poland, and Czechoslovakia, other parties are allowed and indeed function as semi-autonomous organizations, while in East Germany the Communist party has merged with the socialist party to form a Socialist Unity party. But in all cases, the Communist party is the leading element, as witnessed by the fact that, where other parties are allowed and the assembly is composed of a number of groups, members are elected from a single joint list, which always gives the majority to the Communists. Other parties (Christians or agrarians, for instance) are said to exist as long as there are still classes with somewhat distinct characteristics, but the official view is probably that they are doomed to extinction, a process that appears slow to come, however.

Because the Communist party is avowedly an elite, the selection of its members must be careful. Given its over-all mission of controlling and stimulating the society, the party must infiltrate all walks of life. These two aspects are somewhat contradictory: The party must be extensive enough to "swim" within the state and society, but not so large that it ceases to be an elite. Over all, Communist parties in radical authoritarian systems have succeeded in doing both adequately, though a tendency toward representativeness has been slowly increasing in the 1960's. In earlier periods, particularly under Stalin in the Soviet Union and under Stalin's influence elsewhere, periodic purges made certain that "undesirable" elements were eliminated from the party at all levels and that the rest were kept on their toes as a result. But large-scale purges have become increasingly rare with the result that the Soviet party has gradually grown to a membership of 13 million. Moreover, it has apparently become increasingly easy to enter the party; the period of "candidate" membership, which was taken very seriously in the past, is no longer a major hurdle.

The party, while thus quite extensive, shows a variety of biases. It extends into the working class, both urban and rural, and Communist party workers act as spurs, for instance, for production drives—though one hears less about them than in the Stalin period. But it is even more present and influential among the intelligentsia at large, that is, the business and administrative classes in factories or offices, among technicians or nonspecialists, military or civilian. Indeed, it often seems as if membership in the Communist party is required for such jobs, or at least that promotion is facilitated for those who belong to the party. Here, the Communist party shows some of the characteristics of a network or an "establishment." It ensures that men and women are at least ostensibly socialized into the goals of the Communist society, and it has the effect of giving these men and women, as a consequence, many advantages.

This educational, elite-formation function of the Communist party accounts for its considerable role in the selection of inputs to go into the system. It is typically stated, as we saw in Chapter 6, that the Communist party operates on the principle of democratic centralism, which means that ideas are first discussed at the bottom levels, then approved by representative organs (ultimately by the party Congress, which meets every four years), and afterward must be accepted and actively supported by all, whatever views had been expressed originally about them. Some questions are debated at length; reforms of various legal codes, for instance, were discussed widely in the Soviet Union. But in general, the existence of the Communist party has the effect of sifting views and demands at the grass roots, particularly those from nonmembers, and indeed preventing not only the enunciation and spread of dissenting views but even consideration of the idea of dissent as an alternative line of conduct. There are marked variations, admittedly, over both time and space. The system was clearly more totalitarian, or closed, under Stalin than in the 1960's in the Soviet Union; it is more closed in the Soviet Union and East Germany than in Yugoslavia and even Poland or Rumania. But over all, the restriction on demands is one of the characteristic features of an extensive single party such as the Communist party.

The Communist party has two other important roles. First, as a framer of policy it makes high-level decisions and, at lower levels, coordinates the work of the various state agencies. This role, of course, is only a more extreme version of the functions all parties tend to have, especially as their structures become more efficient, more extensive, and more centralized. In West European countries, the party in power provides much of the impetus for major decisions as well as the personnel responsible for these decisions. In Communist polities, the same party remains permanently in power and assumes the special role of leading the polity. Much of the decision-making is done by the party, for instance in its central committee, its political bureau (or presidium), or its secretariat, rather than by state organizations. Sections of the party secretariat parallel some of the ministries and oversee activities of these ministries; laws passed by the assembly and government are discussed and approved beforehand by the central committee and its presidium. Hence the somewhat justifiable claim that the real head of the government is the party general secretary, not the chairman of the council of ministers, though it is probably not equally valid everywhere.

This pattern is repeated at the local level, but here the party also helps to solve some of the problems that the vast bureaucracy entails by cutting across vertical links between central ministries and individual factories and by providing a form of coordination that might not otherwise occur. Thus, the party secretary in a region, town, or district (as well as in a republic or other autonomous component of a federal Communist state such as the Soviet Union) plays the part of a regional commissioner or coordinator. Local party meetings and personal connections further the maintenance of the Communist network. The administrative machine of as complex a state as the Soviet Union would probably clog were there no party to help render more informal its many relations, contracts, exchanges, and so forth.

The second role of the party, more specific to single-party systems, is to oversee the implementation of decisions and control the way they are carried out by the bureaucracy. This function is allied with coordination and similar to it but extends more widely throughout the hierarchy. Communist party control plays a special part in the fulfillment of economic plans, the Soviet invention designed to achieve economic growth and to bring about plenty. But the party is also engaged in activities more limited in scope: It may act as an "ombudsman" and protect citizens against the bureaucracy. Though the process takes place within the prevailing normative framework, this redress mechanism is not to be dismissed as a mere paper aspect of the feedback that takes place in Communist systems.

Because the party is *the* crucial organization, various other organizations are naturally dependent on the party. Groups created to prolong the tentacles of the party in all aspects of society, whether of the young (the Komsomol in the Soviet Union), of women, of workers (the very large trade union organizations), athletic organizations, cultural associations, and so on, are composed of both party members and nonmembers but are aimed at mobilizing the population under the party's aegis. The Komsomol is particularly geared to this purpose, since it serves as a preparatory institution from which Communist party members are eventually recruited. Yet these organizations are in their own right instruments of participation. They are becoming increasingly autonomous and are thereby introducing some tension between the party's goals and their own. But they had to be created as dependent associations to break communal ties, particularly religious ones (success on this front has been far from complete, even in the Soviet Union, let alone in other East European countries, especially Poland). The need to prevent the growth of grass-roots organizations is always present, as demonstrated in the late 1960's and early 1970's by the underground Jewish organizations, which the Soviet Union tried to suppress with only moderate success. Clearly, the more the demands channeled by such dependent organizations—for instance, workers' organizations—fall outside the scope of the selection structure that the

Communist party aims at maintaining, the greater the resulting tension. Yet the legitimacy levels of these organizations depend on their ability to channel large numbers of demands effectively.

Groups and the party thus play a major part in the output side of the political process in Communist states, while their role in processing demands has probably increased as well. Conversely, state organizations are perhaps more involved in inputs than in normally expected of a bureaucracy. At the top, constitutional arrangements have led to the establishment, in all Communist countries except Cuba, of an apparatus of government and assembly that is not formally very different from similar bodies in liberal democracies. Lower in the hierarchy, however, the bureaucracy—and even the military—have created tensions that are more reminiscent of Third World polities. It would be wrong to dismiss assemblies in the Communist world, particularly in Yugoslavia or Poland, as we noted in Chapter 7, as mere rubber stamps, because they do play a part in channeling demands, at least in questions affecting particular and not general policy. The degree of decentralization that exists in the three federal Communist states—the Soviet Union, Yugoslavia, and Czechoslovakia—also should not be discounted as purely formal. Nevertheless, the convention system of government adopted by Communist states has clearly given easy dominance to the Communist party. In all these states, the assembly presidiums and the councils of ministers are composed overwhelmingly of Communist party members. Meanwhile, the really difficult problems Communist states have had to face, both for economic development and for their ideological unity, have concerned the bureaucracy and the military.

Communist systems must achieve economic development at sufficient speed to enable them to distribute goods and services widely among the population. Thus the bureaucracy, the technical bureaucracy in particular, is given prominence, high status, and much autonomy. But this must not be at the expense of the over-all policy goals, so the party must be a watchdog of the technicians' actions. As a result, the notion of the dependence of the bureaucracy on the political masters, an axiom adopted everywhere in the early part of the twentieth century, is a basic and particularly crucial principle of Communist systems. Decisions on priorities are made by political men, as for instance the choice of capital investment over consumer goods, as well as the many less important decisions resulting from this choice.

In practice, however, clashes are unavoidable between the political masters and the technicians, who feel they know best what is good for their service. As we noted in Chapter 8, technicians might disagree among themselves if left alone; but difficulties arise when young men with talent begin to discover that the party needs their services more than they need the party. This led to a celebrated conflict between Malenkov and Khrushchev in the mid-1950's, when Khrushchev sided with the party and won on its behalf. Party dominance was maintained and reaffirmed. But the problem is always present. The "new class" criticized by Djilas in Yugoslavia may have comprised party men as well as other members of the middle classes,[1] but the role of the bureaucracy, the technical bureaucracy in particular, will unavoidably increase and the weight of Communist party secretaries will diminish. Political socialization needs to be carried on continuously on a wide scale, but probably nothing short of a Chinese-style cultural revolution, emphasizing the primacy of fundamental attitudinal changes rather than the primacy of economic development, can profoundly alter the basis of the problem. And such cultural revolutions may be too costly in men and resources to be allowed to recur.

The same type of tension involves the military. With the army too, the prevailing principle has been that civilians must remain masters. To ensure that the principle was applied, the Soviet military from the start included many political officers, whose function was to "educate" the army and to report officers and men of questionable loyalty. The nationalistic character of Russia's World War II effort made loyalty a less critical problem, at least for the great bulk of the Soviet Army. But the large amount of imposition on which Communist states rely has the effect of placing a key responsibility on the army, while external dangers in a cold war environment both enhance the status of the military and raise the question of the reliability of the East European Communist allies. On at least two occasions, in Hungary in 1956

[1] Milovan Djilas, *The New Class* (New York: Praeger, 1957).

and in Czechoslovakia in 1968, the Soviet military has been directly involved in the maintenance of a Communist system outside the country's borders. In other cases, involving China and East European states, the Soviet military has had to be relied upon for possible action. Thus it is not surprising that its involvement in politics should at times have been fairly deep.

Indeed, the mid-1950's debate between technicians and party was solved to Khrushchev's and the party's advantage thanks to military leaders who gained in importance as a result (though efforts were made afterward to reduce their influence). On other occasions and in a less conspicuous fashion, the role of the army has also seemed large. The Soviet system is too complex, admittedly, for an army takeover to be more than a remote possibility; even an army-backed change of civilian leaders is quite unlikely. But in the structural configuration that characterizes this system, the party's role seems likely to decrease at the expense of the bureaucracy and, both in the Soviet Union and in East European Communist states, as well as in China, the military has been called on and will be called on again to act as an arbiter in a variety of circumstances.

This is especially likely because, as we suggested, the bureaucracy (along with the military) has become an increasingly important means by which demands are channeled into the system. Demands are in the first instance those of the "new class" and those which technicians and administrators receive from the population while on duty, particularly outside the capital. The bureaucratic machinery allows demands to be fed in without raising problems of public presentation, particularly if the demands are couched in technical terms and are shielded against outright rejection by ostensible references to the norms and policy goals of the political system. In this way, control of the system may to some extent escape the leadership. The Yugoslav experiment of workers' control at the grass roots appears to be one ultimate conclusion of such a development. Each productive unit is at least in theory so independent that the Communist party machine has almost nothing to do with the over-all process. As a result, technocracy may gain more than appears perhaps at first sight, for many local decisions are likely to be influenced by immediate technical, administrative, or commercial considerations rather than by the norms and policy goals of the polity. Clearly, Communist systems find themselves confronted with practical problems that were only in small part theoretically anticipated—and then were often attributed to purely "bourgeois" attitudes, which Communism would easily eradicate. The future development of Communist polities thus depends on a series of choices, though the choices open to leaders are usually much smaller than is readily assumed.

The Future of Communist Systems: Liberalization or Cultural Revolution?

In the Soviet Union first, and in a number of East European States later, radical authoritarian norms led to major economic changes and to new social structures. Communist systems have clearly been able to bring about large shifts in policy goals and moderate changes in participation over a short period. But, since the early reforms, these systems have found it easier to preserve the "conquests" than to undertake further reforms, and the division of the Communist bloc into at least three and possibly more groups is an indication of some lack of assurance in facing the future.

In the Soviet Union and possibly East Germany, Czechoslovakia since 1969, Bulgaria, Mongolia, and North Korea, the stress is on the maintenance of achievements; there is little ability or will to move further, apparently for fear of toppling the whole system. There is in fact little danger that the system might be toppled in the Soviet Union, Bulgaria, or Mongolia, but the response of Soviet leaders to events in Czechoslovakia can be understood only if one assumes that the notion of possible chain reactions entered into their calculations. The system needs time to digest earlier changes, and such a *status quo* attitude is proof that still higher legitimacy levels are needed, that it will take time gradually to bring over members of the polity hitherto lukewarm or plainly unfavorable and to engage the allegiance of citizens whose low level of education renders them generally passive.

The newly urbanized proletariat is likely to be more conscious about the future development of society than was the largely illiterate peasantry Lenin inherited from the Tsars. As we saw, these relatively immobilist policies vis-à-vis the basic structure of society, the organization of the Communist party, and the position of the bureaucracy do not suppress tensions altogether. But the rationale is to reduce tension by making few further changes and thus diminishing the credibility of alternative courses of action. The perpetuation of a semi–cold war type of competition—particularly if developments like Vietnam periodically occur, contributing to the belief in a potential confrontation—also helps to reduce internal tension levels by lending credibility to nationalistic appeals.

The other two lines of development in the Communist world, the Chinese and the Yugoslav (the Cuban line is in some ways modeled on the Chinese, and several East European efforts move somewhat half-heartedly in the Yugoslav direction), involve further changes in the structure of the political system. Both have the ultimate and indeed similar aim of achieving greater participation outside the rigid corset provided by the Communist party in "orthodox" Communist states. But the two lines differ as to most of the means and in the hopes placed in the nearness of the solution.

The Yugoslavs are more optimistic (or naïve) in that they appear to believe in the possibility of a fairly rapid disintegration of the state machinery, in accordance with the early Communist canons regarding the "withering away of the state." Workers' control of factories, the increased role of the component republics in the determination of social and economic policy goals, the apparently much more genuine role of groups, particularly trade unions, in the elaboration of policy (epitomized by the existence of five assemblies at the federal level), the large amount of discussion in the chambers of the republics and of the federal government, the emphasis on compulsory rotation of personnel —all these measures suggest a concern on the part of Tito and the Yugoslav Government with breaking up the "new class," with realistically analyzing and remedying the bureaucratic defects of a Communist party in which many leaders fight to maintain their positions. These participatory measures are also popular, and the legitimacy of the political system as a whole is fairly high (of course, nationalistic distrust of the Soviet Union and the popularity of the Yugoslav leader also have much to do with its legitimacy). But it is not obvious that these measures amount to much more than liberalization in the conventional sense, which would be the same in a liberal democracy or an authoritarian conservative state. The effect is also to enhance the business or commercial side of the country's life, since factories become increasingly committed to profit, which ensures their autonomy; participation may not appear to be much higher than in other polities.

The much more limited moves in other East European countries, such as Poland (in a zigzag fashion) and Hungary (in a slower but apparently more regular way), have been almost entirely directed toward liberalization. These systems seem to become less authoritarian in the means of government, apparently somewhat at the expense of the radical nature of the policy goals. They have maintained the socio-economic achievements previously attained, but the impact of Western "consumer values" seems slowly to bring policy goals toward a center position. Demands for social equality appear weaker than demands for an opening up of the society, and, in a relatively muted form, the latter demands begin to be accepted. Some of the groups (unions, cultural organizations) have started to acquire autonomy, their legitimacy increases as a result (in Poland they have supported strikes), and the "weight" of the Communist party consequently diminishes in the decision-making process.

The apparent inability of these systems to go farther in the direction of radical policy goals possibly justifies the *status quo* character of the Soviet system. But it gives even greater value to the attempts made by China (and to a lesser extent Cuba) to modify the entire society through a "cultural revolution" aimed at reforming the whole personality of the people. If it is true that the Communist party, by becoming established, necessarily acquires bureaucratic attitudes, if its goals are steadily reduced to maintenance of the *status quo* and steering the society away from tension, then it becomes logical to try to break up the Communist party and to do periodically what the Communist party itself did when it first came to power. An attack against structures ceases to be directed against the bourgeois structures of the past and turns against all structures as containing within themselves the seeds of bourgeois society: an emphasis on status differences, custom and tradition as the bases for decisions, and overemphasis of technical achievements and technical decision-making. Clearly, the Chinese revolution succeeded in shaking up structures and in bringing about the idea of permanent criticism and questioning as a universal means of political education.

It remains highly questionable, however, whether such a shakeup can become a permanent system of government and whether the requirements of cultural change can be combined with minimum requirements for economic growth. The cultural revolution had serious consequences for China's economy. It is clear that, in Cuba, desires to achieve targets in sugar production have led to a considerable toning down of the cultural aspects of Castroism. This is not the place to discuss the relative merits of economic development versus cultural achievements, but it appears empirically true that, for underdeveloped societies like China or Cuba, the dilemma is so acute as to be inescapable. It seems particularly difficult to tilt policy away from economic development when the country is poor, and when the ultimate goal of personality change is not in any case certain to be achieved. It has clearly not been achieved in the East European states, and evidence from Cuba and China does not suggest that a difference has indeed come about there either, although such a vast experiment will take a long time to produce results.

The questionable character of long-term developments on either the Yugoslav or the Chinese pattern is intensified when one notes that in both countries, as in Cuba, maintenance of the political system appears due in large part to the presence of popular, charismatic leaders who owe their popularity to the nationalistic appeal of their original rule. In most other Communist systems, personalization of power has at times been instrumental in developments: Lenin's appeal was probably one of the main reasons for the survival of the first Communist state. On balance, however, personalization of power has been somewhat secondary in the continuation of most Communist systems. Stalin's bizarre charisma and Khrushchev's personal appeal helped the Soviet state, but the system also had structures that were "anonymous," and efforts were made repeatedly to limit the "personality cult" (though these efforts were of course somewhat half-hearted, as if personalization were unconsciously felt to help maintain the system). In China, Cuba, and Yugoslavia on the contrary, the founders of the system are those who periodically introduced the new changes. Changes have probably been possible only because these leaders raised legitimacy levels higher than they would otherwise have been. The question of the development of these polities after the leaders' disappearance therefore arises. They may well turn toward a *status quo* position on the Soviet model, with perhaps some liberal measures in the East European states. The cost of more drastic changes might very well be—as Soviet leaders appear to fear—the total disappearance of the system, particularly in Cuba, which, unlike the other Communist states, is not within the direct sphere of influence of the Soviet Union.

Radical authoritarian regimes appear to be at the crossroads. Change seems not to be possible at more than a certain rate. If considerable change takes place at one moment in time, much time has to be spent later in consolidation—in other words, legitimizing the change among the population. Moreover, accidents of various kinds, particularly the emergence of leaders through nationalistic movements resulting from world events, account for the maintenance and possible furtherance of radical policy goals. The achievements of Communist systems have been considerable. In particular, the Soviet Union's ability, on its own, to develop an alternative model of government to that of liberal democracies amounts to one of the major social transformations of all times, especially in light of the characteristics, both economic and political, of Tsarist Russia. Whatever the current extent of admiration for China in many quarters, China would not have had its revolution but for the Soviet Union. Besides, it is not yet certain that China has brought about a system truly different from the one in the Soviet Union. This is precisely why Communist systems are at the crossroads and why, as we have noted, their prestige is no longer as high as it was in 1945 in the West and in the Third World. Radical authoritarian states appear to have achieved some kind of equilibrium, which apparently can be modified only at the expense of the whole system.

12

Populist Systems

Neither Communist systems nor liberal democratic systems have made decisive inroads in the Third World. Liberal democratic systems are found mainly in some Commonwealth and Latin American countries, and Communist systems, apart from Cuba, are exclusively confined to North and East Asia. Elsewhere, there are, as we saw, a small number of traditional systems, mainly monarchies, which are usually older countries in which the state organization is of long standing and is backed by communal groups. These are the Third World states where conflict levels remain low because the legitimacy base has not been broken, often because of the isolation or the smallness of the polity.

Where the legitimacy base has been markedly eroded by the appearance of new groups which challenge the traditional norms of the polity, or where no legitimacy base has ever existed in the polity (as in truly new nations), conflicts take the form of confrontations between sharply opposed groups, some locally implanted and some seeking to build or buttress a sense of national identity. The issue is social and economic development, which the more modern elements press for, while communal groups attempt to uphold the traditional norms and the traditional patterns of political leadership.

The conditions under which the conflict develops and the ways in which it is resolved will vary markedly. The number of variables is so large that even in examining an individual polity we cannot expect to account for all the specific norms and structures or all the specific structure-function relationships that have a bearing on the conflict. But we can at least look for some general lines in the current characteristics of these polities and in the dynamics of their evolution.

Let us start from the premise that these countries include both elements pressing for socio-economic development and elements trying to retain the traditional system. Depending on who wins, we can distinguish between populist and authoritarian conservative systems. In the former, the policy goals are halfway between conservatism and radicalism, while emphasis will be placed on greater participation than occurs in traditional systems. In the latter, the policy goals are conservative and there will be little emphasis on participation. In both cases, means are likely to be authoritarian if conflict levels are high and legitimacy is low. Opposition over goals will often be such that the systems may be able to maintain themselves only by not allowing any voice to dissenters, or at best by tolerating a relatively ineffective form of criticism. These systems are all in some way imposed; indeed, for the wholly new countries the national unit itself is imposed. But the extent of authoritarianism obviously varies with the way in which opposition presents itself, with the right of potential dissent, and with the degree of implantation of the structures of the political systems. As populist systems differ in a number of ways, not only in goals, from authoritarian conservative systems, we shall consider them separately. Indeed, authoritarian conservative systems have at times been created in reaction not only to populist systems but also to Communist and even liberal democratic forms of government.

The Origins and Spread of Populist Systems

We can expect to find differences among populist systems in their goals and, possibly more markedly, in their structural organization. Development is a key goal, but countries vary in resources, traditions, and background. They also tend to imitate different structures elsewhere. Some countries choose the path of socialism, others that of capitalism. Since Third World countries in the large majority of cases have a limited industrial infrastructure, the question of private property versus the public ownership of means of production does not constitute as important a cleavage as it does in economically more advanced countries. This is not to suggest that there are no differences between, for instance, Ivory Coast and Guinea or between Kenya and Tanzania, but the stress in all four countries on socio-economic development and the way in which the structures of the polity are geared toward the achievement of this goal makes these countries more similar than might at first be assumed. These four countries are, moreover, extreme cases of capitalist and socialist polities. In the large majority of the thirty or forty countries that can be classified as populist, a mixture of state capitalism and private capitalism, often linked through mixed-economy enterprises, and a variety of social benefits given to the whole population or at least to the employed sector make the policy goals of the political systems relatively similar.

There are perhaps more important differences in the origins of populist systems. They can be roughly divided into two groups —perhaps at two poles—with intermediate positions. To simplify, it can be said that one-third or two-fifths of the countries (mostly located in the Middle East and North Africa or in the northern part of Sub-Saharan Africa) have a Muslim culture and are older nations in the cultural and psychological senses. Algeria, Tunisia, and Sudan may have only recently acquired their independence, but there is a sense of cultural identity among the members of the polity (this may, however, be modified by divisions among ethnic groups, like the Kabyls in Algeria or, more seriously, the rift between the Arab North and the black South in Sudan). Similar points could probably be made about Senegal or Tanzania. Over all, these countries constitute political entities where the main cleavage concerns the development of an existing nation. However, the question of the unity of the nation can re-emerge in terms of the degree of centralization some segments of the population are prepared to allow, which may lead to increased imposition and therefore authoritarianism on the part of the central government.

At the other extreme, there is a group of countries, located mainly in Africa south of the Sahara, that show almost a complete absence of national identity. This may be because the country is large and very populous and includes truly different nations within its borders, in which case unity is maintained only with great difficulty and precariously. The cases of Zaïre—previously Congo (Kinshasa)—and Nigeria spring to mind immediately. But national identity may also be lacking because belief in the idea of the "nation" is spread among only a very small section of the population and because the country itself results from an arbitrary decision by a colonial power about administrative boundaries, as in many of the former French territories of West and Equatorial Africa, which has proved a very unsatisfactory basis for nationhood. A similar case is Gambia, an enclave in Senegalese territory which has maintained itself as a polity for a mixture of linguistic and commercial reasons. The same happened in other parts of the world in the past, particularly in Europe, but there the process of nation-building was slower and a sense of national identity had much more time to grow. Indeed, many Latin American countries, despite their 150 years of independence, still have a low level of national identity, particularly where the Indian population has been left outside the political system and is involved in a subsistence economy on a quasi-autonomous basis.

The Structures of Populist Systems

Whether these polities are new nations or simply new political systems emerging with independence or after a coup (as in Libya, Sudan, and Egypt in 1952), the question of structures, particularly acute for populist systems, cannot be considered successfully solved by comparison with the development of party and group structures in radical authoritarian states. Hence a variety of solutions exist, and there is a tendency for many countries to oscillate from one type of structure to another.

The problem posed by the creation of structures is particularly serious in populist states because, basically, the leaders of the political system are confronted with a group configuration that resists, at best, or opposes firmly, at worst, the aims of socio-economic development these leaders seek to implement. As in traditional conservative systems, the groups that are legitimate among the population, particularly the rural population (usually 80 to 90 per cent or even more of the total) are of a tribal or ethnic character. Some new African states south of the Sahara have many quite small tribes that wish to uphold the values of the past without change; indeed, they are not likely to understand the political changes that have come about. This accounts in part for the low level of national cultural identity. If a country comprises a large number of tribes dispersed geographically, and if prior to independence the colonial power left these tribes intact and unchanged, having no interest in upsetting the equilibrium among them, the new national leaders may experience great difficulty in making themselves understood by the population. They will sometimes be viewed as members of other tribes attempting to move in and to impose their will. Moreover, it often happens in Africa that the same tribe dwells on both sides of a national boundary (the Ewes in West Africa, for example), and the pressure to divide the loyalty of the tribe between nations may increase tension and lead to permanent boundary problems (one nation may try to use the tribe to influence events in the neighboring polity). Where one tribe is much larger than the rest, as in Uganda, a sense of national unity can be fostered by that tribe, but the others may resent the predominance of the major tribe. As a result, as precisely in Uganda, the political system is weak and is periodically confronted with crises that may ultimately lead to its downfall.

As populist systems face strong latent or overt opposition, their strategy is to counteract it by building the nation, if required, or the political regime at all events, through structures that extend widely in the population. This suggests the creation of an extensive party, supplemented by various dependent associations, which eventually will constitute a network of organizations able to buttress the political system. The model is clearly that of Communist systems, and one can understand why, in a number of populist states, a single-party system of this type has in fact been constructed. Such parties can be found in some of the new African states, the best examples being Tanzania and Kenya among the former British, and Senegal, Ivory Coast, and

Guinea among the former French territories. In the Arab world, Tunisia has the only true example of such a party, and it was built indeed before independence.

But the build-up of a party and its dependent associations is possible only when a number of favorable circumstances are present. First, the party will be extensive only if it is not wholly imposed on the population, that is, it must have the loyalty of at least some members of the population. If there are substantial areas where the political system has no support at all, the party will be stronger on paper than in reality. The situation confronting Lenin and the Communist party in Russia was more favorable than that in most African states: National unity existed, tribal sentiment was low, and industrial development had begun on a large scale in a number of centers. Indeed a type of "national party system" had emerged in the period immediately preceding World War I, during the checkered existence of the assemblies (dumas). Similarly, those new states that are already somewhat united and whose tribal problems are not overwhelming are likely to be able to create a party system.

Second (and this does indeed foster the kind of national unity we just examined), the party will be more likely to grow up and gain strength among some segments of the population if it was started in colonial times and was instrumental in bringing about independence. If the population has come to identify with the party on grounds of national unity, this party is likely to have acquired a capital of trust that will enable it to remain influential in the future. If we consider the examples mentioned earlier, all were characterized by the development prior to independence of a party that was solidly implanted in the colonial territory and was visible to the population.

Even so, these cases of strong party implantation differ from the Soviet experience in important ways. Possibly because national unity was an immediate requirement, and possibly also because of the absence of industrialization, these parties are essentially parties of national unity, not elite groups aiming overtly at leading the polity toward a new era. It would be wrong to suggest that the single-party systems (or in some cases near-single-party systems) in these countries have no long-term aims of education of the population. But the educational aspect is pressed less strongly and is geared toward the creation or maintenance of a national unit as well as the promotion of new ideals. It is usually stressed in the Third World that problems are different from those of the Soviet Union because there is no class basis in African countries; the imperialists are said to be outside the system, not within it. In practice the development of these parties is designed to reduce or even eliminate the tribal or ethnic basis of the society, but tribal and ethnic differences are not viewed in the same black-and-white terms as the opposition between bourgeoisie and proletariat in a Communist country (it could be argued that the coalitions in some Communist countries, such as East Germany, reflect a similarity to the African attitude, but even there the Communist elite is kept distinct from the other parties). Over all, African socialism aims at incorporating all groups into the system. Tribal battles (as in Ghana under Nkrumah) are rarely overt, and their objective may be to convert tribal leaders to new ideas of development. There is often an element of pride in the "consensual" basis of tribal decision-making, possibly mixed with a fear that, if clashes with all the tribes were direct, the imposition of the system would be too harsh and the system might be toppled.

Thus the populist single party is more a compromise between old and new society than the Communist single party. What appears to make the compromise possible is the fact that nearly all these parties have charismatic leaders who acquired their appeal among the general population during the battle for independence. Hence these parties are not likely to be truly extensive unless they can be built around a leader, and the very influence of the personalized leaders prevents the parties from being extreme in their battle with traditional groups. In Ivory Coast, Guinea, Kenya, Tanzania, and Tunisia the party was created by and around a leader (though in the case of Guinea the strength of the party dwindled markedly in the 1960's, as it had in Ghana before the military coup toppled Nkrumah). The legitimacy of the party is therefore in large part indirect: The population supports the party mainly because it supports the leader.

Hence the conclusion that it is impossible, or at least very difficult, for a populist party to become extensive in the context of a Third World situation unless it originally was backed by a leader with considerable strength among the population. And not every national leader will feel it possible or necessary to build a party. In some of the smaller African countries, particularly in Equatorial Africa, the single party is not extensive: Either these countries are too small to require a strongly implanted party, or the leader's personal appeal is not large enough to enable the structures built around him to extend widely among all sections of the population. As long as the government can rule without the support of the whole population, the system may indeed be able to last. But the regime is on a razor's edge; it may soon be replaced by another populist regime, or the traditional groups may be strong enough to force a return to a traditional conservative regime or, more probably (because of the weight of populist elements that will have to be countered), to install an authoritarian conservative system.

Since the existence of an extensive party depends so heavily on the existence of a popular leader, many new countries do not have extensive parties; they are not likely to be built in countries previously ruled by traditional conservative regimes, in which conditions do not favor the emergence of popular leaders. Yet these countries, as we know, have groups that favor development, in particular the institutional groups, primarily the bureaucracy and secondarily the military. Of course, if such groups are not large, their attitudes will make no impact on the polity. But if we assume that they are large, an *esprit de corps* is likely to emerge among members of the bureaucracy, especially if they have been educated abroad and are acutely aware of the country's lag in development. The military may come to favor development if it feels frustrated by the traditional conservative regime and considers the future of the country to be at stake. As these groups increase in strength, the legitimacy of the old regime decreases and the propensity of the military to intervene thereby increases. The combination of resentment from the bureaucracy and capability in the military to take over by using the weapons and personnel at its disposal therefore constitutes a prima facie basis for a coup.

Thus coups will occur to topple traditional conservative regimes, and we should not be surprised to see them occur in the older nations where the legitimacy base has been eroded, such as

Egypt in 1952 or Lybia in 1970; the situation in Mexico during
World War I was of the same character, as was that in Turkey
after World War I. But a coup can also occur in a new country
with a populist regime whose leadership does not have a sufficiently broad popular base and (consequently, as we saw) the
single party is not really implanted in the population. We are
of course referring not to situations of an authoritarian conservative character (the coup in Nigeria in 1966 or in Uganda in
1971) but to situations like those in Dahomey, Mali, and Zaïre,
as well as in Algeria, Somalia, and Sudan, where a new populist
regime either supplanted another populist regime but hoped to
achieve better results, or wanted to lead the country away from
party squabbles and toward greater unity of purpose in the direction of development.

Yet, as we indicated in Chapter 8, the lack of legitimacy makes
such an intervention temporary, because the new regime either
is itself toppled in turn (coups have occurred with considerable
regularity in Dahomey, as they did in Mexico before 1916) or
changes in character to a more civilian regime. We showed earlier in this section that a populist regime could be built on the
basis of an extensive party (with aims and characteristics different
from those of a Communist single party), provided a charismatic
leader existed. The intervention of the military may constitute
one way in which the charismatic leader–extensive party sequence takes place. When it comes to power the military has a
breathing space during which either (and preferably both) of the
essential elements of the sequence can emerge. If no charismatic
leader appears and no strong and extensive party is built, the
regime will be toppled and a succession of military regimes will
occur. If, on the other hand, a strong personality emerges from
within the military, possibly after one or several palace revolutions, and if this leader builds an extensive party, the system may
acquire some legitimacy in the long run and be more able to face
the future.

In populist systems which started out as military regimes and
maintained themselves, the military indeed quickly civilianized
the regime and formed a party, while one leader emerged as the
hero of the country. The best example is of course Nasser, who,
after having fought a palace revolution that pushed aside Neguib,

the leader of the 1952 revolution, acquired prestige (through his nationalistic postures and his championship of the Arab cause) and built a political party which, though with difficulty, succeeded in having at least some of the characteristics of a mass party of the populist (not Communist and elitist) type. The emergence of such a popular leader from among the military does not often occur, however, and many military regimes produce "revolutionary councils" in which no one succeeds in establishing his dominance over his colleagues or in creating a popular image for himself in the country. The problems that faced successive regimes in Iraq and Syria in the 1960's stemmed largely from the inability of any of the leaders to establish themselves in this way. They were toppled from power before they were able to achieve popularity, probably because of their inability to find a line— nationalistic or otherwise—to help to build their image among the population in the critical first years after coming to power. The same may happen to military leaders in Mali or Burundi, though the countries are more isolated. On the other hand, Mobutu of Zaïre succeeded in creating a following for himself and in building a party, though perhaps at the cost of moving the regime some distance away from radical goals.

The building of structures, essentially a party structure and dependent associations, is thus a major problem for all populist regimes, particularly in view of the ideal of greater consensus toward which, unlike Communist regimes, Third World leaders strive. Given the short time span of the development of many new states and the fact, moreover, that many charismatic leaders who created the party and even the state still rule the country, it is difficult to be clear about the extent and duration of success. There are ostensibly good results, the best and most durable having occurred in Mexico, which moved from a situation of repeated and almost continuous disruption of government to one of considerable stability under the aegis of a dominant party. Egypt remained under the same system after the death of Nasser, and the Arab Socialist Union seems to have shown strength there despite the purges Nasser's successor apparently felt obliged to carry out. The Tanzanian and Tunisian parties seem solid and well implanted, more so than those of Kenya, Senegal, and even, possibly, the Ivory Coast, while the shakiness of the Guinean regime and party may indicate that, as with Ghana, a populist leader, even if popular, cannot go beyond a certain point in putting pressure on a tribal society. Over all, the build-up of new structures should probably be seen as a success, given the difficulties we listed at the start and if we compare (which is too rarely done) the results achieved in Africa, for instance, with those in Latin America in the nineteenth century and in Europe throughout the several centuries during which nationhood had time to develop.

We began the analysis of Communist states by considering the role, however symbolic, of constitutions. Although it is true to say that in many populist states the government and the assembly abide by constitutional rules inherited from or at least based on European and American models, the constitutional structures appear to be recognized as secondary in the quest for development of a stable system. Constitutionalism is not viewed as the prime element. The goals of the regime are to foster development at the expense of liberal forms and procedures that may slow down this process. For instance, the danger of allowing opposition to grow out of the tribal structures is seen as so large that it needs to be repelled. Nor are constitutions seen as symbols of future achievements and means by which the people can be made to act with greater unity toward a common goal. Populist regimes probably consider them generally as valuable symbols and, on the whole, to be cherished, provided they do not create problems or lead to serious risks for the system as a whole.

Institutions and procedures characteristic of a constitutional system, therefore, are not disregarded or established purely for show. Their implementation is closely dependent on the build-up of party structures. Where the regime is well established, with a popular leader and an extensive party, constitutional structures exist, and their life may not be markedly interfered with. The assembly is likely to meet fairly often, for instance, and debates over legislation or policy will occur. Though these will be less frequent than in liberal democracies, they will be more so than in Communist states. Other aspects of the machinery of states are likely to be fairly open. Legislators will question the bureaucracy and defend individuals or promote demands from the constituencies. Courts will be independent and will guarantee rights. The mass media may offer criticisms, though probably discreet, of government measures.

Where the system is not established, for instance in the early period of a new military regime, no constitutional forms will be followed at all. There will be no constitution and no assembly, and even the courts may be closed or suspended. All powers will be in the hands of the revolutionary council, which may or may not declare that the period of revolutionary government is to be limited and temporary. These regimes gradually come to establish some constitutional structures, usually (though not always) after a party has been created and the basis for maintenance of the regime appears greater. Where no constitutional structures have been created over a long period (as in Syria or Iraq, though even there the situation is proclaimed as temporary), the instability of the military leadership in government confirms the general rule that constitutional "niceties" come after, and only after, the period of stabilization. It is not the case, then, that populist regimes discard constitutional arrangements and have discovered alternative ways of running the polity. Consciously or not, leaders of populist regimes simply feel that the creation of a legitimacy base is a prerequisite. And they look for this legitimacy base at a "consensual" middle point, where traditional leaders will agree to "development" in response to some, but not unlimited, pressure.

The Future of Populist Systems

The dependence of populist regimes on charismatic leadership, whether directly or indirectly by way of the military, poses the question of the future of these regimes after the disappearance of their leaders. The apparent success of the transition in the United Arab Republic and the stability of Mexico over a generation do not in themselves constitute indications that the future of all such regimes is assured. Those two cases may be exceptional or, as in the Mexican example, further problems can arise when the regime has lasted for a sizable period.

In theory, among the conditions that must be fulfilled if a smooth transition is to take place after the disappearance of a popular leader, a sufficient time span under that leader is perhaps paramount. The party and the dependent associations must have had the opportunity to acquire at least some legitimacy of their own. But this condition can be met in a number of ways. The traditional groups may be relatively weak, or tribal pressure may not pose a constant threat to national unity and the developmental goals of the regime. On the other hand, if these pressures are strong, the extensiveness of the party and of its dependent associations may still have markedly changed the attitudes of a large section of the population. It may be that socio-economic changes have reduced tribal influences and increased the desire for development among the population, for instance, through urbanization and the growth of new institutional groups, such as the bureaucracy (though this may create further problems, as the expectations of these groups may rise more rapidly than the regime is able to "deliver"). If as a result of these various developments, the leader's strength is no longer a requisite for maintaining the party, and if the party has both cohesion and genuine influence in the country, the chances of a smooth transition are reasonably large. They will increase if the problems facing the polity at the time of the transition are not very serious. They will of course be much more difficult to overcome if the nation-building process has not been completed. As a rule, it follows that a populist regime in a new state is less likely to survive the succession than a populist regime that has taken root in a well-established polity.

But a populist regime faces problems other than mere survival. They include those of upholding populist goals, namely development and a relatively large dose of participation, even if authoritarian means of government are the price to be paid. Yet the internal dynamics of a populist system lead in due course to more conservative goals, though not necessarily liberal means as well. Unlike radical authoritarian parties, populist parties aim at achieving some consensus and are not based on the idea of an elite that drives the country toward some promised land. This is not to say that there is no promised land, which in many ways is what the goal of development is, but it is to be reached with the acceptance of all concerned. It is perhaps achieved if elite groups drawn from the bureaucracy and the intellectual middle classes of the towns join forces with the traditional leaders of the countryside. But conflicts are likely to arise within the party, for instance on agricultural methods or on priorities between rural and urban development. If consensus is to prevail, the decision-making process will be based on compromises rather than on clear-cut but imposed choices. If, over a period, this process is formalized and institutionalized, if, as in Mexico, structures are established within the party to represent each subgroup on a corporate basis, there will be a tendency for the system to maintain the *status quo,* while groups that did not partake in the original sharing of power will be excluded. The regime may thus become more pluralistic but also more conservative; indeed, conservatism may be strengthened by the fear that any major change in the distribution of benefits would upset the equilibrium and bring about the downfall of the system.

Populist governments can achieve a middle way and avoid both the danger of repeated regime changes and marked confusion (on the Syrian or Iraqi model) and the danger of "immobilism" on the Mexican pattern. But the requirements of legitimacy and change are in large part contradictory. The contradiction can be avoided only if, somewhat accidentally, leaders emerge who carry enough personal legitimacy to make changes acceptable to the population and therefore harmless for the regime. On a different plane, the dilemma is similar to the one faced by Communist systems, which leads supporters of the Soviet middle way to be generally content with maintenance rather than policy change. But the danger for populist regimes is greater than for Communist systems, because the Soviet Union did achieve a level of development (after starting from a higher level, admittedly) that made it possible for the system to maintain its normative position without developing intolerable tensions. In populist regimes, a static position will lead to greater tensions. Many populist systems are therefore likely to be marked, and for long periods, by chronic instability.

We must always remember that populist regimes often emerge in countries that are very new, and that they must attempt to lift the population from traditional modes of living in a short time. Thus the task must be seen as truly monumental, greater even than the task undertaken by Lenin and his successors in the

Soviet Union. This perspective is sometimes lacking, as we noted earlier. No such task was ever accomplished in such a short time in West European countries in the past, even though European regimes benefited from a larger legitimacy base and were not confronted with the high expectations that have begun to spread among large sections of the population in the developing states. The path toward development chosen by populist regimes remains narrow, and it is also long. We have little experience on which to base an "optimal" rate for development with various types of group configuration and various levels of legitimacy. This is why the measurement of these problems on a dynamic basis is of major importance for the well-being of large numbers of countries and, ultimately, of the world. Solution of the fundamental equation of populism is therefore a vital task and a real challenge for scholars and practitioners of politics, across political systems and across generations.

13

Authoritarian Conservative Systems

The types of political systems examined in the last three chapters are concerned, in one way or another, with moving away from traditional forms of government and trying to build new structures. The development of stable liberal democratic systems requires the transformation of the traditional groups and their use as the bases of new legitimate bodies, especially parties. Radical authoritarian and populist systems attempt to silence traditional groups by pressing against them the weight of the single party and its dependent associations. It is not surprising that there should also be a number of political systems that go in the opposite direction and endeavor to return to more traditional policies. These are the authoritarian conservative systems, which differ from traditional systems in that the maintenance or restoration of old values requires imposition—sometimes a great deal—though the two types are broadly similar in policy goals and levels of participation.

Origins and Spread of Authoritarian Conservative Systems

The ability of a system to prevail on the basis of authoritarian conservative norms depends on the extent to which it can rely on at least some support among the traditional structures of the polity. The problem these systems face is the converse of that of populist systems: Their difficulties increase with the size of the groups that favor socio-economic development and change. The system must be imposed, and there will be a point at which the amount of imposition required exceeds the short-term and longer-term means of coercion at the system's disposal. Authoritarian conservative systems therefore tend to appear when demands for socio-economic development (and indeed for participation or liberalization) begin to be fairly large and constitute a challenge of some magnitude, though not when this challenge is so strong and so buttressed by an extensive party and groups, or when change has become so widely accepted, that the legitimacy of the traditional communal groups has effectively dwindled.

If this point is not reached, the emergence of an authoritarian conservative system may be brought about by a variety of circumstances. It may stem directly and without a break from a traditional conservative system in which a challenge to the leadership has begun to manifest itself, in which case the same leaders need a much greater level of imposition than in the past. In other cases, leaders of traditional regimes are replaced by new men who consider the traditional system incapable of preserving the values of the polity. Through such a "pre-emptive strike," the new leaders allege they are preventing a coup from the left from taking over the polity. The Nigerian coup of 1966 fitted this description somewhat. Finally, an authoritarian conservative regime may emerge in reaction to an already implanted liberal democratic, populist, or radical authoritarian system (no clear example of a move from a radical authoritarian type of situation exists at present, but reactions to left-wing regimes in Central Europe, particularly in Hungary after World War I, were perhaps a prototype). The new regime must be installed by a coup, and the more complex the society and the more established the regime, the more the coup is difficult to organize, and the more uncertain it is in its results. It was easier for Salazar and the Greek military leaders to take power than for Hitler and Mussolini.

Authoritarian conservative regimes must be distinguished conceptually—and indeed in reality—from the takeovers, in particular military takeovers, that profess to have, sometimes truthfully, a "temporary" character. The best recent example of the latter is perhaps the first military coup in Ghana, which led to the ousting of Nkrumah and the introduction of a liberal democratic regime. Several coups in Argentina, Brazil, and other Latin American countries have also been temporary. George Monck played a similar part in England in 1660, prior to the Stuart Restoration. In such cases, the role of the military in the coup and immediately afterward may be large, but the regime is viewed as an interregnum and is accepted as long as the belief that it is temporary and is helping the return to "normalcy" holds up. The military has no legitimacy *per se* but holds in fact as much legitimacy as the regime it proposes to establish or reinstate.

But the provisional regime may endure, and the boundary between really and seemingly temporary regimes may sometimes be unclear. Some regimes may not overtly declare themselves provisional (in particular, no date for the surrender of power may be given) yet may convey the impression that the system is transitional, precisely in order to attract support from groups and from sections of the population who opposed the previous regime and could not be counted on to support the current regime if it established itself permanently. Thus supporters of liberal democracy may accept a military regime that will bring back freedom "in due course." This situation has characterized a number of Latin American military regimes, including those of Brazil and Argentina in the second half of the 1960's, and the same impression has been conveyed by the Greek military leaders who took power in 1966. Indeed, all of Franco's efforts to legitimize his regime after 1945 (and his abandonment of a positive defense of a fascist form of government) were directed at giving the impression that the system was in some form provisional; the monarchy was thus re-established in principle in 1949!

Such indefinitely provisional regimes have to be counted among authoritarian conservative systems, particularly when the provisional character of the regime does not prevent its leaders from making policy and building up structures and procedures designed to help maintain the system. Only in cases where the leaders of the takeover expressly state that they do not wish to stay in power any longer than is necessary for the creation of, for instance, a liberal democratic system, as in Ghana after Nkrumah, and indeed only when a realistic but short timetable is given in advance, is it possible to suggest that the new government genuinely borrows its support from the very regime it hopes to promote.

The conditions leading to the appearance of authoritarian conservative systems help to suggest where they are likely to spread. Of the twenty-five or so countries that should be labeled authoritarian conservative, the large majority are in the Third World, particularly Africa and Latin America. Some of the smaller countries in Africa, either immediately after independence or in the following few years, showed authoritarian characteristics combined with a conservative policy. Malawi from the start and Upper Volta and Mali after coups are examples of such polities. To these must be added South Africa and Rhodesia because of their harsh racial policies imposed on the majority of the population. Authoritarian conservative regimes have followed traditional systems in some Central American states, such as Honduras and Nicaragua, or replaced populist systems as in Guatemala. They displaced liberal democracies, albeit unstable ones, in Argentina and in Brazil, where the regime emerging from a coup attempted, somewhat half-heartedly, to bring the polity back to more traditional values. Elsewhere, authoritarian regimes are less widespread, despite the fact that some of the best-known examples (Chiang's Taiwan, Franco's Spain, and Salazar's Portugal) are in Asia and Europe. But systems of this kind were of course very common in Europe in the past, particularly when crises of legitimacy occurred. While Napoleon's regime should probably be labeled populist in policy goals and in the levels of participation allowed, those of Hitler, Mussolini, and a number of Central and East European states in the interwar period were authoritarian conservative, for all the "progressivism" of their professed policy goals. They needed a wide appeal to the population at large because of the nature of the political systems they sought to control, but once in power they did not increase participation or change the distribution of social and economic benefits in an egalitarian direction. And if they (somewhat half-heartedly) built party and other structures reminiscent of those in Communist or populist systems, it was only because of the need to combat Com-

munism. Indeed, this situation suggests the dilemma in which
authoritarian conservative systems are placed, which makes their
long-term position shakier than that of other systems.

The Structures of Authoritarian Conservative Systems

An authoritarian conservative system aims at returning to past
values and therefore to a configuration of structures that characterized previous political systems (in some cases mythical). Typically, this should be achieved by placing considerable emphasis
on communal group structures, and authoritarian conservative
systems indeed attempt to use existing or previous social structures and social relationships as much as possible. But two sets
of circumstances can reduce the possibility. First, the system faces
a challenge in which the traditional social structure undergoes a
crisis in legitimacy, with the result that it cannot play a part in
decision-making and communication without being buttressed.
The farther the society has moved away from traditional legitimacy patterns, based on ethnic, tribal, or even religious groups,
and the more the new groups (institutional groups or parties) replace the old ones as instruments through which demands are
made, the more difficult it is to use the communal group structure
as an assured basis for the political system. Second, to compound
the problem, some of the communal groups may not lend themselves to buttressing the authoritarian conservative system: Loyalty
to a deposed leader or king or a dislike for imposition may create
oppositions and tensions within the group structure.

A conservative authoritarian system cannot expect to be maintained by relying only on traditional patterns of social relationships. Yet, unlike populist or radical authoritarian systems, conservative authoritarian systems are often reluctant to create a
party. A party can be effective only if it is well implanted in the
polity and therefore extensive, which might threaten the oligarchical character of the polity. The typical party structure favored
by authoritarian conservative leaders is one that is superimposed
on the social structure and, like the National Union in Portugal,
has few roots in the population. True, the Nazi and Italian
Fascist systems were based on parties, and even mass parties, but,
as we already noted, this was due to the political context in

which those systems were created. The Nazis had to compete in elections with other parties before coming to power, for instance. The level of socio-economic development of the polities concerned and the challenge presented by Communism were also factors. In Germany and, to some extent, Italy, the new regimes could not have come about merely by attempting to reimpose an "old order" that had collapsed. They needed also to control complex political, social, and economic systems, for which they required a powerful set of structures. But these two European examples are limit-cases of authoritarian conservative systems (those of other Central and East European States at the same period had a substantially less developed party structure). Indeed, the two regimes were particularly authoritarian—and the Nazi system had to be more authoritarian than its Italian counterpart—because they were confronted with a strong challenge from a large number of existing groups of an associational character. They consequently had to rely on a party and a whole range of dependent organizations, which gave these dictatorships a more "participationist" and less oligarchical appearance than other authoritarian conservative systems. As a result, and also to some extent because of the policy goals they had to accept, they were in some ways nearer to populist systems. Their defense of old values had to include the support of some new ideas.

Other authoritarian conservative systems do not normally create party structures and dependent associations. Interestingly, the Falange, which was Spain's equivalent of the Nazi and Fascist parties, slowly lost importance as the system became more established (in contrast with developments in Communist and populist countries, where parties remain strong or increase in strength over time). But the neglect of party-building means that authoritarian conservative systems are hampered—and to some extent hamper themselves. An extensive party would provide the main means of educating the population and of gaining support over the long term. Authoritarian conservative systems therefore condemn themselves to attempts to impose their norms and goals by short-term means while hoping that, in the long run, the traditional structures will regain the influence and support they had in the past. This is why the main type of new structure on which these systems can count is the military, possibly with the help of the bureaucracy, along with a popular leader who embodies a pattern of hierarchical and disciplined authority consistent with the over-all goals and norms of the regime.

Some conditions must be fulfilled if the military is to be counted on to support the system. The military is capable of becoming an institutional group and forming the nucleus of a challenge to traditional norms, as we know, if its members are separated socially and intellectually from the political leadership and if its nationalistic vision of the country's destiny is frustrated by the lack of development typical of a traditional conservative system. Thus, for an authoritarian conservative regime to be backed by the army, at least a section of the military must remain tied, personally and ideologically, to the communal groups, and tribal, ethnic, or religious feelings must remain strong among it. Second, the military is likely to feel embittered against an existing populist regime that praises development in principle but is confronted in fact with social and economic difficulties that it cannot solve. A coup against a populist regime may prove easier than a coup against a traditional system. Over all, however, authoritarian conservative systems have one specific asset: They emphasize hierarchical values, which populist radical authoritarian or liberal democratic regimes tend to combat. As a result, if the other conditions are present to tilt the military away from the previous regime, authoritarian conservative norms will probably satisfy the soldiers and ensure their loyalty, particularly that of the senior officers, while lieutenants and captains are more likely to press for development. This indeed suggests that, if the military has been well organized over a long period and if discipline is tight, a coup from the authoritarian Right, civilian or military, has a chance of success and duration.

Yet the military alone cannot, as we know, maintain its influence in a complex polity. It needs both the technical support of the bureaucracy and some legitimizing strength from other sources. The help of the bureaucracy is sometimes difficult to obtain, because technicians will press for development rather than for traditional goals. The collaboration of administrators may be easier to obtain through a mixture of fear and patronage; it is likely to be enlisted if the previous regime was unsuccessful in developing the country and at the same time very demanding

of the bureaucracy. In particular, where inflation has been ram-
pant for long periods, as in Latin America, the more conservative
among the administrators (those precisely who are more closely
associated by family or other ties with communal groups) are
likely to support the return to a less dynamic form of economic
management for the sake of achieving normalcy. In general, authoritarian conservative systems are more likely to find support
among generalist administrators than among specialists, among
those who place great emphasis on economic stability rather than
those who wish to develop the industrial infrastructure, among
the managers of economic enterprises rather than social administrators. But relations will remain uneasy: Ongania's regime in
Argentina was faced with many difficulties with technicians who
seemed originally supportive but who, logically enough, became
increasingly skeptical because of the small economic growth of
the country. In Spain, an uneasy truce between modernizers and
traditionalists was maintained for decades, largely because of the
"fear of the unknown" that formed the basic, though negative,
support of Franco's "provisional" regime. Over all, authoritarian
conservative systems are less likely to build the strong structures
that would positively buttress their regimes than to rely on the
maintenance of negative feelings about other systems as well as
on short-term and makeshift arrangements.

Not surprisingly, these systems must rely to a marked extent
on a leader's popular appeal. Indeed, the leadership requirement
is even more pronounced than in other types of political systems,
for both positive and negative reasons. Positively, as we saw,
these systems are based on oligarchical norms—hierarchy and discipline are at a premium. This is perhaps even more the case
than in traditional conservative systems, at least ostensibly and
overtly, because in traditional conservative systems the leadership of the communal groups is accepted naturally by all and
therefore need not be emphasized. In authoritarian conservative
systems the restoration or maintenance of oligarchical values is
the practical proof that a leader can be the guide that the society
requires to save it from "chaos and subversion."

But the positive emphasis on leaders is combined with the
fact that, negatively, no long-term means, as we saw, are available
to help maintain the system. Even in the short term, the support

of the military may become shaky unless soldiers can be made to look up to their leader, preferably a military leader or at least one who uses the trappings of military dress and command to impress civilians and military alike. Thus the future of these systems is little assured if the leader has no charismatic pull among at least a large section of the population and if he cannot spread the belief among his supporters that, with time, the old structures on which society was based will be once more widely recognized and accepted, hence that it is worth working with him to quicken the pace of the return to normalcy.

Given these general characteristics, the part played by constitutional institutions and procedures is perhaps smaller in an authoritarian conservative system than in any other. There is no call for a real development of constitutionalism (since the emphasis is on authoritarianism, not on liberalism) or even for the symbolic emphasis on certain values that formalization in a constitution would provide (as in radical authoritarian systems). In traditional conservative systems, constitutional structures may develop slowly from the acceptance of a number of customary procedures, by which, for instance, participation is gradually enlarged. In populist systems, the role of the leader is accidental, though necessary, and the aim remains an "anonymous" system. Therefore, as we saw, constitutional structures emerge, sooner or later, as the populist system is better established. In authoritarian conservative systems, on the contrary, constitutional structures are logically viewed as a constant danger. When they are created, if only on paper, their purpose is often to give the system an appearance of normalcy in the eyes of the world. In Greece and Spain, among others, large parts of the constitution have gone unenforced for long periods, and some military regimes (those that claim to be provisional, as well as many others that remain obscure on this point) do not even create constitutional structures, any more than they do when they form the first stage of a populist system. The low priority of constitutions, like other aspects of authoritarian conservative systems, makes for a profoundly transitional character, reinforced by the fact that the leader's influence can last only for a finite period. Thus, the future of authoritarian conservative systems is, more than that of other systems, in question.

Can Authoritarian Conservative Systems Survive Their Leaders?

Authoritarian conservative systems are largely a reaction to changes taking place in a polity. Even if it is not always possible, with the means at our disposal, to know in advance which of the countries of the world are likely to be ruled by this type of regime, we can state with assurance that the grounds for the appearance of such regimes exist in many countries and that in some the conditions are maximized. When the legitimacy of the current system is low (whether the system is traditional conservative, liberal democratic, radical authoritarian, or populist) and is decreasing fairly rapidly, when the long-term instruments on which to base a new legitimacy are not powerful, when the current leader does not have a strong personal appeal, when traditional group structures are still relatively influential but their role in the decision-making process is decreasing, and when socio-economic conditions contribute to a loss in the apparent effectiveness of the system as well as in its long-term justification, the potential for an authoritarian conservative system exists. If, furthermore, the military is dissatisfied but well organized and averse to radical policies, and if it is headed by a popular general, the probability of a takeover is high. Yet the authoritarian conservative system that might then come to power will probably suffer from an inability to be more than a stopgap arrangement. Dependent on structures designed to ensure short-term survival, leaders are reluctant to create new structures capable of maintaining the system for a long period, for such an act is incompatible with their goals. Indeed, as we saw with the Nazi and Italian Fascist regimes (which did not survive their leaders, incidentally), the nature of the system changes if a long-term structure is created. The disappearance of authoritarian conservative regimes appears as logical and inevitable as their recurrence.

In a manner of speaking, an authoritarian conservative regime exists in order to disappear. If successful, it will turn into a traditional conservative regime as the old communal groups become able once more to constitute the legitimacy base and the channels of communication in the polity. Such developments were not unknown in the past, nor are they totally unknown at pres-

ent. When a "usurper" took over a country, gradually established his influence among a variety of groups, and passed his
office along to his son, he could be said to have created an authoritarian conservative regime that, by lasting, became traditional conservative. New dynasties were often of this kind, for
instance the Tudors of England at the end of the fifteenth century and possibly the Bourbons in Spain and elsewhere in the
Mediterranean in the eighteenth. But in these cases, the new
authoritarian conservative regime did not develop in an environment of populist or liberal democratic systems. It was the consequence of a fight with a traditional conservative system that
had ceased, at least in the eyes of some, to be legitimate because
the monarch was not accepted, while the monarchical basis of
legitimacy was not in question. The authoritarian conservative
"usurper" had simply (though it was not always easy) to ensure
that the universal principle of legitimacy of communal groups
and hereditary leader would work to his advantage and not to
that of others.

The future of authoritarian conservative leaders is far more
uncertain in the contemporary world because communal groups
as such have come to be challenged. As a result, authoritarian
conservative systems are engaged in a paradoxical behavior: Their
attempts to re-establish the strength of communal groups rest on
direct imposition and on the popularity of the leader, but the
leader's personality or charisma gives the system a modicum of
"democratic" basis, which is contradictory to the aims of the regime. If the leader is popular, he does not draw his strength from
the groups alone, hence it is unlikely that he will contribute to
restoring the strength of communal groups whose structure of influence is oligarchical. It is true that, as we saw, an effort is made
to assert the hierarchical nature of the leadership and in this way
to reintroduce oligarchical values in the polity. But the long-
term success of such an effort is questionable. It may succeed
moderately well in small, isolated polities, where it is possible to
control, if necessary by sheer force, the challenges that occur. It
is not surprising that one of the more successful efforts has been
in Haiti, where, indeed, the dead leader was followed by his son.
(Similar developments have occurred in other Central American

states.) But it is not likely to succeed in a more typical polity, which is internally dynamic and subjected to outside pressures.

There appear to be only two normal outcomes for authoritarian conservative systems in the contemporary world. One is the change that takes place after the death of the leader, and whether it is relatively slow or rapid will depend on the continuing ability of the social structure to control a large part of the population. Changes following Salazar's disappearance have been slow but significant; changes after Franco's are likely to be more rapid. The other outcome is the displacement of the authoritarian conservative leaders either by a coup or through a more or less voluntary surrender of office by the leaders themselves, after finding they are unable to stay in power, pursuing the fiction that their regime was temporary from the outset. Argentinian, Nigerian, and Ugandan military rulers have been, are, or will be subjected to this "rule" in the 1970's. When it does not happen, movements like those that displaced Trujillo in the Dominican Republic, Batista in Cuba, and Perez Jimenez in Venezuela are likely to occur. Authoritarian conservative systems have proved unable, through many attempts, despite the use of a variety of techniques and often much intellectual effort as well, and in a number of cases despite a reliance on the strongest physical weapons, to overcome the legitimacy problem. Given the part played in the contemporary world by populist regimes, as well as radical authoritarian and liberal democratic systems, they are unlikely to find in the future a more satisfactory way of doing so.

Authoritarian conservative systems can be labeled an aberration among types of political systems, but this judgment overlooks the fundamental problem these systems attempt to tackle, even if they do not succeed in dealing with it, and even if (though perhaps not more than some radical authoritarian and even populist systems) they use means of government that are repugnant to what are commonly thought to be "civilized" polities. The problem is a decrease in influence of some groups and of the values these groups extolled. Tribal or regional allegiance, ethnic feelings, and religious commitments have led and continue to lead to the demand for a return to the type of society that, actually or mythically, existed when these groups prevailed. The pace at which value changes have taken place has been "unbearable" for the supporters of the older values in many societies; the failures of many systems professing "modern values" have constituted an argument, in the eyes of many, for a return to the past, even if the failures of populist and other systems cannot be objectively attributed to the systems or their leaders. Authoritarian conservative systems must therefore be considered facts in a world environment, whether they are stable or not and whether or not they achieve, in the long run, the goals they pursue. By examining them, it becomes possible to see more clearly the reasons for some of their excesses as well as many of their contradictions. By examining them in comparison with other systems, the excesses and contradictions of other systems can also be noted.

14

Government and People in the
World Today

Although the problems facing the countries of the contemporary world are numerous and varied, and although the structures that exist or are created *ad hoc* have many different characteristics, a cross-national study shows common elements and helps to identify a number of general conditions. As we said in Chapter 2, we are not suggesting whether men can or cannot change the course of their destiny through political means. What we examined here were simply the conditions under which changes occur, whatever the cause or source of the change. The norms of leaders and people are in large part the result of socio-economic forces, but to conclude that individuals are incapable of putting forward different norms in similar socio-economic conditions is risky. If certain norms are put forward by the leaders of a political system, and depending on how closely these norms correspond to those of the whole population, a number of consequences will follow for the structures of the polity and the stability of the regime, and therefore the extent to which these norms will be implemented. The extent of imposition in a political system depends on the "distance" between the norms of the leaders and those of the people, which is not an absolute distance but varies according to the educational levels in the polity. For a given distance, some types of structures will be more successful than others in helping to bring about some norms and some policy goals, though time is also required. Pressure on the polity will have to increase if normative changes are to be implemented more quickly. There is thus a relationship among norms, structures, pace of change, and original support, which gives the study of comparative government its unity—and importance—in the contemporary world.

Changes in Normative Configuration and the Problem of Legitimacy

One of the key problems of political life is the pace at which changes can occur without endangering the framework of the polity. The question is not one of stability in the narrow sense, whether the stability of particular leaders or even of a regime. The problem is broader: It relates to the point at which change may so shake the customs of a population that a reaction will automatically set in and either the change will not be implemented or a "backlash" effect will reduce the efforts of leaders to nothing. We do not know as yet the exact shape of the curve, nor indeed is change or its acceptance easily quantifiable. But we can clearly state, on the basis of accumulated evidence, that there are limits to the amount of normative and policy goal change that can be brought about in a given amount of time. The problem facing politicians (and political scientists) is to find out how to maximize the amount of change that will "stick" in a given period.

The pace of change will affect the over-all maintenance of the system and ultimately the amount of change possible by its impact on the extent to which leaders and political arrangements will be accepted. As we have noted, the problem of legitimacy cannot be avoided, but because the nature of the movements between legitimacy levels in a system is so complex, a number of strategies can be devised and have been tried, often purely empirically, to meet this problem. These strategies can be summarized, and somewhat oversimplified, under three headings, though there are many variations around the main theme.

The first strategy is the *immobile society.* A given capital of legitimacy exists in a polity, as a result of the immemorial existence of a number of structures that have come to be accepted, typically passively, and often because no alternative springs to the minds of leaders and the population. Because it depends on an existing capital of legitimacy, the immobile strategy prevents those who adopt it from even suggesting that a new political system can be established. It is rarely used in practice, as its successful pursuit depends not only on the polity and its members but also on the environment in which the polity exists. Difficult to pursue in the past because communications and influence existed across countries, it is even less practicable in the contemporary world, because these influences have multiplied, mobility is greater, and the world has become, more truly than ever before, one large meeting place and one large exchange market for norms and structures. Thus we should not be surprised that systems embracing this strategy—traditional conservative systems —should be less numerous, and that, except for some cases where, indeed, some change does take place or where accidents of geography or leadership make a static system tolerable, the contemporary world should become less and less characterized by immobile polities.

The second strategy is *controlled change,* where it is assumed that changes will be accepted only if they are gradual. On the surface, this philosophy appears to coincide with the nature of legitimacy and with the way in which a capital of trust can be built and be spent. Structures and leaders are accepted up to a point; the views of men are modified slowly, and potential opposition members can be won over only if they are slowly made to see that new arrangements and new policies are not in fact prejudicial to their life and well-being. Let us not consider what rate is held best for such a controlled change. No one knows this optimal rate, admittedly, but it is wrong to criticize the strategy simply because its exact terms are not yet well known. But with controlled change the danger is always that, depending on attitudes or temperament, changes will appear to be too slow in the eyes of some men, while they appear too rapid in the eyes of

others. Basically, the premise of the strategy is that the legitimacy with which systems are endowed can be modified only by
changes that have previously occurred in the minds of individuals. At a given point in time, some views, goals, or polities
are or are not acceptable to a population; strictly speaking, they
are acceptable to some particular group and are acceptable at
some intensity level.[1] This is the given, and changes in polities
will have to take note of this basic acceptance. Structures will
help; trust will be passed from one group to another, from one
leader to a group, from a group to a leader. But the basic axiom
is that psychological acceptance always has to precede basic
policy change. It is therefore right to call this a strategy of "reconciliation" between groups and individuals.[2] One leaves to
members of the polity the duty to change their own attitudes
themselves—and if they do not, this fact will form the limit of
the attempts made.

This strategy, of course, characterizes liberal democratic polities, or is at least the genius and principle of that type of government. Liberalism is crucial in such a system, as the views of
everyone on policies and structures have to be taken as givens. No
one has any right to a greater weight than any other. It is true
that liberal democratic polities do not often follow the principle
in reality. It is also true that many polities, though overtly
liberal and democratic, in fact constrain discussion within narrow
limits or do not extend participation to the whole polity. But in
essence liberal democratic polities are primarily reformist and
reconciliatory. They accept legitimacy as a prior condition to the
implementation of change. Procedures and institutions couched
in constitutions are the embodiment of this basic creed. In order
to develop and change, one must first "lift the curtain" and let
every individual express what he feels. Slowness in the rate of
change may be the consequence, but it stems both from the
modesty of leaders who do not feel entitled to change men more
than they wish and from a certain pessimism, that is, a belief that
a rapid rate of change will always boomerang and that caution
is preferable to imagination.

1 See Dahl, *Preface to Democratic Theory, passim.*
2 David E. Apter, *The Politics of Modernization* (Chicago: University of
Chicago Press, 1965), p. 25.

The third strategy is *rapid change*. Given that there is little justification for the idea that some men or some polities should indefinitely be ahead of others and reap greater benefits, it is indeed difficult to oppose in principle the idea that rapid and sizable change should be pressed by leaders of some polities. But efforts at rapid change have shown, empirically and with regularity, that problems of legitimacy cannot be avoided and that acquiring support requires major efforts. Brute force and sheer physical imposition have seldom been successful and, after a period, come to be repugnant as well as inefficient. Thus leaders of political systems wishing to achieve large normative changes as quickly as possible have turned to education as their major ally. Rather than suggest that man must be taken always as he is today, and rather than believe that a man's view of a policy change can truly be acceptable before the fact (which is, in effect, what the liberal democratic strategy ultimately contends), supporters of rapid change assume that people modify their norms as policies unfold, that they come to realize the value of reforms, and that "human nature" is no more immutable or operative than any other "material" that exists in this world. Evidence indeed supports such a dynamic view. What is not known is how much man changes and exactly under what pressures this change is best brought about. But it is known that man varies in different contexts, different environments, or different conditions.

In order to be effective, this strategy has to be based on the faith of the populations, however, because education in the conventional sense will not be sufficient, or quick enough, to provide the legitimacy base the system requires. Some imposition will have to be introduced. But the system also demands that the population accept the idea that conditions will change under the new norms, that life will be better and arrangements more suitable if only it will believe, for the time being, in the future as the leaders portray it. The missionary zeal of leaders must go further: It must convince the people that working toward the new goals will bring about their benefits more quickly. Hence the notion that this strategy is one of mobilization of energies toward a change of the environment and of mankind itself.[3] This requires that certain structures and certain men be taken on

[3] Apter, *Politics of Modernization*, pp. 43–80 and *passim*.

faith initially and be trusted for some time when they say that the "millennium" will come. Such systems are not truly legitimate, but they have enough legitimizing potential to support a "take-off" and to increase legitimacy by the very benefits they provide.

This strategy describes, in broad and somewhat idealized terms, the goals that radical authoritarian and populist systems attempt to bring about. It explains why these systems need organizations, such as parties, and often need leaders of a personalized type to hold the polity together during the intermediate period. This is why, too, such systems are fragile. Ultimately they are based on a gamble that, after the transitional period, the people will indeed have accepted the normative and policy changes put forward by leaders. This is why, too, these leaders have to be seen as prophets of a new society. Unless they are seen in this role, the system will collapse and the change to be brought about will never take place, with further consequences in popular disillusionment.

The real difficulty with the rapid change strategy, however, is that, by its very nature, it is applied only up to a point and for specific goals. Indefinite change is difficult to conceive, and leaders tend to set forth goals whose achievement appears to mark the end of the strategy, as if society could then dedicate itself either to no change or to controlled change. Thus mobilizing regimes have an innate propensity to become reconciling. Or else, the goals may seem too distant and the legitimacy levels required too large. Many radical authoritarian regimes have turned reconciliatory; the process is probably unavoidable, sooner or later, though we still do not know how long it takes for a mobilizing regime either to achieve its goals (and thereafter seek merely to maintain prior achievements) or to decide that the goals are too distant and that it is better to settle for what has been achieved. Meanwhile, as this happens, problems of legitimacy become increasingly difficult to solve within the framework of a legitimizing philosophy. The capital of trust may seem to melt away suddenly in a population that has become accustomed to believing in the benefits of change. The strategy of *permanent revolution,* which a mobilizing system logically entails, has not yet been defined, but if the revolution is not permanent, the logic of reconciliation becomes, once more, inescapable.

People and Policies

We have considered the relations between people and leaders and the effect that popular support may have on the maintenance of regimes and broad policy goals in global terms. But, particularly where the system is of a reconciling type, the question of the relationship between people and government regarding policies in detail is of major importance. If leaders are to be responsive to the population, if the system is to be democratic in any real sense, it should not only involve the whole population in decision-making but also be attentive to some of the specific contours of the people's desires.

Yet it is clear that the participation of the people in detailed policies is nowhere very marked. Neither the structures we examined, such as groups and parties, nor procedural arrangements devised through constitutions, such as the referendum, allow a very widespread involvement of the people in policy determination. Arguments have been put forward against referendums in various parts of the world: The level of participation is sometimes so low that the groups supporting a particular cause can have their way with the participation of a very small fraction. This is of course not always the case, but the more specific and complex the issue and the more repeated the demands made on the people to agree on specific laws, the smaller the turnout appears to be. Moreover, referendums are usually criticized on the grounds that, rather like associational groups, they tend to "atomize" the political system. It becomes difficult to follow policies because each referendum is on a particular question, which may or may not fit well with the rest of the program. The populace itself becomes inconsistent: It can vote for policies and later vote down the financial backing needed to carry them out.

These arguments are probably exaggerated, and they are all the more widespread because the procedure of direct popular participation through referendums has not been adopted on a very broad scale, not even in liberal democracies, and not even on paper. Switzerland is the only country in which referendums take place regularly (as well as popular initiatives, which allow the population to force government and assembly to consider a problem and introduce a law). Elsewhere the people are rarely consulted at the national level for legislation, though they may be increasingly involved in the constitutional process. There are sometimes more occasions for popular participation at the regional or local level. Many states of the United States, for instance, regularly involve their citizens in referendums, often with very low participation, on complex taxation and legislative issues. Over all, the limited development of referendums has in part been due to the criticisms raised against the value of the technique, as well as its misuse. Hence many plebiscites are designed merely to ratify and give symbolic approval to a popular leader, and the measures for ratification, common in populist states, relate to broad policies or, indeed, norms and policy goals, not to the detailed problems found in Swiss referendums and the propositions offered in U.S. state ballots.

The limited use of, and the criticisms leveled at, the referendum are typically offered as proof that, in liberal democracies at least, participation in detailed issues should be channeled through groups and through the development of "responsible" party systems to provide competition between programs that are detailed and coherent enough to give some meaning to the electors' choice. Yet we saw that the formula of "competitive mobilization," prevalent in some countries of Western Europe in the early part of the twentieth century, rarely exists today. As a result, opportunities for broad choices have come to be restricted. Moreover, the number of countries in which the mechanics of the system offer real possibilities of choice is in fact very small, as the party system must be both sufficiently simple and sufficiently balanced for the election to lead to the selection of the executive. In many countries, opportunities for a variety of coalitions among the parties represented in the assembly are large. Elsewhere, one party is so overwhelming that there is little chance, if any, to dislodge it from power. Thus the involvement of the people in the choice of policies or programs is always quite small, even in polities where, with two-party systems on the U.K. model, it has long been recognized by both electors and leaders that the function of elections is to help choose between programs, and where efforts are ostensibly made to abide by this rule.

Popular participation therefore takes place in a more indirect fashion, and some of the desires and aims of the people come to be channeled through associational groups and even to some extent through communal groups. But this leads to a more atomized political system than a well-organized party system would create, and the effects are in some ways similar to those of referendums. Participation is therefore "static," and reconciling systems are thus even further differentiated from mobilizing systems, whose leaders view associational groups as likely to create difficulties and insoluble oppositions and as not truly embodying the will of the people. Thus the relationship between government and people remains, to a large extent and everywhere, on the most general footing. An indirect relationship through groups and, to some extent, parties sometimes causes demands to be pressed upon the system and to become policies, but this is surely only a toned-down and "realistic" version of the ideal of democracy and participation, which reconciling and, in the end, mobilizing systems claim to pursue.

The Study of Comparative Government and the Relationship Between People and Politics

The debate between description and prescription has been one of the more long-standing controversies in political science. For many, modern developments in political science have tended to overemphasize the study of behavior to the neglect of the scholar's obligation to guide practitioners toward the "good society" and to choices among alternatives based on moral principles and an idealistic vision. Some of the modern studies of governments, individual and comparative, indeed appear to show too much concern for a description of the minutiae of arrangements and structures. But it is dangerous to overstress the distinction, or to deem it possible to prescribe for government without knowledge of the internal mechanics and constraints that result from the structural configurations, the types of normative pressures, and the levels of support existing in a polity. We suggested in the introduction to this chapter that a basic relationship existed relating the various components of all political systems. If prescription is to be effective, efforts must be made to define most accurately the parameters of this relationship and thus to determine the conditions that relate structures, norms, and support in their concrete variations.

The study of comparative government on a cross-national basis provides the framework within which this relationship can slowly be discovered. In the course of the last decades, partial or middle-range[4] theories relating to groups, parties, the role of the military and the bureaucracy, the conditions under which leadership is likely to be personalized or charismatic, and the effect of personalized leadership have gradually been discovered. It is simply not possible, as we noted repeatedly in this book, to expect a *fiat* to abolish communal groups or make a party a viable and extensive structure. It is plainly wrong to expect the military to obey the civilian power in all circumstances and for any policies. The conditions under which these structures operate now begin to be known. Further descriptions of phenomena in all types of countries are required—even by those who have basically a prescriptive goal—as we often must proceed by induction or must test hypotheses in a number of fields where our knowledge is lacking. The number of variables is large, and the "functional equivalents" are numerous. We saw that the military could under some conditions replace parties, that the bureaucracy could take the place of groups, and that charismatic leadership could make up for failing party support. An examination of detailed structures will help to build a more complex network of middle-range theories and thereby help to build a more rigorous analysis of comparative government than has been at our disposal in previous generations.

Clearly, however, the ultimate goal must be a general theory that will relate the various problems and will constitute the true basis for prescription. Up to now, general analysis has been mainly confined to model-making. We have a model of the political system. We have some ideas of functions (in the sense of "operations" assigned to the system). We know that there are

4 See Joseph LaPalombara, "Macrotheories and Microapplications in Comparative Politics," *Comparative Politics*, 1 (1968): 52–78.

norms, and we realize that they are ordered according to different dimensions. It seems that some locations in the space of the normative dimensions are more likely to be occupied than others. We can infer from descriptions the universal part played by legitimacy and support, though we are rather hazy about the dynamics of support development, support transfer, and, in particular, opportunities for the establishment of a legitimizing process. Because of these difficulties, comparative government has been repeatedly subjected to a number of contradictory attacks, ranging from, at one extreme, the consideration of specific historical or contextual problems, allegedly on the grounds of the importance of culture, to, at the other extreme, the build-up of further general theories stressing the role of the economic substructure, the role of culture, and the influence of attitudes. Ultimately, neither approach is likely to be satisfactory, not because general theories should not be built nor individual cases analyzed, but because individual cases cannot help us to cope meaningfully with future problems or with prescription, and because general theories, in a field where so many variables are involved, have to be oversimplified and are of little use if developed too rapidly and with too little middle-range support.

The hope for the future of comparative government lies in the slow emergence of a general theory on the basis of the partial or middle-range theories that have been "discovered" and generally accepted, if only under special conditions or with specific assumptions. Problems relating to functional equivalents must be explored, as they will provide linkages among structures hitherto too little studied. An examination of the interrelationship between norms will suggest to what extent some types of normative configurations are possible and the reasons for the pre-eminence of these configurations. The analysis of imposition and of natural development will lead to the assessment of the extent to which change is possible in given types of polities and thus go some way toward suggesting the parameters of the fundamental relationship in comparative government. None of these types of analysis are impossible, though the precise measurement will always raise difficulties, and one will therefore have to accept, for a period at least, some vagueness, some lack of rigor, and many difficult choices in the comparisons.

Yet it is because of this mixture of theoretical difficulty and profound practical importance that the study of comparative government, undertaken systematically on a cross-national basis, should have a wide appeal, extending beyond the strict confines of political science. All social scientists are involved in the study of comparative government, both because the tools of economists and psychologists, as well as a sociological approach, are clearly of importance to the understanding of problems and because efforts of social scientists in their own disciplines can have no practical effect unless the political system can bear the strains and stresses of new policies and new ideologies. Politics has often been called an art, usually the art of the possible. Comparative government must study what the possible is, where its limits are, and the various ways for turning it into reality. To marry description and prescription is thus to look for the art where art can operate but to look scientifically at what is recognized as scientific. It is, after all, the only hope for mankind, because on the politics of men and their governments ultimately depend the world's well-being and survival.

Appendix

The following table gives some of the basic characteristics of the countries of the contemporary world as of January 1, 1972. Eight characteristics are given:

1. Normative configuration:
    TC = traditional conservative
    LD = liberal democratic
    RA = radical authoritarian
     P = populist
    AC = authoritarian conservative
2. Existence of a party system:
    No = no parties
    Single = single-party system (or forced coalition, as in East Germany, or overwhelming strength of a party)
    Two + = more than one party
3. Monarchy or Republic
4. Unitary or federal
5. Assembly:
    Yes = one or more chambers
    No = no chamber
6. Military:
    Yes = the military is in power, or exercises very strong influence
    No = limited influence of the military
7. Personalization of power: High, medium, or low
8. Economic wealth of country, as based on per capita GNP:
    Rich = over $750
    Intermediate = $250–$749
    Poor = below $250

Where the position is ambiguous, the characteristic is preceded by the symbol (?)

Appendix

SOME CHARACTERISTICS OF THE COUNTRIES OF THE
CONTEMPORARY WORLD

	1 Norms	2 Party	3 Mon/Rep	4 Unit/Fed	5 Assembly	6 Military	7 Person.	8 Wealth
ATLANTIC AREA								
Australia	LD	Two+	Mon	Fed	Yes	No	Low	Rich
Austria	LD	Two+	Rep	Fed	Yes	No	Low	Rich
Belgium	LD	Two+	Mon	Unit	Yes	No	Low	Rich
Canada	LD	Two+	Mon	Fed	Yes	No	Low	Rich
Denmark	LD	Two+	Mon	Unit	Yes	No	Low	Rich
Eire	LD	Two+	Rep	Unit	Yes	No	Low	Rich
Finland	LD	Two+	Rep	Unit	Yes	No	Low	Rich
France	LD	Two+	Rep	Unit	Yes	No	Low	Rich
West Germany	LD	Two+	Rep	Fed	Yes	No	Low	Rich
Greece	AC	No	?Mon	Unit	No	Yes	Low	Interm
Iceland	LD	Two+	Rep	Unit	Yes	No	Low	Rich
Italy	LD	Two+	Rep	Unit	Yes	No	Low	Rich
Luxembourg	LD	Two+	Mon	Unit	Yes	No	Low	Rich
Malta	LD	Two+	Mon	Unit	Yes	No	Low	Interm
Netherlands	LD	Two+	Mon	Unit	Yes	No	Low	Rich
New Zealand	LD	Two+	Mon	Unit	Yes	No	Low	Rich
Norway	LD	Two+	Mon	Unit	Yes	No	Low	Rich
Portugal	AC	Single	Rep	Unit	Yes	No	Low	Interm
Spain	AC	Single	?Mon	Unit	Yes	No	Medium	Interm
Sweden	LD	Two+	Mon	Unit	Yes	No	Low	Rich
Switzerland	LD	Two+	Rep	Fed	Yes	No	Low	Rich
United Kingdom	LD	Two+	Mon	Unit	Yes	No	Low	Rich
United States	LD	Two+	Rep	Fed	Yes	No	Low	Rich

EASTERN EUROPE AND NORTH ASIA

Albania	RA	Single	Rep	Unit	Yes	No	Low	?Interm
Bulgaria	RA	Single	Rep	Unit	Yes	No	Low	Interm
China	RA	Single	Rep	Unit	Yes	?No	High	?Poor
Czechoslovakia	RA	Single	Rep	Fed	Yes	?No	Low	Rich
East Germany	RA	Single	Rep	Unit	Yes	No	Low	Rich
Hungary	RA	Single	Rep	Unit	Yes	No	Low	Rich
North Korea	RA	Single	Rep	Unit	Yes	No	?Medium	?Interm
Mongolia	RA	Single	Rep	Unit	Yes	No	Medium	?Poor
Poland	RA	Single	Rep	Unit	Yes	No	Low	Interm
Rumania	RA	Single	Rep	Unit	Yes	No	?Low	?Interm
U.S.S.R.	RA	Single	Rep	Fed	Yes	No	Low	Rich
North Vietnam	RA	Single	Rep	Unit	Yes	No	Low	?Poor
Yugoslavia	RA	Single	Rep	Fed	Yes	No	High	?Interm

MIDDLE EAST AND NORTH AFRICA

Afghanistan	TC	No	Mon	Unit	Yes	No	Low	?Poor
Algeria	P	Single	Rep	Unit	No	Yes	Low	?Interm
Bahrein	TC	No	Mon	Unit	No	No	Low	?Interm
Cyprus	P	Single	Rep	Unit	Yes	No	Medium	Interm
Iran	TC	No	Mon	Unit	Yes	No	Medium	Interm
Iraq	P	Single	Rep	Unit	No	Yes	Low	Interm
Israel	LD	Two+	Rep	Unit	Yes	No	Low	Rich
Jordan	TC	No	Mon	Unit	Yes	?No	?Low	Poor
Kuwait	TC	No	Mon	Unit	Yes	No	Low	Rich
Lebanon	LD	Two+	Rep	Unit	Yes	No	Low	Interm
Libya	P	No	Rep	Unit	No	Yes	Low	Interm
Morocco	TC	No	Mon	Unit	Yes	No	Medium	Poor
Muscat and Oman	TC	No	Mon	Unit	No	No	Low	?Poor
Qatar	TC	No	Mon	Unit	No	No	Low	?Poor
Saudi Arabia	TC	No	Mon	Unit	No	No	Low	Poor
South Yemen	P	Single	Rep	Unit	No	No	Low	?Poor
Syria	P	Single	Rep	Unit	No	Yes	Low	Poor

	1 Norms	2 Party	3 Mon/Rep	4 Unit/Fed	5 Assembly	6 Military	7 Person.	8 Wealth
Tunisia	P	Single	Rep	Unit	Yes	No	High	Poor
Turkey	?LD	Two+	Rep	Unit	Yes	?No	Low	Interm
UAR	P	Single	Rep	Unit	Yes	No	Low	Poor
Yemen	P	No	Rep	Unit	No	Yes	Low	?Poor

SOUTH AND EAST ASIA

	1 Norms	2 Party	3 Mon/Rep	4 Unit/Fed	5 Assembly	6 Military	7 Person.	8 Wealth
Bangladesh	P	Single	Rep	Unit	?No	No	Medium	Poor
Bhutan	TC	No	Mon	Unit	Yes	No	Low	?Poor
Burma	P	No	Rep	Unit	No	Yes	Low	Poor
Cambodia	AC	No	Rep	Unit	Yes	Yes	Low	Poor
Ceylon	LD	Two+	Rep	Unit	Yes	No	Low	Poor
China (Taiwan)	AC	Single	Rep	Unit	?Yes	No	High	Interm
India	LD	Two+	Rep	Fed	Yes	No	Low	Poor
Indonesia	P	Two+	Rep	Unit	?Yes	Yes	Medium	Interm
Japan	LD	Two+	Mon	Unit	Yes	No	Low	Rich
South Korea	LD	Two+	Rep	Unit	Yes	No	Low	Interm
Laos	TC	No	Mon	Unit	Yes	No	Low	?Poor
Malaysia	TC	Two+	Mon	Fed	Yes	No	Low	Interm
Maldive Islands	TC	No	Mon	Unit	Yes	No	Low	?Poor
Nepal	TC	No	Mon	Unit	?Yes	No	Low	?Poor
Pakistan	AC	?Single	Rep	Unit	?Yes	Yes	?Low	Poor
Philippines	LD	Two+	Rep	Unit	Yes	No	Low	Poor
Singapore	P	Single	Rep	Unit	Yes	No	Medium	?Interm
Thailand	AC	No	Mon	Unit	Yes	Yes	Medium	Poor
South Vietnam	AC	No	Rep	Unit	Yes	Yes	Medium	Poor
Western Samoa	TC	No	Mon	Unit	Yes	No	Low	?Poor

AFRICA SOUTH OF SAHARA

	1 Norms	2 Party	3 Mon/Rep	4 Unit/Fed	5 Assembly	6 Military	7 Person.	8 Wealth
Botswana	TC	Two+	Rep	Unit	Yes	No	Low	Poor
Burundi	P	Single	Rep	Unit	No	Yes	Low	Poor

Country								
Cameroon	P	Two+	Rep	Fed	Yes	No	Low	?Poor
Central Afr. Rep.	P	No	Rep	Unit	No	Yes	Low	Poor
Chad	AC	Single	Rep	Unit	Yes	No	Low	?Poor
Congo (Brazzaville)	P	No	Rep	Unit	No	Yes	Low	Poor
Dahomey	AC	No	Rep	Unit	No	Yes	?Low	?Poor
Ethiopia	TC	No	Mon	Unit	Yes	No	Medium	Poor
Equatorial Guinea	P	Single	Rep	Unit	Yes	No	?Medium	?Poor
Gabon	P	Single	Rep	Unit	Yes	No	Low	Poor
Gambia	LD	Two+	Mon	Unit	No	Yes	Low	?Poor
Ghana	AC	No	Rep	Unit	Yes	Yes	Low	Interm
Guinea	P	Single	Rep	Unit	Yes	No	High	Poor
Ivory Coast	P	Single	Rep	Unit	Yes	No	High	Interm
Kenya	P	Single	Rep	Unit	Yes	No	High	?Interm
Lesotho	?TC	Two+	Mon	Unit	Yes	No	Medium	Poor
Liberia	TC	Single	Rep	Unit	Yes	No	Medium	Poor
Madagascar	P	Single	Rep	Unit	Yes	No	Low	Poor
Malawi	AC	Single	Rep	Unit	Yes	Yes	Medium	Poor
Mali	?AC	No	Rep	Unit	No	No	Low	Poor
Mauritania	P	Single	Rep	Unit	Yes	No	Low	Poor
Mauritius	P	Two+	Mon	Unit	Yes	No	Low	?Poor
Niger	P	Single	Rep	Unit	Yes	Yes	Low	Poor
Nigeria	AC	No	Rep	Fed	No	No	Low	Poor
Rhodesia	AC	Single	Rep	Unit	Yes	No	Low	Interm
Rwanda	P	Two+	Rep	Unit	Yes	No	Low	?Poor
Senegal	P	Single	Rep	Unit	Yes	No	Medium	Poor
Sierra Leone	LD	Two+	Mon	Unit	Yes	No	Low	Poor
Somalia	P	No	Rep	Unit	No	Yes	Low	?Poor
South Africa	AC	Two+	Rep	Unit	Yes	No	Low	Interm
Sudan	P	No	Rep	Unit	No	Yes	Low	Poor
Swaziland	TC	Single	Mon	Unit	Yes	No	Low	Poor
Tanzania	P	Single	Rep	Unit	Yes	No	High	Poor
Togo	P	No	Rep	Unit	No	Yes	Low	Poor
Uganda	AC	No	Rep	Unit	No	Yes	Low	Poor
Upper Volta	AC	No	Rep	Unit	No	Yes	Low	?Poor
Zaïre	P	Single	Rep	Unit	?Yes	Yes	Medium	Poor
Zambia	P	Two+	Rep	Unit	Yes	No	Medium	Poor

LATIN AMERICA

	1 Norms	2 Party	3 Mon/Rep	4 Unit/Fed	5 Assembly	6 Military	7 Person.	8 Wealth
Argentina	AC	No	Rep	Fed	No	Yes	Low	Interm
Barbados	LD	Two+	Mon	Unit	Yes	No	Low	Interm
Bolivia	AC	No	Rep	Unit	No	Yes	Low	Poor
Brazil	AC	Two+	Rep	Fed	Yes	Yes	Low	Poor
Chile	LD	Two+	Rep	Unit	Yes	No	Low	Interm
Colombia	TC	Two+	Rep	Unit	Yes	No	Low	Interm
Costa Rica	LD	Two+	Rep	Unit	Yes	No	Low	Poor
Cuba	RA	Single	Rep	Unit	No	No	High	Interm
Dominican Republic	AC	Two+	Rep	Unit	Yes	?No	Low	Interm
Ecuador	AC	Two+	Rep	Unit	Yes	?No	Low	Poor
El Salvador	TC	Two+	Rep	Unit	Yes	No	Low	Interm
Guatemala	AC	Two+	Rep	Unit	Yes	No	Low	Interm
Guyana	P	Two+	Rep	Unit	Yes	No	Low	Interm
Haiti	AC	Single	Rep	Unit	Yes	No	High	Poor
Honduras	AC	Single	Rep	Unit	Yes	No	Low	Poor
Jamaica	LD	Two+	Mon	Unit	Yes	No	Low	Interm
Mexico	P	Single	Rep	Fed	Yes	No	Low	Interm
Nicaragua	AC	Single	Rep	Unit	Yes	No	Low	Interm
Panama	?P	Two+	Rep	Unit	Yes	?No	Low	Interm
Paraguay	AC	Single	Rep	Unit	Yes	?No	Medium	Poor
Peru	P	No	Rep	Unit	No	Yes	Low	Interm
Trinidad and Tobago	?P	?Two+	Mon	Unit	Yes	No	Medium	Interm
Uruguay	LD	Two+	Rep	Unit	Yes	No	Low	Interm
Venezuela	LD	Two+	Rep	Fed	Yes	No	Low	Rich

Selected Bibliography

General Works on Comparative Government

ALMOND, G. A., and J. S. COLEMAN, eds. *The Politics of Developing Areas.* Princeton, N.J.: Princeton University Press, 1960.

ALMOND, G. A., and G. B. POWELL. *Comparative Politics.* Boston: Little, Brown & Co., 1966.

APTER, D. E. *The Politics of Modernization.* Chicago: University of Chicago Press, 1965.

ARISTOTLE. *The Politics.* Baltimore: Penguin Books, 1962.

BLONDEL, J. *An Introduction to Comparative Government.* New York: Praeger, 1970.

CARTER, G. M., and J. H. HERZ. *Government and Politics in the Twentieth Century.* Rev. ed. New York: Praeger, 1965.

DAHL, R. A. *Modern Political Analysis.* Englewood Cliffs, N.J.: Prentice-Hall, 1963.

————. *Polyarchy.* New Haven, Conn.: Yale University Press, 1971.

DEUTSCH, K. W. *The Nerves of Government.* New York: Free Press, 1963.

EASTON, D. *A Framework for Political Analysis.* Englewood Cliffs, N.J.: Prentice-Hall, 1965.

————. *A Systems Analysis of Political Life.* New York: John Wiley & Sons, 1965.

ECKSTEIN, H. H., and D. E. APTER, eds. *Comparative Politics.* New York: Free Press, 1963.

FRIEDRICH, C. J. *Constitutional Government and Democracy.* Boston: Ginn & Co., 1950.

HOLT, R. T., and J. E. TURNER. *The Political Basis of Economic Development.* Princeton, N.J.: Van Nostrand, 1966.

MONTESQUIEU, C. *The Spirit of Laws.* New York: Hafner Publishing, 1965.

VERNEY, D. V. *The Analysis of Political Systems.* New York: Humanities Press, 1960.

Bases of Political Systems and Political Development

BANKS, A. S., and R. B. TEXTOR. *A Cross-Polity Survey.* Cambridge, Mass.: MIT Press, 1963.

COLEMAN, J. S., ed. *Education and Political Development.* Princeton, N.J.: Princeton University Press, 1965.

DOWNS, A. *An Economic Theory of Democracy.* New York: Harper & Row, 1957.

FINKLE, J. L., and R. W. GABLE, eds. *Political Development and Social Change.* New York: John Wiley & Sons, 1966.

GREENSTEIN, F. I. *Children and Politics.* New Haven, Conn.: Yale University Press, 1965.

JACKSON, R. J., and M. B. STEIN. *Issues in Comparative Politics.* New York: St. Martin's Press, 1971.

KORNHAUSER, W. A. *The Politics of Mass Society.* Glencoe, Ill.: Free Press, 1950.

PYE, L. W. *Aspects of Political Development.* Boston: Little, Brown & Co., 1966.

PYE, L. W., and S. VERBA. *Communications and Political Development.* Princeton, N.J.: Princeton University Press, 1963.

ROSTOW, W. W. *The Stages of Economic Growth.* New York: Cambridge University Press, 1960.

RUSSETT, B. M., *et al. World Handbook of Political and Social Indicators.* New Haven, Conn.: Yale University Press, 1964.

SHILS, E. *Political Development in the New States.* New York: Humanities Press, 1962.

Groups

BENTLEY, A. F. *The Process of Government.* Ed. by PETER H. ODEGARD. Cambridge, Mass.: Harvard University Press, 1967.

EHRMANN, H. W., *Interest Groups on Four Continents.* Pittsburgh: University of Pittsburgh Press, 1958.

EISENSTADT, S. N., ed. *The Political Systems of Empires.* New York: Free Press, 1963.

GALENSON, W. G. *Comparative Labor Movements.* Englewood Cliffs, N.J.: Prentice-Hall, 1962.

S<small>TORING</small>, H. J., ed. *Essays on the Scientific Study of Politics*. New York: Holt, Rinehart & Winston, 1962.

Parties

A<small>LLARDT</small>, E., and Y. L<small>ITTUNEN</small>. *Cleavages, Ideologies and Party Systems*. Helsinki: The Academic Bookstore, 1964.

C<small>OLEMAN</small>, J. S., and C. G. R<small>OSBERG</small>. *Political Parties and National Integration in Tropical Africa*. Berkeley and Los Angeles: University of California Press, 1964.

D<small>UVERGER</small>, M. *Political Parties*. London: Methuen & Co., 1955.

E<small>PSTEIN</small>, L. D. *Political Parties in Western Democracies*. New York: Praeger, 1967.

H<small>ODGKIN</small>, T. *African Political Parties*. Baltimore: Penguin Books, 1961.

L<small>IPSET</small>, S. M., and S. R<small>OKKAN</small>, eds. *Party Systems and Voter Alignments*. New York: Free Press, 1967.

M<small>ACKENZIE</small>, W. J. M. *Free Elections*. New York: Humanities Press, 1958.

M<small>ICHELS</small>, R. *Political Parties*. Glencoe, Ill.: Free Press, 1949.

N<small>EUMANN</small>, S. *Modern Political Parties*. Chicago: University of Chicago Press, 1955.

O<small>STROGORSKI</small>, M. *Democracy and the Organization of Political Parties*. 2 vols. 1902; reprint, New York: Haskell House, 1970.

R<small>AE</small>, D. W. *The Political Consequences of Electoral Laws*. New Haven, Conn.: Yale University Press, 1967.

Governmental Structures: Federalism, Executives, Assemblies

A<small>NDREWS</small>, W. G., ed. *Constitutions and Constitutionalism*. Princeton, N.J.: Van Nostrand, 1961.

B<small>LONDEL</small>, J. *Comparative Legislatures*. Englewood Cliffs, N.J.: Prentice-Hall, 1972.

B<small>RZEZINSKI</small>, Z., and S. B. H<small>UNTINGTON</small>. *Political Power USA/USSR*. New York: Viking Press, 1965.

D<small>UCHACEK</small>, I. D. *Comparative Federalism*. New York: Holt, Rinehart & Winston, 1970.

D<small>UVERGER</small>, M. *De la Dictature*. Paris: Juillard, 1961.

E<small>DINGER</small>, L. J., ed. *Political Leadership in Industrialized Societies*. New York: John Wiley & Sons, 1967.

F<small>RIEDRICH</small>, C. J., ed. *Totalitarianism*. Cambridge, Mass.: Harvard University Press, 1954.

K<small>ORNBERG</small>, A., and L. D. M<small>USOLF</small>. *Legislatures in Developmental Perspective*. Durham, N.C.: Duke University Press, 1970.

L<small>ASSWELL</small>, H. D., and L<small>ERNER</small>, D., eds. *World Revolutionary Elites*. Cambridge, Mass.: MIT Press, 1965.

M<small>ARVICK</small>, D., ed. *Political Decision-Makers*. New York: Free Press of Glencoe, 1961.

Neustadt, R., ed. *Presidential Power.* New York: John Wiley & Sons, 1960.

Truman, D. B. *The Congressional Party.* New York: John Wiley & Sons, 1950.

Wahlke, J. C., et al. *The Legislative System.* New York: John Wiley & Sons, 1962.

Wheare, K. C. *Federal Government.* London and New York: Oxford University Press, 1963.

———. *Legislatures.* London and New York: Oxford University Press, 1963.

———. *Modern Constitutions.* London and New York: Oxford University Press, 1966.

Bureaucracies, Military, Judiciary

Chapman, B. *The Profession of Government.* New York: Humanities Press, 1966.

Finer, S. E. *The Man on Horseback.* New York: Praeger, 1962.

Huntington, S. P. *The Soldier and the State.* Cambridge, Mass.: Harvard University Press, 1957.

Janowitz, M. *The Military in the Political Development of New Nations.* Chicago: University of Chicago Press, 1964.

Kirchheimer, O. *Political Justice.* Princeton, N.J.: Princeton University Press, 1961.

La Palombara, J., ed. *Bureaucracy and Political Development.* Princeton, N.J.: Princeton University Press, 1963.

Rostow, E. V. *The Sovereign Prerogative.* New Haven, Conn.: Yale University Press, 1962.

Rowat, D. C. *The Ombudsman.* Toronto: University of Toronto Press, 1968.

Schubert, G. *Constitutional Politics.* New York: Holt, Rinehart & Winston, 1960.

Simon, H. A. *Administrative Behavior.* New York: Free Press of Glencoe, 1957.

Strauss, E. *The Ruling Servants.* London: George Allen & Unwin, 1961; New York: Praeger, 1961.

Tullock, G. *The Politics of Bureaucracy.* Washington, D.C.: Public Affairs Press, 1965.

Studies of Individual Countries or Regions

Europe

Beer, S. H., and A. B. Ulam, eds. *Patterns of Government: The Major Political Systems of Europe.* New York: Random House, 1962.

BRYCE, J. *Modern Democracies.* London: Macmillan, 1891.
DAHL, R. A. *Political Oppositions in Western Democracies.* New Haven, Conn.: Yale University Press, 1966.
MACRIDIS, R. C., and R. E. WARD. *Modern Political Systems: Europe and Asia.* Englewood Cliffs, N.J.: Prentice-Hall, 1963.

Communist Countries

BARGHOORN, F. C. *The USSR.* Boston: Little, Brown & Co., 1966.
FAINSOD, M. *How Russia Is Ruled.* Cambridge, Mass.: Harvard University Press, 1953.
IONESÇU, G. *The Politics of the European Communist States.* New York: Praeger, 1967.

Near East and North Africa

HARARI, M. *Government and Politics of the Middle East.* Englewood Cliffs, N.J.: Prentice-Hall, 1962.
LERNER, D. *The Passing of Traditional Society.* New York: Free Press of Glencoe, 1958.

South and Southeast Asia

PYE, L. W. *Politics, Personality and Nation-Building.* Cambridge, Mass.: MIT Press, 1962.
SCALAPINO, R. A., ed. *The Communist Revolution in Asia.* Englewood Cliffs, N.J.: Prentice-Hall, 1965.
WARD, R. E., and D. A. RUSTOW. *Political Modernization in Japan and Turkey.* Princeton, N.J.: Princeton University Press, 1964.
WEINER, M. *Party Politics in India.* Princeton, N.J.: Princeton University Press, 1964.

Africa South of the Sahara

CARTER, G. M., ed. *African One-Party States.* Ithaca, N.Y.: Cornell University Press, 1962.
DODGE, D. *African Politics in Perspective.* Princeton, N.J.: Van Nostrand, 1966.

Latin America

KANTOR, H. *Patterns of Politics and Political Systems in Latin America.* Chicago: Rand McNally, 1969.

LAMBERT, J. *Latin America*. Berkeley and Los Angeles: University of California Press, 1967.

TOMASEK, R. D., ed. *Latin American Politics*. Garden City, N.Y.: Doubleday, 1966.

VÉLIZ, C., ed. *Obstacles to Change in Latin America*. London and New York: Oxford University Press, 1965.

Index

and groups, 76–77, 206–7
leadership of, 212–13
and military, 210–12
and norms, 42–43, 203–4
origins of, 204–6
and parties, 207–10
Portugal, 63, 100, 219, 221–22
Powell, G. B., 17*n*, 28*n*, 39
Presidential systems, 125–26
and liberal democracies, 178–79
Probabilistic theory, 27–30
Promotional groups, 73–76; *see also* Associational groups
Proportional representation, 106–7
and executives, 120–22
Protectional groups, 75–76; *see also* Associational groups
Protestantism, 74, 78–79
and political parties, 85–86
Pye, L. W., 45*n*

Quasi-federalism, 114–16

Radical authoritarian systems:
and groups, 76–77
and norms, 41–42; *see also* Communist systems
Radicalism, 36–37
Rae, D., 196*n*
Referendum, 237–38
Regional authorities and federalism, 113–17
Religious groups, 74, 78–79, 85–86; *see also* Communal groups
Religious parties, 85–86
Rhodesia, 221
Roman Catholicism, 74, 78–79
and political parties, 85–86
Rotation of executives, 120–21
Rousseau, J.-J., 68*n*, 173
Rule-adjudication, 20–21
and judiciary, 147–52
Rule-application, 20–21
Rule-implementation, 136–41
Rule-making, 20–21
Rumania, 193
Russia, 208
Rwanda, 160

Saudi Arabia, 24, 89
Second chambers, 131

Selection, 18–19
Senegal, 205, 207, 212
Sierra Leone, 105, 169
Singapore, 89, 100, 164
Socialization, 22–23
Socio-economic development, 45
and dictatorship, 57–60
and liberal democracies, 169–70
Somalia, 156
South Africa, 221
South Korea, 88–89, 169, 178
Soviet Union, 97, 99–101, 114, 117, 131–32, 186–90, 192–95, 198–99, 202, 209, 216–17
Spain, 63, 74, 100, 220–21, 225–26
Structural dictatorships, 60
Structural functional analysis, 24–25
Structures, 9–12
differentiation of, 28–29
Sudan, 170, 205–6, 211
Support, *see* Legitimacy
Swaziland, 159–60
Sweden, 87, 103, 183
Switzerland, 103, 114–15, 117, 119, 238
Syria, 212, 214

Taiwan, 221
Tanzania, 63–64, 101, 120, 205, 207, 209
Technical dictatorships, 60–61
Technicians:
and Communist systems, 195–96
role of, 137–41
Technocratic state, 139–41, 152
Tocqueville, A. de, 175
Trade unions, 79–80
and political parties, 91–96; *see also* Associational groups
Traditional political systems:
and assemblies, 161–62
and change, 233
and development, 155–56
future of, 163–66
and groups, 76–77
and legitimacy, 157–59
and military, 162–63
and norms, 42, 159
and parties, 159–61
Truman, D. B., 68*n*
Tunisia, 101, 205, 208–9
Turkey, 89, 169–70, 177, 211

25-302